T0319963

Central Bank Reserve Management

Central Bank Reserve Management

New Trends, from Liquidity to Return

Edited by

Age F.P. Bakker

At the time of writing Director of the Financial Markets Division at De Nederlandsche Bank. He now is Executive Director at the International Monetary Fund and Professor of Money and Banking at Vrije Universiteit Amsterdam

Ingmar R.Y. van Herpt

Senior Economist, Financial Markets Division, De Nederlandsche Bank, Amsterdam

Edward Elgar
Cheltenham, UK • Northampton, MA

Published by
Edward Elgar Publishing Limited
The Lypiatts
15 Lansdown Road
Cheltenham
Glos GL50 2JA
UK

Edward Elgar Publishing, Inc.
William Pratt House
9 Dewey Court
Northampton
Massachusetts 01060
USA

Reprinted 2009

A catalogue record for this book
is available from the British Library

ISBN 978 1 84542 957 7

Printed in the UK by the MPG Books Group

Contents

PART TWO: RESERVE MANAGEMENT: RETURN VERSUS
    LIQUIDITY

PART THREE: IMPLICATIONS FOR CENTRAL BANK
    BALANCE SHEETS

Contributors

Age F.P. Bakker
Director Financial Markets Division
De Nederlandsche Bank
Professor of Money and Banking
Vrije Universiteit Amsterdam

Heung Sik Choo
Head of Planning Team, Reserve Management Department
Bank of Korea

Joachim Fels
Chief Global Fixed Income Economist
Morgan Stanley

Hervé Ferhani
Deputy Director Monetary and Financial Systems Department
International Monetary Fund

Roberts Grava
Principal Financial Officer, Reserves Advisory and Management Program
World Bank

Pentti Hakkaraïnen
Member of the Board
Bank of Finland

Ingmar R.Y. van Herpt
Senior Economist, Financial Markets Division
De Nederlandsche Bank

Matthew Higgins
International Officer, Emerging Markets Group
Federal Reserve Bank of New York

Donna Howard
Chief Financial Markets Department
Bank of Canada

Esteban Jadresic
Director Financial Operations
Central Bank of Chile

Jennifer Johnson-Calari
Senior Manager, Reserves Advisory and Management Program
World Bank

Adam Kobor
Senior Investment Officer, Reserves Advisory and Management Program
World Bank

Hans-Helmut Kotz
Member of the Board
Deutsche Bundesbank

Robert Litterman
Managing Director, Director of Quantitative Resources
Goldman Sachs Asset Management

Robert N. McCauley
Chief Representative BIS Asian Office
Bank for International Settlements

Luděk Niedermayer
Vice Governor
Czech National Bank

Francesco Papadia
Director-General Market Operations
European Central Bank

Avinash Persaud
Chairman Intelligence Capital Limited

Mika Pösö
Chief Dealer, Market Operations Division
Bank of Finland

Vinod Kumar Sharma
Executive Director
Reserve Bank of India

Hidehiko Sogano
Deputy Director-General International Department
Bank of Japan

Isabel Strauss-Kahn
Head Market Operations Division
Banque de France

Flemming Würtz
Senior Economist, Directorate-General Market Operations
European Central Bank

Amy Yip
Executive Director Reserves Management Department
Hong Kong Monetary Authority

Preface

The rapid growth of foreign reserve holdings of central banks has raised considerable interest in the issue whether yield considerations should play a larger role in the investment of these reserves. Whereas traditionally liquidity has been the main objective in the choice of investment instruments as reserves needed to be readily deployable for intervention purposes, governments as shareholders of central banks have increasingly taken a keen interest in the returns on what are essentially public funds. Nowadays many central banks have set up separate investment portfolios where the asset mix is determined largely by return considerations. At the same time central banks as monetary institutions with primary responsibility for monetary policy face considerable limitations with respect to the optimization of portfolios. Therefore, some countries have gone a step further in setting up a separate investment fund for the management of national wealth.

The changed perspective on the trade-off between liquidity and return was the main motive for organizing a round-table on Trends in Central Bank Reserve Management at the Nederlandsche Bank in Amsterdam, October 2005, which brought together academics, financial market practitioners and central bankers from around the world, including some of the Asian countries which have experienced the most rapid growth of official reserves. Also key experts from international organizations, such as the Bank for International Settlements, the International Monetary Fund and the World Bank gave presentations. The various contributions and discussions at the round table proved to be of considerable interest as the topic had not been tackled before in such a diverse group of experts. The editors have selected participants to expand on their notes and prepare contributions under three headings: trends in the size of central bank reserves; central bank reserve management; and implications for central bank balance sheets.

The editors are grateful for the willingness of the authors to contribute to this volume and are thankful for their willingness to take editing comments on board with a view to making the volume suitable for a wider audience. The enthusiastic response underlines the growing preparedness on the part of central banks to be transparent about their reserve management practices. We would like to express our thanks also to Tijs de Bie, Han van der Hoorn, would like to express our thanks also to Tijs de Bie, Han van der Hoorn, Saskia Link-Broekzitter and Marja Kooijman from the Nederlandsche Bank for co-organizing the round table. Finally, our thanks go to Keejet Philippens-Stants who prepared the typescript and to Peter Keus for preparing the figures.

1. Central Bank Reserve Management: Trends and Issues

Age F.P. Bakker and Ingmar R.Y. van Herpt

1.1 INTRODUCTION

Reserve management at central banks has been a relatively under-researched area of the finance literature. Whereas there is an extensive research on optimal asset allocation, only a very limited part of this literature takes account of the specific monetary and institutional restrictions that central banks are faced with in the management of their foreign exchange reserves. Now seems an appropriate time to take a more in-depth look at the role of central banks as asset managers. Over the past decade central bank reserves have grown exponentially. Global reserves are today exceeding $4 trillion, having more than doubled since 2000 (see Figure 1.1). Much of these reserves are concentrated in Asian emerging markets and oil-exporting countries. This creates important challenges for the public institutions that are responsible for managing this accumulation of national wealth. Also, foreign assets held by central banks have grown to such an extent that changes in their investment behaviour are sometimes perceived having the potential to move market prices.

To a considerable extent the growth of foreign exchange reserves is associated with global imbalances. The accumulation of foreign exchange reserves is largely the by-product of policy choices regarding exchange rate regimes. Several countries in Asia have for some time resisted upward pressure on their nominal exchange rates vis-à-vis the US dollar by absorbing the inflow of foreign currency and investing the proceeds in predominantly US assets, but probably also increasingly in euro assets. In other countries, reserve accumulation has been the result of high current account surpluses stemming from a price boom in the markets for their primary export products, the most important one being crude oil.

Figure 1.1 Development of global central bank reserves

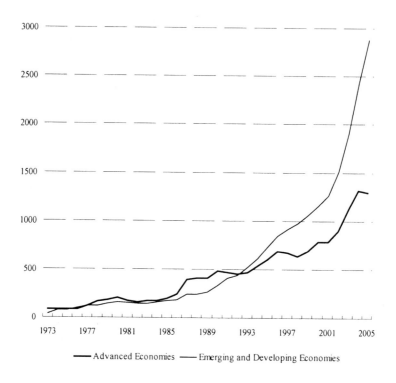

— Advanced Economies —— Emerging and Developing Economies

To some extent, the accumulation of reserves apparently is also motivated by the desire to build large buffers against financial contingencies, such as a crisis of confidence causing a sudden strong outflow of capital. More generally, the volatility in the funding costs for many emerging markets and their sensitivity to changes in the global interest rate environment may have triggered a need for foreign liquidity in excess of what used to be considered an adequate level based on traditional indicators such as reserves as a ratio of imports or of a domestic monetary aggregate. Earlier experiences, notably the Asian financial crisis of 1997–8 have reinforced this type of argument.

The steep rise of foreign reserves held by central banks has been an important contributing factor to the increased attention for reserve management at central banks, but it has not been the only factor. In general, the increased focus on transparency and accountability has also affected the central banking community and has raised pressure on central banks to get a decent return on what are essentially public funds. Of course, the increase in foreign exchange reserves has given added flexibility to focus more on returns as the need to keep them all in liquid assets has become less pressing.

Also, higher returns can compensate for the costs of carrying large foreign exchange reserves.

Central banks, being institutions performing a public policy task in which credibility is crucial, are relatively constrained in their risk tolerance, which limits their investment opportunities. However, within these constraints, there has been a gradual trend in which central banks have broadened the boundaries of their investment universe, for example by extending the duration of their fixed-income portfolios and moving gradually down the credit curve into non-government fixed income assets. Important connected issues are whether central banks, apart from changing their strategic asset allocation, should also aim at generating excess returns through active asset management and whether central banks should manage their reserves in-house or outsource part or all of the reserve management to external fund managers.

An often neglected aspect of thinking about asset management of central banks is related to the liabilities side of the balance sheet. The composition of liabilities of the central bank may have important implications for the asset allocation. Major components on the liability side of the central bank balance sheet are the outstanding banknotes as well as the deposits placed by commercial banks under reserve requirements. Also the financial buffer provided by capital and reserves determines the ability of central banks to absorb losses on assets and therefore is a major factor in the risk tolerance of central banks. An increasing number of central banks within the euro zone have engaged in ALM studies to get a better insight in their risks.

This chapter discusses some of the key themes emerging from the contributions to the book. The following section briefly considers the underlying causes of the tremendous reserve build up in emerging markets, including the academic debate on its sustainability. Section 1.3 captures the main trends that can be observed in the reserve management by central banks, including the gradual shift in the objectives of asset management from liquidity to return. Also the policy challenges faced by central banks aiming to be risk-return optimizers in a very special institutional environment are discussed. Section 1.4 analyses the asset management function in the context of the central bank balance sheet and the relation with the institutional setting in which the central bank operates, including the relationship with the shareholder, i.e. the government. The last section concludes.

1.2   RESERVE ACCUMULATION: SUSTAINABLE OR NOT?

In a number of oil-exporting countries, the accumulation of foreign exchange reserves reflects the proceeds of oil exports which have steeply increased together with the rise in oil prices. A striking example is Russia, where official foreign exchange reserves have increased from $24 billion in 2000 to $198 billion in March 2006. Still, the foreign reserves of these oil-exporters are dwarfed by the size of accumulated reserves in for example Japan, China, Taiwan and Korea. Their foreign exchange reserves now account for slightly more than half of world foreign reserves held by central banks.

There is a significant literature on the recent rise in foreign exchange reserves, and it is not the purpose of this chapter to assess this literature in depth. However, for the sake of better understanding the consequences for the management of reserves it is useful to have some insight into the causes of the steep rise in foreign reserves at central banks. The accumulation of foreign claims by central banks reflects global current account imbalances, with the US current account deficit being mirrored by surpluses in a number of Asian and oil-exporting countries (see Table 1.1). In some countries, like China, the impact on foreign reserves is exacerbated by strong capital inflows, some of which are speculative in nature. Although investment in emerging economies is running at a high pace, there is still a lack of domestic allocation opportunities for excess domestic savings. Therefore, these excess savings are invested abroad in the form of reserve accumulation by central banks in the absence of well developed domestic financial markets.

Table 1.1 Current account balances as percentage of world GDP

	1995	2000	2005
US	− 0.4	− 1.3	− 1.8
Euro area	0.2	− 0.1	0.0
Japan	0.4	0.4	0.4
Other advanced economies	0.0	0.2	0.3
Newly industrialized Asian economies	0.0	0.1	0.2
China	0.0	0.1	0.4
India	0.0	0.0	0.0
Latin America	− 0.1	− 0.2	0.1
Oil exporters	0.0	0.5	0.8

Sources: IMF, World Economic databases.

Exchange rate regimes play an important role in perpetuating this reserve accumulation. Most emerging Asian economies follow export-led growth policies, of which a fixed exchange rate to the US dollar is an important element. Maintaining the exchange rate peg requires interventions by the central bank in the foreign exchange markets, leading to an accumulation of foreign exchange, predominantly dollars. The recycling of funds back to the US, where these funds are invested, allows that country to maintain relatively low interest rates and high levels of consumption, providing a growing market for Asian exports. The result is manifest in large global current account imbalances.

In analysing this recycling mechanism, two main schools of thought can be distinguished, which differ as to its sustainability. According to the first school the status quo is sustainable, and is in some ways akin to the Bretton Woods system, which existed from 1945 until 1973. The reason for this is that both parties have a keen interest in keeping the system running; the US profits because it is allowed to structurally consume more than it produces, whereas the Asian emerging markets profit because the system enables them to continue their export-led strategy, generating economic growth and employment. As a welcome by-product of this policy, emerging Asia has been able to build a considerable financial buffer that is considered as a necessary contingency fund to withstand adverse shocks such as they experienced during the Asian financial crisis in 1997–8.

Opponents of this 'Bretton Woods II' view usually point to the deteriorating net international investment position of the US, which reached a record negative amount of $3.7 trillion, or around 30 per cent of GDP in 2005. As interest payments on this worsening position grow, the current account deficit increases ever further to clearly unsustainable levels. Most observers, including international institutions as the IMF, believe that some adjustment in current account imbalances will be needed in order to keep the system sustainable. Economic policies could be helpful in bringing a gradual adjustment about, such as policies to open up financial markets in Asia, whereas the US would need to trim its budget deficit and pursue policies that promote private saving. However, such an effort of coordinated economic policies would be rather unique and could not be hoped for, at least not in the short term. A more likely scenario would be that at some stage the accumulation of dollar assets reaches saturation point. This would trigger a dollar decline and probably higher US interest rates, which would help towards global current account adjustment.

In this volume Higgins (Chapter 7) discusses the measurement of US dollar reserve accumulation. US data may actually understate the pace of accumulation since they do not include official dollar deposits held offshore. However, substantial as this accumulation may be, when scaled against the global and US financial markets, Higgins argues that it is not immediately obvious that the cumulative inflows of foreign official capital into the US has a large impact on dollar asset prices or the exchange rate of the US dollar.

A related debate rages on the question whether exchange rate realignment could contribute to this global current account adjustment process. The argument that is mostly heard in this context is that the lack of flexibility of the Chinese exchange rate regime presents the main obstacle to global readjustment, as it keeps the Chinese renminbi undervalued, thus contributing to the US current account deficit. This argument has been exceedingly popular in circles of policy makers, not least within the US government. However, there are also dissenting voices. Persaud (Chapter 3) points at the limited role that the Chinese current account surplus plays as a counterpart to the US deficit. He pointedly recalls the experience of Japanese surpluses in the 1980s and 1990s, in which constant US pressure to revalue the yen contributed to the slowing of economic growth in Japan and the start of a deflationary spiral, while hardly contributing to trimming the trade imbalance with the US.

Alternatively, the theory of the 'savings glut', of which Fed chairman Bernanke has been one of the leading advocates, does not explain global imbalances as mainly the result of policy choices but rather sees them as the by-product of an imbalance in investment opportunities, which has resulted in excess savings from Europe and Asia being exported to the US. As economic growth picks up in Asia and Europe, this would redirect savings away from the US in a process that by all means is expected to be gradual and smooth.

As the accumulation of foreign exchange reserves continues in the meantime, it has increasingly put into question the relevance of traditional indicators for reserve adequacy. Among these indicators are the level of reserves in terms of number of months of imports, the ratio between reserves and short-term external debt, and the ratio between reserves and the monetary base. Many foreign reserve portfolios at central banks have by now far exceeded some if not all of these conventional measures of reserve adequacy. This may indicate that in some cases the level of reserves is suboptimal and may become a source of rather than a protection against financial instability. In particular, central banks have occasionally found it difficult to cope with the domestic monetary implications of a large-scale absorption of foreign currency inflows. The typical policy reaction by central banks has been to stem the growth of domestic money resulting from the foreign exchange accumulation by selling or issuing securities but, as the case of China indicates, this may be only partly successful. These sterilization policies may also involve considerable cost, depending on the spread between domestic interest rates and the return earned on foreign assets. However, this need not always be the case: Sogano shows in Chapter 5 that in Japan the foreign reserves holdings, which are largely invested in US Treasury securities, earn a positive net return due to the extremely low domestic interest rates. Apart from the costs of sterilization there are two other drawbacks connected with large reserve accumulation. First, if eventually the exchange rate has to appreciate, very substantial losses on US dollar holdings may occur. Depending on the institutional arrangements for absorbing these losses, this may have negative consequences for the financial position of the central bank and may lead to fiscal losses. Second, large reserve buffers may be a 'curse in disguise' because they may temporarily insulate the country involved from market discipline and thus may allow bad economic policies to be pursued longer than would normally have been the case. When finally the adjustment has become inevitable the negative output shock may be just the larger.

In this book several attempts are made to bring the thinking about reserve adequacy a step further, building on recent experience and making use of marginal cost and benefit analysis. Yet, as McCauley argues in Chapter 2, it remains difficult to explain the recent reserve accumulation in terms of these classical economic concepts, all the more as foreign reserves often seem to be the by-product of other macro-economic policies rather than the outcome of a conscious optimization process. An interesting exception to this observation is provided by the Central Bank of Chile, where a reserve optimization exercise was done, using estimates for both marginal costs and benefits of holding reserves. As Jadresic describes in Chapter 4, this has led to the decision to actually reduce the level of foreign reserves.

1.3 TRENDS IN CENTRAL BANK RESERVE MANAGEMENT

The role of the asset management function at a typical central bank has traditionally been to invest the foreign exchange reserves in a portfolio of highly liquid assets that is exposed to as little market and credit risk as possible. The main rationale behind this investment policy is that foreign reserves represent a contingency buffer to support an exchange rate policy, to be able to service foreign currency debt or, in a currency board, to cover the monetary base. In this philosophy, foreign currency assets need to preserve their value, even in the short term, and must be held in instruments that can be liquidated quickly and against minimal prize concessions. These safety and liquidity criteria have been typically translated into portfolios consisting of high quality government bonds with a maturity of less than one year.

Over the past few years this classical image of central bank reserve management has started to show some cracks, which can be attributed to several factors. The first one, as already mentioned in the previous paragraph, has been the accumulation of reserves to unprecedented levels in central banks predominantly located in Asia and in oil-exporting countries. As the size of foreign reserves grows larger, the likelihood that they are all to be needed for financial contingencies decreases. The traditional consideration of keeping reserves in liquid form in order to stand ready for interventions has waned somewhat into the background. This creates opportunities to invest at least part of the reserves in less liquid and safe assets and earn a premium by assuming more liquidity, market and credit risk.

Secondly, the creation of the single currency in Europe not only profoundly changed the balance sheets of participating central banks but also changed the rationale for holding reserves. Whereas in the ERM, there was a clear need for liquid foreign reserves in order to be able to defend the fixed exchange rate if necessary, with the disappearance of the national currencies the need for liquid reserves to back up the exchange rate policy moved to the background. Also, the division of responsibilities within the Eurosystem triggered a rethinking of the role of reserves within the National Central Banks (NCBs). As the ECB, with the reserves that were transferred to it at the start of EMU, takes primary responsibility for possible foreign exchange interventions, the NCB's reserves can be seen as a second line of defence, with only a limited chance of being called upon. As Hakkaraïnen and Pösö put it (Chapter 12), EMU has perhaps not reduced the level of macroeconomic risk, but it has expanded the range of tools to manage this risk mainly because the European institutional framework has taken over part of this burden. This has lessened the need for NCBs to invest all of their reserves in assets of the highest quality and liquidity categories. As a by-product of the conversion of the national currencies into the euro, a substantial part of what used to be foreign reserve portfolios (mainly Deutschemarks) now consists of domestic currency assets. This has obviously changed the nature of these assets, which have again moved considerations of liquidity and safety somewhat to the background.

A third trend that has affected the thinking about reserve management has been the increased demand for transparency and accountability of central banks, both by the shareholder and the public at large. Mounting pressures on government budgets and the low yield environment worldwide provided incentives for some central banks to look more critically at the underlying objectives of their foreign reserve holdings and the implications for asset management. An illustrative case is provided by Yip (Chapter 9) who described how in 2000 the Hong Kong government ran into a fiscal deficit situation and the Hong Kong Monetary Authority (HKMA) came under increasing pressure from the Treasury as well as from public opinion to generate a return to help cope with the fiscal deficit. In general, it has made many central bank boards more conscious of the returns that are earned on foreign reserve assets and the opportunity costs of investing only in the safest and most liquid assets. Of course, the steep rise in the size of foreign exchange reserves has reinforced this trend. As reserves grow, the pressure on the central bank to exert prudent stewardship over what is essentially a national store of wealth increases. Finally, the sterilization operations to counter the monetary effects of foreign reserve growth may have made central banks more conscious of the cost of carrying reserves, especially when this cost exceeds the return earned on these reserves.

At the same time, being public institutions performing a public policy task in which credibility is crucial and the loss of reputation potentially devastating to their effectiveness, central banks are more constrained in their investment opportunities than their private sector counterparties. There are other specific factors at play: central bank shareholders (i.e. governments) display a relatively low tolerance for losses and the arrangements with the government on profit transfers often provide central banks with very little freedom when it comes to dividend policy. This limits the options for compensating losses in one year by retaining profits in the next year.

Obviously, the extent to which central banks have been susceptible to the factors just described varies considerably, depending on specific circumstances. Nevertheless, some trends can be observed, although most of them have been confined to only a part of the central banking community.

First, central banks have been looking at ways to expand their universe of possible investments to earn higher returns with only minimal concessions to liquidity and safety. The most obvious way in which this is done is by performing a portfolio optimization exercise, which points at opportunities for improving the risk–return trade-off through diversification. Johnson-Calari, Grava and Kobor in Chapter 8 convincingly show that starting from a short duration government portfolio the risk–return trade-off can be dramatically improved when duration and credit risk constraints on the strategic asset allocation are relaxed. Second, a critical assessment of the objective of foreign reserves has in some cases led to the split of these reserves into two kinds of portfolios with different purposes. The liquidity, or intervention portfolio, whose purpose is to function as a classical contingency buffer, meets the highest standards of safety and liquidity and typically consists of high quality government bonds with a short maturity. The investment portfolio, which reflects a store of national wealth rather than a contingency buffer, universally bears the characteristics of a long-term investment portfolio, relaxing the constraints on market, credit and liquidity risk. The central banks of Korea, Russia, India and the Hong Kong Monetary Authority are known to adopt such a dual approach. As Choo describes in Chapter 6, the Bank of Korea has classified its reserves into three tranches, setting up a new 'long-term investment tranche' in addition to the already existing liquidity and investment tranches. Some countries have gone a step further by setting up an independent reserves management agency outside the central bank with an explicit mandate to manage part of the national wealth on a more long-term horizon and within a more relaxed set of investment constraints. Singapore has been a long-lasting example with the establishment already in 1981 of the Government Investment Corporation (GIC); recently Korea has launched a similar agency, the Korea Investment Corporation (KIC), to which a small part of its foreign currency reserves have been allocated. Also Norway has set up a separate investment fund, to invest the proceeds from oil exports. This Government Pension Fund, the successor of the former Petroleum Fund, is invested in a wide range of foreign financial instruments, including bonds, equities, money market instruments, derivatives and emerging market assets.

The increased attention to returns has first of all translated into extending the duration of fixed income portfolios to capture more interest rate risk. Also, many central banks have expanded their range of investable assets, by moving down the credit curve and investing in less liquid assets. For example, in the RBS Reserve Management Trends Survey 2006 which covers exclusively central banks, one-third of respondents indicated that they are currently invested in A-rated bonds, whereas one-quarter invested in ABS, and one-quarter invested in MBS (Pringle and Carver, 2006). Some central banks also invest in corporate bonds and equities.

Moreover, central banks in general have upgraded their risk management techniques, becoming more conscious of the overall risks in their balance sheet and the allocation of risk across various asset classes. Central bank boards have become more involved in taking strategic asset allocation decisions in annual benchmark exercises. Also, many central banks have over the past few years devoted more resources to reserve management and upgraded IT systems to support their asset management.

Deciding to extend the range of possible investable assets has involved the question of whether or not to outsource the management of these relatively new and unknown asset classes to an external manager. Important considerations for outsourcing have been the lack of expertise within the central bank concerning the particular asset class or market or the fact that the building-up of expertise itself can be prohibitive in terms of the cost and time involved. For this reason, central banks often outsource their MBS portfolios to specialized managers, because they do not feel comfortable dealing with the complexity related to the embedded optionality in these instruments. A second reason may be efficiency: for a central bank that seeks exposure to the equity market it may be more cost-efficient to outsource this exposure to a large passive index manager than to set up the portfolio management function itself. A third reason may be that pursuing an active portfolio management strategy may be seen as potentially conflicting with other responsibilities of the central bank, such as setting interest rates. However, this has to be weighed against the implied cost of outside management.

Indeed, a major issue that central banks face in reserve management is whether they should passively manage their portfolio once the strategic asset allocation has been decided or whether they should seek to earn an excess return by actively managing their portfolio. In the finance literature the passive management is associated with *beta*, which is the return received on exposure to the market portfolio, whereas *alpha* is the return earned by active management and thus outperforming the market portfolio. Opinions differ widely on the pros and cons of active management. Advocates of *alpha* would argue that being more conscious of return should also involve actively managing the portfolio within certain risk constraints. In fact, many central banks, while being very conservative when it comes to determining their strategic asset allocation at least until recently, have pursued active management strategies for quite a long time.

Opponents typically argue that active management is a relatively costly strategy because it involves setting up a department of well trained portfolio managers, and additional risk management expertise, including expertise on operational risk, or mandating an external manager involving an expensive fee structure. Within this line of reasoning, central banks are well advised to look at ways to improve the total return on their assets by improving the risk–return characteristics of their strategic asset allocation rather than to aim at outperforming an overly conservative benchmark. Also, ultimately alpha is a zero sum game; with foreign exchange reserves held by central banks now exceeding US$ 4 trillion, this becomes an issue. According to Kotz and Strauss-Kahn (Chapter 16), as to the question whether it is possible to generate consistently above-average returns, empirical research provides sobering results. However, central banks may want to engage in active management for other reasons than seeking excess returns. Being an active market player may facilitate the access to market intelligence that central banks need for exercising their responsibility to safeguard financial stability. In practice, especially in the case of central banks pursuing a financial stability mandate, this argument is a forceful one. It may also partly explain what Litterman in Chapter 15 calls the active risk puzzle, at least when central banks are concerned: if central banks are confident that they can outperform the market they should take much more active risk than they do now; alternatively, if one recognizes that alpha is a zero sum game and that there are inefficiencies and transaction costs to carry, so that the average investor will underperform, then one should not take active risk at all.

The increased consciousness of central banks towards risk–return considerations has triggered more attention to the issue of currency composition. It is difficult to gather a complete picture, as central banks, especially those in emerging market economies, usually do not disclose adequate information on the currency composition of their reserves. Although the IMF periodically constructs and publishes estimates of the currency composition of reserve holdings, a large and growing part of reserves is registered as invested in unspecified currencies. Based on these, albeit incomplete, figures it arises that the US dollar still accounts for more than two-thirds of total central bank foreign reserve holdings (see Table 1.2). However, with the accumulation of central bank reserves the threat of prospective changes in currency composition has become a market-sensitive issue: over the past two years public statements by central bank officials that hint at possible currency diversification away from the US dollar have occasionally led to significant, albeit not long-lasting, exchange rate volatility.

This raises the question what criteria determine the currency composition of central bank reserves? First, in the case of a fixed exchange rate, when the domestic currency is pegged to one currency or a basket of currencies and the foreign reserves act purely as an intervention portfolio to defend the currency peg, one would typically expect the nature of the exchange rate peg to be reflected in the currency composition of central bank reserves. However, as the size of reserves grows beyond what should reasonably be available for intervention purposes, this argument becomes less forceful, and other considerations, such as diversification, become more important. Second, if foreign central bank reserves are seen as a contingency buffer to cover the external liabilities of the economy, then the currency composition of reserves should primarily reflect the currency composition of the external debt. Emphasizing developing countries with large external debt, Sharma argues in Chapter 10 that the currency allocation of reserves should closely mirror the currency denomination of external debt. Finally, liquidity considerations can also affect the optimal currency allocation, especially for central banks with sizable reserves, because only markets for financial assets denominated in the major currencies are sufficiently deep and liquid to meet their criteria.

As foreign reserves rise and as they are domestically financed, either by an expanding monetary base, or through the issuance of domestic central bank securities or an increase in treasury balances, currency risks increase. A simple risk budgeting exercise based on VaR calculations typically shows that currency risk easily outweighs all other quantifiable risk in the central bank balance sheet. As currency risk increases, the issue of whether to manage, and possibly mitigate, this risk becomes more pertinent. Here again, central banks are particularly constrained.

The classical view has been that holding foreign currency reserves on its balance sheet is one of the key responsibilities of the central bank, and currency risk is an inevitable by-product of this responsibility that is subordinated to more overriding macro-policy objectives, such as maintaining price stability and/or a competitive exchange rate.

Table 1.2 Share of national currencies in total identified official holdings of foreign exchange

	2003	2004
All countries		
US dollar	65.8	65.9
Japanese yen	4.1	39
Pound sterling	2.6	3.3
Swiss franc	0.2	0.2
Euro	25.3	24.9
Industrial countries		
US dollar	70.5	71.5
Japanese yen	3.8	3.6
Pound sterling	1.5	1.9
Swiss franc	0.2	0.1
Euro	22.1	20.9
Developing countries		
US dollar	60.7	59.9
Japanese yen	4.4	4.3
Pound sterling	3.9	4.8
Swiss franc	0.2	0.2
Euro	28.9	29.2
Unallocated reserves[1]		
All countries	29.8	32.6
Industrial countries	0.2	0.3
Developing countries	47.2	50.2

1 Foreign exchange reserves whose currency composition is not submitted to the IMF, in percentage of total official holdings of reserves.

Source: IMF, Annual Report 2005, Appendix I, Table 1.2.

This still seems to be the predominant view, also among central banks with very large foreign reserves. However, there are exceptions. The Bank of Canada is an example of a central bank where foreign assets are fully funded by foreign-currency liabilities. According to Howard (Chapter 11) a framework of well-defined asset and liability matching minimizes both interest rate and currency risk incurred by the Bank of Canada. Another example is provided by De Nederlandsche Bank, which has fully hedged the currency exposure on its US dollar portfolio by means of forward transactions. However, these approaches are not universally applicable. Foreign currency funding may be very costly in countries with a low credit rating, resulting in a substantial negative spread on carrying foreign reserves. As the size of reserves increases, both issuing paper in foreign currency and selling foreign currency in the forward market may counteract the exchange rate policy, as in both cases the supply and demand dynamics in the foreign exchange cash market are affected putting upward pressure on the domestic currency. As Fels rightly argues (Chapter 13) a separate target for the level of dollar reserves would conflict with the exchange rate target.Therefore, those central banks that carry large reserves and that have become more sensitive to currency risk are likely to pursue an approach of gradual currency diversification.

1.4 IMPLICATIONS FOR THE CENTRAL BANK BALANCE SHEET

Appropriate capitalization or a sufficient level of financial buffers is of relevance for the reserve management function of the central bank, because a lack of financial autonomy may lead the central bank to engage in overly conservative, and hence suboptimal, investment policies. In addressing this issue, not only the amount of risk is important; the institutional setting in which the central bank operates may also be of considerable importance. As Papadia and Würtz show in Chapter 17, central bank balance sheets come in very different shapes and sizes and there is not a clear relationship with the effectiveness of the central bank. What counts in the end for a central bank in order to perform its policy functions effectively, is that it has a sufficient degree of financial autonomy so that it can pursue its policy objectives without being constrained by balance sheet or profit and loss statement concerns. Central banks are special institutions because the prospect of future seignorage income based on their monopoly to issue banknotes allows them to operate even with negative capital. Periods of undercapitalization may not pose severe problems for the functioning of the central bank, depending on the source of undercapitalization and provided there is a clear plan for remedying the situation. For example, Niedermayer argues in Chapter 14 that the negative capital at the Czech National Bank is exclusively the result of the appreciation of the Czech koruna, which has been a beneficial development from a macroeconomic viewpoint. Because of this, the lack of capital has not hampered the credibility and effectiveness of the CNB in conducting its policy tasks.

The degree to which sufficient capital may play a role in establishing financial autonomy depends on its relationship with the government and how this relationship is reflected in the arrangements for financing central bank operating expenditure and for sharing risks. It is also depends on the rules for the distribution of profits and losses that may over time affect the accumulation of capital. Typically, profit remittance arrangements are of an asymmetric nature in which losses have to be borne by the central bank. Financial independence of central banks can be substantially strengthened by agreeing on symmetric profit distribution rules which could allow central banks to retain earnings in order to recoup earlier losses.

The spectrum of possible institutional settings in which a central bank operates can be seen as limited by two extreme end-points – one in which the central bank is a pure agent of the government and another where the central bank as the principal has complete discretion over how it acts and is responsible for the losses it incurs. A key difference between the two models, which can be called the agent model and the principal, or corporate, model, is the extent to which a central bank bears the risks associated with its activities on its own balance sheet. In the agency model, the central bank acts as an agent for the government and may require very little capital either because the main risks associated with its activities are borne by the government or because its mandate is narrow and hence its operating costs are low. In the principal or corporate model, the central bank has a clear mandate that requires it to assume certain risks in the conduct of its operations through its own balance sheet. In this case, the central bank may need a fairly large capital base to support its activities and absorb potential future losses.

The preservation of capital over time not only depends on the risk profile of the central bank but is also influenced by accounting standards and the profit distribution rules agreed with the government. Bakker (Chapter 18) shows that the adoption of fair value accounting, without a simultaneous adjustment in profit distribution arrangements, may result in an asymmetric situation in which unrealized valuation gains are transferred to the government whereas losses have to be absorbed by the capital stock of the central bank. This will lead to an erosion of central bank capital over time. It may also create incentives for central banks to limit the volatility in their reported profits under fair value based accounting standards, by pursuing overly conservative investment strategies, where the investment horizon is governed by the financial reporting cycle. This would provide an obstacle to more rational reserve management strategies, aimed at generating adequate returns over a long-term horizon.

A possible solution that some central banks adopt is to use fair value accounting standards for their assets and liabilities but to exclude unrealized valuation gains or losses from appearing in the profit and loss account. However, Ferhani argues in Chapter 19 that for the sake of transparency it would be better if full recognition of gains and losses, both realized and unrealized, would be supported by proper income distribution arrangements with the government, in which the preservation of central bank capital over a multi-year horizon takes centre-stage. However, this may require education of the shareholder, in terms of explaining the investment strategy and the risks involved in pursuing such a multi-year strategy.

1.5   CONCLUSION

Whatever their precise causes, the enormous accumulation of central bank foreign exchange reserves over the past years has substantially raised the likelihood that a considerable part of these reserves are here to stay for quite some time. This reserve accumulation, together with the increased demand for transparency and accountability, and the decline in global bond yields, has made central banks more conscious of their responsibility to earn a decent return on what are essentially public funds. Central banks have reacted in various ways, depending on the size and purpose of their reserves, but nevertheless a gradual trend towards more rational investment strategies can be observed. A typical feature of this trend is the broadening of the universe of possible investment instruments, with central banks extending the duration of their fixed income portfolios and relaxing constraints on credit risk. In several cases, the organizational structure of the reserve management function has been changed, involving a split between a liquid intervention portfolio and a long-term investment portfolio, or transferring part of the reserve management to a completely new agency. With the increasing size of reserves and the rationalization of the reserve management, the risk awareness of central banks has increased as well. Risk budgeting sometimes even leads to a reduction of exchange rate risk by diversifying the currency composition or by hedging exchange rate risk, but here the institutional constraints for central banks are still viewed as particularly strong. More rational investment policies may lead to higher volatility in the profit and loss account under fair value accounting. Depending on the institutional setting in which the central bank operates, this may heighten the need to revise the profit distribution arrangements with the government in order to preserve the financial autonomy of the central bank in the long term.

PART ONE

The Size of Central Bank Reserves

2. Assessing the Benefits and Costs of Official Foreign Exchange Reserves

Robert N. McCauley

2.1 INTRODUCTION

The growth of official foreign exchange reserves in Asia has led many to the view that the costs of holding such reserves must now exceed the benefits. Yet it remains very difficult to conceive of the benefits and costs with any clarity and no less difficult to measure them with any accuracy. This is particularly the case insofar as foreign exchange reserves to many eyes represent a by-product of other policies rather than a separate outcome of some optimization process that weighs benefits and costs. On this view it becomes hard to know where to stop the analysis of benefits and costs.

This chapter attempts to bring some order to this subject without pretending to settle many of the issues. A general result is that the costs, and therefore the welfare, associated with official foreign exchange reserves need to be assessed in relation to the mode of financing. A more specific result is that borrowed reserves are inexpensive to credit-worthy sovereigns. It would seem to follow that their benefits could be quite marginal while still leaving a balance of increased welfare. Another result is that the carrying ('quasi-fiscal') costs of reserve holdings appear generally low in the large reserve holding economies in East Asia.

The balance of this chapter is organized as follows. First, benefits of reserve holdings are discussed. Secondly, costs are discussed. These have been conceived as a net intermediation margin in foreign currency, as a quasi-fiscal cost in the case of foreign exchange reserves financed with domestic currency debt, or as foregone domestic investment. In addition, one can conceive of another cost arising from having risk-averse officials manage foreign assets on behalf of the economy. Different notions of cost are then associated with different cases of reserve management as defined by the financing of reserves. The penultimate section discusses the balancing of benefits and costs. The last section summarizes the proposed associations.

2.2   BENEFITS OF OFFICIAL FOREIGN EXCHANGE RESERVES

In the wake of the Asian financial crisis of 1997–8, it became common to conceive of the benefit of holding sufficient official foreign exchange reserves as one of making less likely a crisis that can lead to a deep recession. A rapid withdrawal of cross-border investment, the reasoning went, could lead to a fall in the value of the domestic currency, a sharp hike in interest rates, or both. These in turn can lead to widespread corporate distress, nonperforming bank loans, layoffs, personal insolvency and recession.

In recent academic treatments, the rapid withdrawal of cross-border investment is known as a 'sudden stop' (Calvo (1998, 2000), Edwards (2004)). This, however, seems an altogether too genteel term for the phenomenon. For instance, BIS banking statistics show a $16 billion decline in international bank claims on Korea in the first quarter of 1998, which scaled to the US economy's GDP would be equivalent to something like a $300 billion withdrawal of bank credit in a quarter. Kindleberger's metaphor of a cracking whip seems more apt.

Such a rapid withdrawal of credit can cost a significant share of output. This has been modelled as resulting from the adjustment cost of liquidating an investment to raise funds before the investment matures (Aizenman and Lee (2005)). In any case, contractions of GDP in the order of 5 per cent were characteristic of the Asian crisis. Holding relatively high levels of official foreign exchange reserves is thus seen as providing a form of self-insurance against the risk to stability and output of a rapid withdrawal of international credit[1].

Against this view, some argue that the hazard of a rapid withdrawal of cross-border investment is not a random event like a typhoon but rather something that becomes likely after a bout of imprudently rapid credit growth and associated misalignment of asset prices. Moreover, the cost of a depreciation of the domestic currency is likely to be higher when firms have borrowed heavily in foreign exchange. Better to craft policies to ensure financial stability and to let exchange rate flexibility discipline foreign currency borrowing than to accumulate foreign exchange reserves, some would say. This perspective can draw support from the highly non-linear relationship between sovereign credit ratings and scaled levels of foreign exchange reserve holdings. The countries thought most credit-worthy do not have such large foreign exchange reserves as those thought to be of middling quality.

An intermediate position is that it takes time to build up the institutions that make an economy more resilient in the face of external liquidity shifts. In the meantime, ample international liquidity has its benefits.

Following Soto, et al (2004) and Garcia and Soto (2006), these benefits can be quantified in a rough manner. These authors build on empirically estimated early warning systems that find that higher levels of official reserves, usually scaled in relation to short-term debt, are associated with a lower probability of a crisis (Berg and Patrillo (1989), Bussière and Mulder (1999), Goldstein, et al (2000) and Berg et al (2003)). This is not surprising given the performance of measures like the 'quick' ratio of short-term assets to short-term liabilities in corporate distress models. Soto et al (2004) use previous results (Table 2.1) while Garcia and Soto estimate their own, using a wide variety of economic and political control variables.

Table 2.1   Estimates of the effect of official reserve holdings on the probability of crisis

Study	Sample	Crisis indicator	Liquidity indicator	Data used	$1 billion reserve change: effect on crisis probability
Radelet and Sachs (1998), probit	22 emerging markets, 1994–7	Rapid change in capital flow	Short-term debt/ reserves	Chilean data	40 bp (from 7%)
Bussière and Fratzscher (2002), logit	20 emerging markets, 1993–2001	Combined exchange rate, interest rate and reserve change	Short-term debt/ reserves	Chilean data	10 bp (from 6.5%)
Milesi-Ferretti and Razin (1998), probit	105 emerging markets, 1973–94	Exchange rate depreciation over 15%	Reserves/M2	Sample average	51 bp
Berg and Patillo (1999), probit	100 emerging markets, 1970–96	Exchange rate depreciation over 25%	Reserves/M2	Sample average	69 bp
Kamin and Babson (1999), probit	Argentina, Brazil, Chile, Colombia, Mexico and Venezuela, 1980–98	Combined exchange rate, interest rate and reserve change	Reserves/ short-term debt	Sample average	9 bp

Source: Soto, et al. (2004), Table 10, as adapted by author.

consistent estimates of the contribution of higher foreign exchange reserves in relation to short-term debt (as measured by the BIS consolidated international banking data) to reducing the likelihood of crisis using data for 1975–2003. Then, using plausible assumptions about the cost of a crisis in terms of foregone GDP, they measure the benefits of reserves in terms of expected GDP.

In Chapter 4, Esteban Jadresic presents a stylized application of this approach[2]. A decline in reserve holdings of $1 billion would lower Chile's 2002 ratio of reserves to short-term debt from 1.38 to 1.29 (Soto, et al (2004), page 17). This would raise the estimated probability of crisis by 20 basis points, or one-fifth of 1 per cent. A crisis amounting to 5 per cent of Chile's $80 billion GDP would cost $4 billion. Thus the calculated expected loss of running with $1 billion less in reserves would be $8 million. As noted below, this is close to, but below, the calculated cost of holding the $1 billion.

How does one assess the cost of reserves? It turns out that there are various notions of the cost and that their appropriateness varies with the source of the funding for reserves.

2.3   COSTS OF OFFICIAL FOREIGN EXCHANGE RESERVES

There are three commonly cited but different notions of the cost of holding official foreign exchange reserves and these apply differently according to how a country finances its reserves. This section distinguishes the three notions of cost, which are often confused in discussion of this topic, and adds a new notion. Then the three cases of the financing of reserves are distinguished: those that are borrowed in international currency; those that are financed in domestic currency; and those that represent fiscal surpluses. The burden of the argument is that different notions of cost are appropriate to the three cases.

Notions of the cost of reserves

At least three notions of the cost of reserves can be found in different analyses of the benefits and costs of reserves. Something like the credit spread is to be found in Lee (2005); the gap between domestic and foreign interest rates is to be found in Edison (2003); and the difference between the domestic marginal product of capital and the international risk-free rate is to be found in Aizenman and Lee (2005). Sometimes, as in Aizenman and Marion (2003), the three notions can be found in a single treatment with little guide for the reader as to their mutual consistency or various application. Hauner (2005) is a rare exception in attempting to take all three common notions into account.

A credit spread

In most respects the simplest notion of the cost of reserves is a credit spread. This might be termed instead an intermediation margin, but the latter term suggests that the cost is nonnegative. Often, but not necessarily, associated with a credit spread is a term spread, that is, the premium in the cost of fixed-rate borrowing over the return on short-term deposits. Under modern financial conditions, such a duration difference need not result from the liquidity or maturity difference between medium-term international borrowing by a country and its short-term placement, so a term spread should be considered as secondary and contingent relative to the credit spread.

Old discussion of currency board arrangements raised the issue of the credit spread. Critics of these arrangements alleged that they transferred resources from the colonies to the metropolitan economy, since trade surpluses were necessary to accumulate the sterling or French francs necessary to back the colonial currency. Against this, it was argued that even 19th Century financial markets allowed the colony to borrow in London or Paris. Thus the growth of the colony's money supply could be accommodated with a grossing up of the colony's balance sheet, that is, by international borrowing and depositing, rather than a one-sided accumulation of international assets through the trade surplus. This left open the question of the cost of such grossing up. One of the important achievements of DeCecco's 'Money and Empire' was to demonstrate that the spread paid by the likes of India to the City of London was very wide indeed – some 5 per cent. Under the more competitive circumstances of today's international financial markets and given the much greater possibility of managing duration and maturity separately, this wide a spread would apply only to the less credit-worthy among the significant holders of official foreign exchange reserves.

'Quasi-fiscal' cost

A very different notion of the cost of reserves is known as their 'quasi-fiscal cost'. This refers to the difference between the yield paid on a country's reserves and the domestic cost of borrowing. This might also be termed the carrying cost or running cost of reserve holding. It need not be a cost: the Japanese authorities enjoy a positive carry approximately equal to the yield on their foreign reserve holdings.

The measure involves several choices. One is the base of the calculation: the accumulated intervention over a given period (a flow), or foreign exchange reserves over a certain threshold ('excess reserves', a stock) or total reserves (also a stock). Another is the care taken with regard to the instruments used to sterilize in the domestic market and the instruments purchased on the foreign reserve management side. This latter aspect is important because of the tendency of Asian central banks to employ relatively short-term sterilization instruments while investing in increasingly long-term foreign assets.

Higgins and Klitgaard (2004) have recently drawn attention to the risk of exchange rate losses on reserve holdings, which is not included in the flow measure of 'quasi-fiscal' cost[3]. Of course, one of the major theorems of international finance is that an interest rate premium, over a long horizon, is matched by exchange valuation losses, suggesting that quasi-fiscal costs (benefits) would be matched by valuation gains (losses) on reserve holdings. (Even if this is true, if reserve holders tend to be of lower credit quality than reserve investments, then there may be a net credit spread akin to that described in the previous section.) Much empirical work leaves this theorem suspect. In particular, it has been argued that there are systematically excess returns on higher-yielding currencies (Remolona and Schrijvers (2003)).

The marginal product of capital less the international yield

The widest measure of the cost of reserves is likely to be the gap between the domestic marginal product of capital and the international yield. Two presumptions attached to this notion of the cost of reserves give it the flavour of an equity premium that varies inversely with the level of development. First, emerging market economies are presumed to have lower ratios of capital to labour and hence higher marginal products of capital than industrialized countries. Second, the relevant international yield is taken to be a risk-free rate. As a result, the cost of reserves on this measure is thought to be higher the less developed is the economy.

The cost of official management of national assets

Genberg et al (2005) have suggested another notion of the cost of reserves that emphasizes the difference between the official management of foreign assets and private management of foreign assets. This measure draws on the evident difference in portfolio management of private versus official fund managers. Just as Rogoff has argued that central bankers are selected for a 'conservative' set of preferences vis-à-vis the tradeoff between inflation and other possible goals of monetary policy, so too one can see central bankers as selected for their risk aversion in investing foreign assets. Certainly, the security portfolio of official reserve managers in the United States shows a strong preference for safe securities in the form of Treasury and agency paper, while that of private asset managers shows a strong preference for equities and corporate bonds (see Table 2.2).

Thus, if the counterfactual for official reserve accumulation is increased holdings of foreign assets in private hands in the same country, then it follows that a cost of official management of national assets is the lower returns that can be expected on safer securities. Of course, the difference between official and private risk aversion is not a long-term given. Certain funds for the future in commodity-exporting countries, including that of Norway, and even the Government Investment Corporation in resource-poor Singapore, have a well developed propensity to buy riskier assets.

Table 2.2   Foreign holdings of long-term debt and equity in the United States by official and private investors, as of June 2003

	Official holdings		Private holdings		Total
	Billion dollars	Percent of official	Billion dollars	Percent of private	
US Treasury securities	653	68.1	463	13.1	1116
As % of market	*26.6*		*18.9*		*45.5*
Agency securities	180	18.8	406	11.5	586
As % of market	*3.5*		*7.8*		*11.3*
Corporate bonds	21	2.2	1215	34.3	1236
As % of market	*0.3*		*15.4*		*15.7*
Equities	105	10.9	1459	41.2	1564
As % of market	*0.6*		*8.1*		*8.7*
Total	959	100.0	3544	100.0	4503
As % of market	*2.9*		*10.6*		*13.5*

Source: US Treasury et al (2004).

The three different modes of financing reserves

There are three cases of countries depending on the source of the financing of reserves. Most reserves should be thought of as borrowed, with domestic borrowing seemingly more frequent than international borrowing. But there is also the case of unborrowed reserves that correspond to an accumulation of fiscal surpluses.

Looking across Asia and the Pacific, most reserve financing seems to take the form of domestic borrowing or liabilities (see Table 2.3). Where reserves are below a central bank's note issue, as in Australia, the financing can be taken to be cash. Even so, if the reserves were lower, the central bank would have to hold more domestic assets, however. Thus, the opportunity cost of the foreign exchange reserves is lower holdings of interest-bearing domestic assets. Elsewhere, reserves tend to exceed the monetary base and the marginal financing is done with interest-bearing public debt.

Two exceptions are New Zealand and the Philippines, where reserves are mostly financed with foreign currency borrowing. The obligor is the Treasury in the former case and both the Treasury and the Bangko Sentral in the latter case. Another exception among monetary authorities is Hong Kong, where only a small fraction of reserves are financed with Exchange Fund bills and notes, that is, with domestic currency borrowing. The balance represents the claim of the government, accumulated through general surpluses and unspent, earmarked land sales revenues (fiscal) and the accumulated undistributed surplus of the Exchange Fund itself (quasi-fiscal).

Table 2.3 Means of financing of foreign exchange reserves

Foreign currency borrowing	Domestic currency borrowing or liabilities	Fiscal or quasi-fiscal surpluses
New Zealand	Australia	Hong Kong
Philippines	China	Singapore (GIC)
	India	
	Japan	
	Korea	
	Malaysia	
	Singapore (MAS)	
	Taiwan, China	
	Thailand	

Some countries obtain the foreign exchange corresponding to reserve holdings by borrowing in the international capital market. In East Asia and the Pacific, New Zealand represents an almost pure case of foreign exchange reserves financed with foreign currency debt. In operation, the government's debt office sells debt denominated in foreign currency and passes through the liability to the Reserve Bank of New Zealand (RBNZ). It in turn manages the foreign currency assets with a view to minimizing the cost of holding the reserves. The Philippines raises a substantial share of its reserves through foreign borrowing, both by the Republic and the Bangko Sentral ng Pilipinas. For these economies, one can say that the cost of reserves is the credit spread paid. This turns out to be near zero for a sovereign deemed highly credit-worthy like New Zealand, but quite costly for the Philippines[4].

New Zealand

The RBNZ usefully publishes the net cost of its reserve management (see Table 2.4). Operating income measures the difference between the income received by the RBNZ on the reserves and payments to the Treasury to cover its cost of borrowing the reserves.

Table 2.4 Cost of New Zealand's reserve holdings (NZ$ millions)

	Reserve management				
Year	Operating income	Operating expenses[1]	Operating deficit	*Memo: Foreign currency financial assets*	*Operating income / average reserves (basis points)*
2000		4.1			
2001		4.7			
2002		4.8			
2003	(5.0)	4.4	9.4		
3004	(1.1)	4.3	5.4	4,000	
2005	2.3	4.5	2.3	4,100	5

[1]Formerly cost of service, largely fixed costs.

Sources: Reserve Bank of New Zealand, Annual Report 2004, p. 35 and notes thereto, p. 89; Annual Report 2005, p. 35 and notes thereto, p. 89.

Operating expenses (formerly the 'cost of service') covers the overhead of reserve management: personnel, systems and information costs. The operating deficit is the operating income less operating expenses. The operating deficit has gone down over the last three years as the operating income has swung from a loss of NZ$5 million to a gain of NZ$2.3 million. The reserve managers have been able to earn more on the foreign currency holdings than the government has contracted to pay on its portfolio of foreign currency borrowings.

It might seem that the kiwi reserve managers have had a couple of hot years, but more than good luck is at work. The rolling off of older, higher cost liabilities in the Treasury's portfolio of foreign currency borrowing suggests even better years to come. Nowadays, the Treasury finds it cheaper to sell New Zealand dollar debt in the home market and to swap the proceeds into foreign currency. This is a cheap approach to borrowing foreign currency because the Treasury enjoys access to relatively low yields in its own currency bond market, owing to liquidity considerations as well as a scarcity premium given the strong fiscal position and strong foreign demand.

The average variable cost of reserves has become negative. In the financial year 2004–5, reserves rose from NZ$5.7 billion to NZ$8.1 billion, so the NZ$2.3 million operating income as a fraction of average reserves amounted to about five basis points. Fixed costs apart, New Zealand's reserves are spinning money[5]. If this average result reflects a rolling off of old, higher cost liabilities, then at the margin the New Zealand reserves must be earning a positive operating margin in the double digits.

The Philippines

Reserves are in contrast costly to hold for a sovereign that does not enjoy an investment grade rating from the major agencies. The case of the Philippines is less clear than that of New Zealand, since the government's foreign currency debt is not neatly earmarked for reserve holdings but rather exceeds reserve holdings. The BIS reports government international debt securities outstanding of $20.5 billion as of June 2005, while reserves stood at about $18.6 billion at end-September 2005. Based on the spread history of the Philippine US dollar debt over US Treasuries, it seems safe to say that the cost of reserve holdings for the Philippines is measured in the hundreds of basis points rather than in single basis points.

The case of reserves financed with domestic liabilities

In inflation-prone economies pursuing a strategy of exchange-rate based stabilization of inflation, financing an accumulation of reserves with domestic interest-bearing liabilities (sterilization) can prove a costly and even self-defeating exercise (Calvo (1991)). However, the recent state of affairs in East Asia differs from the Latin American circumstances that have given rise to expectations that sterilization is a very costly operation. Even when US policy rates were held to 1 per cent, major reserve holders Japan, Taiwan and Singapore had short-term interest rates below or at US levels. For China, Malaysia and Thailand, short-term interest rates exceeded those in the United States by little enough so that the combination of short-term sterilization debt and medium-term investment of official reserves (given the upward sloping US yield curve) reduced carrying costs to low or even negative levels[6]. Of the major reserve accumulators, Korea and India had interest rates far enough above US rates that the question of sterilization costs of macroeconomic significance arose[7].

Before turning to the estimates of these costs for these two countries, let it be clear that not only the cases chosen, but also the date chosen and the baseline chosen share a worst case character. We focus on March 2004, the last quarter before the Federal Reserve started to raise dollar short-term interest rates. And we will measure the cost of the entire stock of reserves, before turning to more reasonable baselines of reserve holdings.

Computing sterilization costs requires that a counterfactual be squarely faced. What are the foregone opportunities of holding safe but low-yielding foreign reserve assets? If the central bank were to cease holding foreign assets, what would it hold instead? And how much of a gain would this alternative bring? Generally, instead of holding a unit of foreign assets (earning x per cent), the authorities could have held more domestic asset (earning y per cent), or redeemed costly liabilities (saving z per cent), or done a combination of the two. More specifically, however, the alternative(s) chosen ought to respect the composition of the relevant authorities' balance sheet and realities of institutional constraints.

Sterilization costs for Korea and India

We estimate the stock opportunity costs for Korea and India using institutionally appropriate assumptions (see Tables 2.5 and 2.6)[8]. For Korea, we assume that the Ministry of Finance and the Economy's alternative to holding its share of foreign reserves is to redeem the corresponding amount of so-called foreign exchange stabilization bonds outstanding, while the Bank of Korea's alternative is first to pay off all outstanding so-called monetary stabilization bonds and then to invest the remainder of the proceeds of selling the foreign reserves by acquiring the benchmark three-year government bond. For India, we assume that the alternative is five-year government securities[9].

On the unrealistic baseline alternative of no foreign exchange reserves, Korea and India could have saved carrying costs of something like 0.7 per cent and 0.5 per cent of GDP, respectively. Recall that this statement applies to the perfect storm period of high reserves and very low US dollar interest rates. Retaining the focus on this date, what would the cost be on a more realistic baseline?

Table 2.5 Estimated holding cost (per annum) for Korea

	Dec 2002	Mar 2003	Dec 2003	Mar 2004
Quantities (% of 2003 GDP):				
Net foreign assets	16.08	17.96	21.42	22.54
Foreign liabilities	4.23	4.51	5.83	9.21
Yield differentials over US Treasury 2–5 year (%) (average over the previous 12 months):				
MSB 1-year	2.02	2.27	2.14	2.06
Government bond 5-year	2.41	2.47	2.47	2.48
Government bond 3-year	2.61	2.66	2.27	2.23
MOFE's gains from alternative (% 2003 GDP):				
Pay off bonds associated with FX acquisition	0.10	0.11	0.14	0.23
BOK's gains from alternatives (% of 2003 GDP):				
Pay off MSBs, then acquire 3-year bonds	0.36	0.43	0.47	0.47
Switch all to 3-year bonds	0.42	0.48	0.49	0.50

Table 2.6 Estimated holding cost (per annum) for India

	Dec 2002	Mar 2003	Dec 2003	Mar 2004
Quantities (% of 2003 GDP):				
Net foreign assets	12.50	13.17	16.98	18.28
Yield differentials over US Treasury 2–5 year (%) (average over the previous 12 months)				
Indian government securities 5-year	3.46	3.62	3.03	2.75
RBI's gains from alternative (% of 2003 GDP):				
Switch all to 5-year securities	0.43	0.48	0.52	0.50

The problem with answering this question is that there is no agreement on 'necessary' or 'warranted' reserves that would permit a measure of the cost of 'excessive' reserves as a remainder. Our approach therefore is to let the reader 'roll his own' by ranking criteria for reserve adequacy from universally accepted (three months of import cover), to very broadly accepted (100 per cent coverage of short-term external debt), to sometimes proposed (100 per cent backing for foreign currency liabilities of the domestic banking system to residents), to what is most controversial (a third of the stock of foreign-held portfolio investments). This hierarchy of hypothetical warranted reserves yield estimates of the cost of 'excess' reserves. For Korea, this ranges from 0 per cent, on the broadest notion of warranted reserves, to 0.5 per cent of GDP on the most restrictive, down from 0.7 per cent (see Table 2.7).

Table 2.7 Carrying cost[10] of 'excess' reserves for Korea, March 2004

Concept of 'warranted reserves'	'Warranted reserves' $ billions	'Excess reserves' $ billions	Cost of 'excess reserves' as % of GDP
Three months' imports	63	100	0.48/ 0.51
Three months' imports plus short-term external debt	123	40	0.27/ 0.30
Three months' imports plus short-term external debt plus Korean foreign currency deposits in Korean banks	141	22	0.21/ 0.24
Three months' imports plus short-term external debt plus Korean foreign currency deposits in Korean banks plus one-third of foreign holdings of Korean equities	169	– 5	0

Other perspectives on the case of domestically financed reserves

It might be argued that the above perspective is too narrow, and that it is possible to map the case of domestically financed reserves onto the credit spread notion of cost[11]. To do so requires a widening of the consideration to the national balance sheet from the government's alone. Consider the case of a Chinese corporation obtaining a dollar loan and selling the proceeds to the State Administration of Foreign Exchange in return ultimately for a People's Bank of China bill. From the government's standpoint the resulting increase in reserve holdings has been financed by domestic currency debt. But from the national standpoint, the holding of the People's Bank of China bill nets out and one is left with a dollar borrowing (by the corporate sector) matched by, say, a US dollar mortgage-backed security. Any difference in yield results from some combination of a credit difference (the Chinese company's credit versus guaranteed US mortgages) and a duration difference (Libor-based borrowing versus intermediate maturity obligations with call features).

The case of reserves financed with fiscal surpluses

This is the rarest case of international reserves but by no means an insignificant one. In East Asia, Hong Kong and Singapore are examples. Oil exporters are well represented: Abu Dhabi, Norway and perhaps Venezuela come to mind.

This case maps onto two of our measures of cost. If the alternative to foreign asset accumulation is taken to be domestic capital formation, the marginal product of capital measure is the appropriate measure of cost. Where the government has run surpluses, it is particularly easy to imagine that domestic investment in, for instance, infrastructure might have been larger.

It is possible to argue the case differently, however. Under Ricardian equivalence, the forced savings of the state simply substitutes for private savings. In this case, the cost of reserves is simply the difference in the portfolio management behaviour of the public and private sector and our cautious central banker measure of cost is appropriate.

Latter (2003, p. 12) asks whether the resources of the Exchange Fund (EF) could be better used in the territory:

> Could any other part of government use some of this capital and earn a return (in the sense of a social rate of return) higher than what the EF is earning on its investment…? This is the sort of question which deserves some close attention, but doesn't seem to get it. The aim of a transfer of capital would be to put it to potentially more productive use. Of course, this should not be regarded as a recipe for budget handouts – the Financial Secretary has rightly stressed the need to bring recurrent revenue and expenditure back into better balance. Any decision would depend crucially on a proper assessment of whether capital could be employed more profitably outside the EF. If it could, then this option might be preferred to dependence on a revenue surplus to fund capital projects. At the very least it is a question that needs routinely to be asked, and answered.

Mapping reserve financing and notions of cost

In sum, this section has suggested a mapping between these notions of the cost of reserves and the different sources of reserve financing (see Table 2.8). Reserves borrowed internationally lend themselves to the credit spread measure of cost. In the case of reserves financed with domestic debt, the further analysis in this case can make the other notions of cost relevant. Reserves corresponding to government surpluses lend themselves to the generally wider spread between low-risk international yields and domestic returns on real capital. Finally, the conservative central banker cost, which has as its counterpart less risky assets on the national balance sheet, has some bearing on all the cases, but has least relevance in the case of internationally borrowed reserves, where an asset/liability matching is possible (and observed in the case of New Zealand).

Table 2.8 Mapping between reserve financing and cost of reserves

	Relevant cost of holding reserves			
Financing of reserves	Credit spread	Quasi-fiscal	Marginal product of capital	Risk-averse central bank
Foreign borrowing	•			
Domestic borrowing/liabilities		•	•	•
Fiscal/quasi-fiscal surpluses			•	•

2.4 BALANCING BENEFITS AND COST

Jadresic's stylized case can serve as an example of balancing benefits and costs of reserve holdings. Reserves lower by $1 billion implied a foregone benefit in the form of a larger probability of a costly crisis. Reducing reserves would also save their holding cost. In the case of Chile, Jadresic took the relevant cost of reserves to be a spread of 100 basis points[12]. In this stylized case, the cost of the reserves outweighed the benefit ($10 million versus $8 million). And in fact the Central Bank of Chile decided to reduce its reserve holdings (Central Bank of Chile (2005), pages 67 and 74). Because it had financed a portion of its reserves with dollar denominated debt, it was able to reduce reserve holdings from levels that they would have otherwise reached by 'grossing down' its balance sheet, that is, paying down maturing dollar debts. Thus, the reserve reduction entailed no selling of dollars against domestic currency, avoiding any exchange rate market impact.

Using such a cost benefit analysis to determine the appropriateness of reserve levels encounters a problem in East Asia. The usual case in Asia is that the cost is negative. Not only the largest reserve holders, China and Japan, but also Taiwan, Korea, Singapore and Malaysia enjoy quasi-fiscal benefits from the lower yields on domestic currency liabilities compared to US dollar yields (or presumably a blended yield reflecting an allocation to euro and yen). New Zealand is able to make a positive turn by selling government paper, swapping the proceeds into foreign currency and investing the proceeds. Does it follow that the reserves are too low in all these economies?

Putting aside the New Zealand case, one answer would be that the concept of the cost of reserves in the case of domestically financed reserves is materially incomplete. In this case, the public sector has a huge exposure to an upward revaluation of the domestic currency, as highlighted by Higgins and Klitgaard (2004). Where the currency has been allowed to appreciate in Korea, this risk has found expression in central bank losses. To argue that the reserve holding is costly under these circumstances requires that, over some period, foreign exchange valuation losses be foreseen to exceed the cumulated benefits of the interest pick-up. This is inherently a very difficult analysis to perform (what is known as a peso problem).

An important feature of the exposure receives less attention than it deserves, however. Reserves will produce quasi-fiscal losses when the domestic currency appreciates. Such appreciation tends to be associated, however, with terms of trade improvements that raise welfare. Reserves can thus be said not to serve only a self-insurance role in making a crisis less likely. In addition, the exchange valuation changes associated with reserves will tend to deliver losses in good times and gains in bad times, meaning that they serve as fiscal insurance.

2.5 CONCLUSION

This chapter did not begin from the premise that the accumulation of foreign exchange reserves is the result of a separate optimization. Rather, the author subscribes to the 'Mrs Machlup's closet' interpretation of reserves as the cumulated side effects of other decisions. It is a misapprehension, in general, to speak of a demand for international reserves, much less of that demand being the result of a careful weighing of benefits and costs.

Consistent with this view, Matthew Higgins argued during the conference that any assessment of foreign exchange reserve accumulation must address the broader policies giving rise to that accumulation and the risks thereby entailed. Going one step further, participant Sweder van Wijnbergen focused not on the possibly mistaken policies that result in the reserve accumulation but rather on the mistaken policies that large reserves would permit. On the assumption that policy is on an unsustainable course, he argued that larger reserves do not avoid crisis but only delay the day of reckoning and make it more expensive when it arrives. This argumentation is reminiscent of arguments in the late 1980s that high corporate leverage was a good thing because it kept an errant management from wasting corporate resources –

even if it left firms subject to bankruptcy from random events or changes in creditor views.

Despite its rejection of the proposition that reserve levels result from a balancing of benefits and costs, this note has sought to address the question of the measurement of direct costs and benefits. It has thus not engaged the issues of the benefits or costs of exchange rate stabilization, whether in terms of employment, the allocation of investment or the risk of a loss of monetary control.

On the benefit side, this chapter took on board the idea that crisis is more likely when countries have less international liquidity and that such crises can prove expensive. Putting these two regularities together permits some rough measure of the benefit of holding reserves.

On the cost side, this chapter has distinguished different notions of cost and different sources of finance of foreign exchange reserves. In order of ease of measurement, the costs include a credit spread in the global capital market, a quasi-fiscal cost spanning two currencies, the gap between domestic real returns and international low-risk financial returns, and the cost of a public rather than private management of national assets. The welfare effects of reserve holdings will be differently assessed if the cost is taken to be a credit spread for a credit-worthy sovereign, which can be negative, or if the cost is taken to be the excess of the domestic marginal product of capital over the international yield.

The usual case in East Asia is foreign exchange reserves financed with domestic liabilities, so that the quasi-fiscal cost is the most immediate measure of cost. Since this cost is negative for most of the major reserve holders, any assessment that the costs of reserve holdings exceed the benefits will depend on the further analysis of the risk of appreciation of the domestic currency, given the exposure entailed by a long position in foreign currency financed by domestic currency liabilities.

NOTES

1. This way of conceiving of the benefits of official reserve holdings leads to comparisons of holdings to stocks rather than flows. Formerly, the benefit of reserve holdings were thought to arise from the possibility of sudden drop-off of exports or a sudden surge in imports, leading to a rule of thumb for reserve holdings in terms of the flow of imports (months). Now the rules of thumb tend to be couched in terms of stock of short-term debt or portfolio investment in domestic equities.
2. This application abstracts from the effect of reserve holdings on credit ratings and spreads. See Cantor and Packer (1995), Eichengreen and Mody (1998) and Soto, et al (2004). The last argues that marginal changes in reserves have little effect in the case of Chile, given its

investement grade rating. Similarly, the effect of higher reserves in reducing the cost of a crisis, as measured by De Gregorio and Lee (2003), is not explicitly considered.

3. The scenario that Higgins and Klitgaard (2004) offer has the domestic currency dropping in like measure against all currencies. In practice, the non-dollar portion of reserve holdings would make for smaller losses over some horizon in the case of generalized dollar weakness.

4. Aizenman and Lee (2005) consider a case of international borrowing, but assume that it is fixed in amount, so that an extra dollar held in reserves is not invested in the domestic economy. This particular assumption of a fixed supply of international borrowing makes the marginal product of capital less the international yield the relevant cost for these authors.

5. The Commonwealth of Canada similarly finds synthetic foreign currency liabilities relatively inexpensive.

6. At the margin, such a mismatch introduces duration risk that would become evident in the event of a parallel upward shift of domestic and international yield curves. But a full assessment of the central bank's duration risk depends critically on the treatment of the outstanding note issue.

7. Empirical analysis provides little support for this measure of the cost of reserves affecting the level of reserves (Edison (2003)).

8. Our rationale for assuming these alternatives is based on institutional plausibility rather than on optimality (in the sense of achieving the highest possible gain). In theory, the first next-best option is always the highest interest alternative available. If the first alternative somehow cannot accommodate the entire stock of foreign reserves to be disposed of, then the next most costly alternative should be adopted, etc.

9. If the exercise were to continue beyond March 2004, the government, instead of the central bank, would bear the marginal opportunity cost under the Market Stabilization Scheme.

10. Note: cost calculated by subtracting the 'warranted reserves' (evaluated at 1140 KRW/USD) from the stock of $174 billion in Bank of Korea foreign assets. First number is based on alternative of paying off monetary stabilisation bonds first, second figure based on alternative of switching all to three-year bonds. Source: Ho and McCauley (2005).

11. Or consider that the policy of accumulating reserves succeeds in holding down the exchange rate. This may discourage investment in the non-traded goods sector while not inducing any corresponding increase in investment in the traded goods sector. In this case, the cost of the policy could be seen as the difference between the marginal product of capital and the international yield.

12. In particular, the central bank retired dollar-denominated paper issued domestically. First it converted dollar indexed debt that was payable in peso to outright dollar paper (Central Bank of Chile Press Release, 5 November 2003, 'The Central Bank of Chile offers exchange option for dollar denominated debt certificates'). Then it reduced the stock of its outstanding bonds in dollars (BCX) from $3.5 billion in May 2005 to $1.8 billion in March 2006. Overall, the sum of dollar-denominated central bank liabilities (BCD, PRD, CERO in dollars, BCX, PCX, XERO in dollars) fell from $6.1 billion in March 2006, reflecting other non-intervention related flows.

3. The Politics and Micro-Economics of Global Imbalances

Avinash Persaud

3.1 INTRODUCTION

Pressure is building up on Chinese authorities to allow for a large revaluation of the yuan to facilitate an orderly correction of global current account imbalances. This pressure is partly politically motivated and does injustice to the complex economic environment in which these global imbalances have emerged. The short-term solution to global imbalances is a reduction in excess spending in the United States – not forced revaluations in countries flirting with deflation. But there is a less risky long-term solution that rests with a gradual loosening of capital controls in China and the development of well-functioning local financial markets in emerging markets, able to recycle temporary surpluses in an economically more efficient and diversified manner than is possible today.

3.2 THE POLITICS

Pressure by the US administration and others to drive the Chinese yuan higher is political bullying masquerading as economics. It is bad economics too, and potentially dangerous for the global economy.

An assortment of lobbyists, politicians and others have urged the US Treasury and the IMF to declare that China is manipulating its exchange rate and that severe trade and financial repercussions should follow unless it revalues substantially and immediately[1]. In the US Congress, Senators Charles Schumer, a Democrat, and Graham Lindsey, a Republican, have authored Bill 295, proposing a 27.5 per cent tariff on Chinese imports unless the yuan is significantly revalued against the dollar. In other walks of life this would be called blackmail.

The Chinese authorities are too familiar with Japan's economic history not to take the threat seriously. In the late 1980s, US lawmakers worried about US deficits, eyed Japan's current account surplus and threatened unilateral trade retaliation if the yen did not appreciate sharply. Market commentators at the time referred to this financial gun-boat diplomacy as the US administration using the dollar/yen exchange rate as a 'stick to beat the Japanese with', in order to prize open Japan's markets[2]. This was not the only driver of expectations of yen appreciation, but these expectations became self-fulfilling. Between 1990 and 1995, the yen appreciated by 50 per cent versus the dollar, plunging Japan into deflation. A toxic mix of deflation and bad debts in the banking system led to its quick collapse. The economic fall-out was so severe that national spending fell and Japan's imports imploded to such an extent that the current account surplus largely remained unchanged (see Figure 3.1)[3].

Figure 3.1   Yen/dollar exchange rate and current account balances (% GDP)

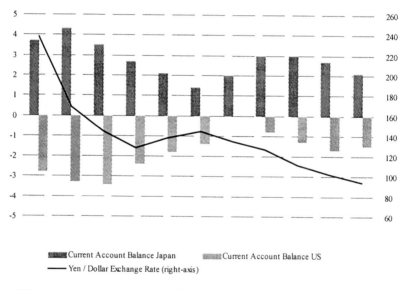

Current Account Balance Japan   Current Account Balance US
——— Yen / Dollar Exchange Rate (right-axis)

When quizzed on how a unilateral appreciation of the yuan or the currencies of other Asian countries can mollify global imbalances, the protagonists retreat to the more moderate position that a yuan revaluation is just part of a package of desirable policies that includes deficit reduction in the US and monetary stimulus in Europe. But political pressures are not evenly balanced between these proposals. Despite deficit-fighting talk from US Treasury Secretaries, President George W. Bush merrily signed in 2005 a

$256 billion highway bill and Congress had not yet made a significant effort to offset the expected $200 billion costs of Hurricane Katrina and the rising costs of the Iraq war. Furthermore, the European Central Bank is tightening its monetary stance. The political realities are that large revaluations in the exchange rates of fast-growing, but poor, Asian countries are more likely than fiscal consolidation in the US or monetary stimulation in Europe.

Indeed the Chinese have already kowtowed to the US Congress and Treasury by abandoning an exchange peg that has been associated with the most successful period of economic expansion of any country in recorded history. In July 2005, after 11 years of a fixed dollar exchange, the Chinese authorities widened the trading band of the yuan. Since then it has appreciated by 10 per cent on a trade-weighted basis and 2.5 per cent versus the US dollar. The National Association of US Manufacturers is calling for a 30–40 per cent appreciation, so they are far from satisfied[4]. The pressure on China continues. Senators Schumer and Lindsey are waiting in the wings.

One of the first questions that need to be answered by those hiding behind the cloak of economic argument, is why the focus on China[5]? The counterpart of the worsening US current account deficit is not China's current account surplus. America's current account position with almost every country has worsened. Since 1990, the US annual current account balance worsened by 1.7 per cent of global GDP while the Chinese surplus improved by 0.25 per cent of global GDP[6] (see Figure 3.2). China's current account improvement accounts for just 15 per cent of the US trade deterioration, which is almost exactly in line with its share of non-US GDP (on a PPP basis). Why is a relatively poor country, accounting for just 15 per cent of the deterioration in the US current account position, the focus of almost all of the attention? Where is the line of Congressional bills pressuring those countries that account for the other 85 per cent deterioration of the US deficit?

The one region or grouping in the world where the current account improvement far exceeds its share of non-US GDP, and far exceeds that of China, is 'oil exporters'. The current account position of oil exporters has improved by 1 per cent of global GDP representing 60 per cent of the deterioration in the US position[7].

A more parsimonious (and less worrying) explanation for the recent deterioration in global imbalances is that oil exporters are running large surpluses as a result of higher oil prices and output. This in turn is largely the result of two things: concern over the security of oil supplies as a result of the Iraq war and above-capacity economic growth – led, in global GDP terms, by the United States. The principal problem with this explanation is that it is politically less appealing than blaming the Chinese for domestic economic imbalances.

Table 3.1   Changes in current account balances 1997–2004

	US$ bn	% of USA	% World GDP ex USA
USA	– 529.0	100.0	26.4
NIAE* + China	160.5	30.1	21.1
Russia + ME	160.0	30.1	6.7
NIAE	124.8	23.5	4.4
Middle East	103.0	19.4	3.5
Japan	75.2	14.2	8.7
Latin America	72.6	13.7	9.5
Euro area	– 64.1	– 12.1	19.3
Russia	57.0	10.7	3.2
China	35.7	6.7	16.7
India	5.1	0.9	7.4

*Newly Industrialized Asian Economies.

Source: IMF, World Economic Outlook Database, April 2006.

3.3   THE ECONOMICS

The protagonists argue that Asian revaluations would be good for Asian economies and they imply various motives for the reluctance of foreign officials to follow the 'right' path. Senator Schumer refers to his pressure on the Chinese to revalue as a 'tough-love effort'.

One myth that is often peddled is that there is something cultural about Asia's savings rate. It is important to remember that East Asia ran massive current account deficits in the region of 5 per cent of GDP during the first half of the 1990s. But back then it was said that there was something cultural about Asian investment.

The reality is far more complex than is suggested by the protagonists and perhaps best seen through the following analogy. Between 1998 and 2003, Japan ran a substantial current account surplus that averaged a sizeable 3.3 per cent of GDP. The consensus recommendation was not that they should not revalue their exchange rate, but devalue it[8]. The argument was that Japan was only running a current account surplus because spending was depressed.

Monetary stimulation was required to boost spending, but with the banking system broken, the only way to do this was by devaluing the exchange rate. A revaluation of the exchange rate on the other hand would have raised unemployment, depressed spending and imports further and was therefore unlikely to reduce the current account surplus. Indeed, the revaluation of the yen between 1990 and 1995 did little to shrink Japan's surplus.

The point is that the correct response to a current account position depends on the underlying economic development, and a tell-tale sign of the appropriate exchange rate response is the inflation rate. Japan's deflation was a sign that revaluation was not the right remedy for its sizeable current account surplus. If Japan was running a high inflation rate and a current account surplus, then a revaluation would have been appropriate. Maybe one day it will, but China is not running an inflation rate that would justify a large revaluation.

In a contemporary context it is worth asking whether Chinese monetary policy would have been tighter (through a revaluation perhaps) or looser (through devaluation) if it was being run by the Bank of England's Monetary Policy Committee with a 2.5 per cent inflation target[9]. Over the course of the past five years, China would have been significantly loosening its monetary policy, not tightening it. Today policy would appear to be in balance. An inflation target of 2.5 per cent would not even allow for a 10–20 per cent revaluation of the exchange rate. Given China's current inflation rate, a revaluation in the order of 10 per cent plus would push China into deflation once more, requiring emergency measures to loosen policy for fear that deflation, amid a banking system with substantial bad debt, would quickly evolve into economic depression. This fear is reinforced by the result of every major global economic model. They all point to Asian consumption falling and unemployment rising if there were revaluations in the order of 30 per cent. How would this be good for fast-growing but poor countries, looking for employment opportunities for the rural poor? It sounds more like a taunt of 'tough-luck' to a trade competitor than 'tough-love'.

3.4 THE FINANCE

But there is another vital point that is ignored by those lobbying for a Chinese revaluation. One cannot think about China's exchange rate management without considering that it exists in the context of capital controls[10]. A question to ask those pointing at China's current account surplus and seeking a large revaluation is, would China still have a current account surplus if it had a fully flexible exchange rate, no capital controls and developed financial markets? The answer is yes. This is because the surpluses are driven by investment rates falling below savings rates (see Figures 3.3a and 3.3b).

An outflow of private sector savings would simply replace official sector reserve growth in keeping external payments balanced, with the exchange rate close to current levels – or if the force of capital outflows was strong enough – at weaker levels. Like Japan before, forced revaluations in this context would only add to an investment shortfall, maintaining a current account surplus and lowering GDP.

China could respond to US pressure by lowering capital controls at the same time as it widens the trading bands. The two effects could cancel each other out in terms of the value of the exchange rate, though the extra flexibility of the exchange rate and looser capital controls could pose unintended risks further down the road if they are not carefully managed.

The real problem, as identified by the Geneva Report study (Genberg et al, 2005), is more macroprudential than macroeconomic. A well-functioning financial system should comfortably recycle temporary mismatches of savings and investment. In 1985 oil exporters' oil revenues were $200 billion. In 2005, they hit $800 billion. It would be economically and prudentially wrong for the oil exporters to invest all $800 billion at home. There is not sufficient local capacity and trying to find it would only lead to deteriorating investment quality. Recent volatility in Middle-East stock markets relate in part to an insufficient diversification of investment abroad and over-investment at home.

The failure of Asian and Middle-East governments to develop deep local financial markets means that their savings are not being invested by the private sector, looking for good, long-term investment opportunities, but instead they are being invested by central banks who are not discerning long-term investors. Central banks are designed and controlled to be price-insensitive buyers of the most liquid and safe instruments. In the name of safety, this concentration in dollar-denominated government securities poses investment risks for Asian and Middle-East central banks and their citizens. It also poses risks for the US by 'artificially' lowering the cost of capital and therefore encouraging investments that would not otherwise be justified. Low cost of capital may have contributed to a US property bubble.

The solution to this self-reinforcing mechanism is to accelerate efforts to develop the local financial markets and loosen capital controls, but in the mean time, to put a large proportion of excess reserves into investment companies, with long-term benchmarks, managed both internally and externally.

This in itself would prove an important boost to the development of a local financial sector. There will be substantial pressure to allow these investment companies to invest at home. Developing countries often suffer from a shortage of long-term risk capital. However, there are a number of problems with such an idea. The two most notable being that foreign exchange reserves have a foreign exchange liability, and so for prudential reasons should not be converted into an illiquid domestic current asset, and investing public money

Figure 3.2 Ratio of foreign exchange reserves (growth to current account surplus)

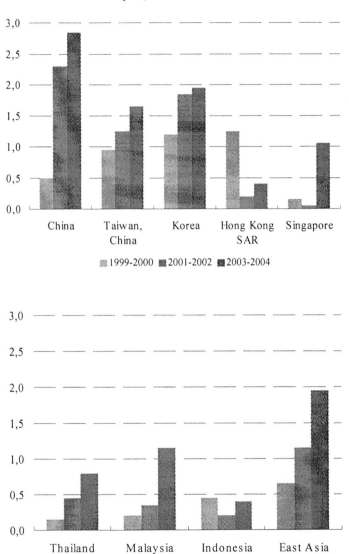

at home will generate substantial political pressures.

Better would be for a group of developing countries to form a loose corporation where they would agree to invest within the group, but not at home. Such funds would boost the safety and return for Asian and Middle-East investors, would provide better discipline for US and other borrowers and would reduce threats posed by the unwinding of large and concentrated imbalances.

3.5 CONCLUSION

The solution proposed above would take time. There are those who argue that time is running out and the international financial system is jeopardized by these growing surpluses. These people clamour for exchange rate adjustment but they have the cart before the horse. The dollar will fall as a consequence of taking the only policy measures that would curb global imbalances immediately: a reduction in domestic spending relative to potential in the US and an increase in Europe and Asia. Once these measures have been initiated, a dollar decline would naturally and voluntarily occur, not least because it would follow fundamentals and be in everyone's interest: it would moderate economic slowdown in the US and inflation in Europe and Asia.

The critical problem is not that the dollar adjustment may prove too narrow tomorrow, but that the necessary policy measures are not being taken today and do not look like happening soon. This is partly because too many economists have colluded with protectionists to blame China for the policy mistakes of the world's richest economies. As we have mentioned above, this is not only morally questionable; it is a factual fallacy. In dollar terms, the US trade deficit dwarfs China's surplus.

It is important to remember the fundamentals. The US trade deficit is caused by the US spending 7 per cent of gross domestic product more than it is producing, largely as a result of consumer optimism, spurred by rising house prices and tax cuts. Would devaluation reduce US domestic spending? No. As the late Rudiger Dornbusch often reminded me, dollar devaluations boost domestic spending as net exports rise. Without the kind of fiscal or monetary tightening currently unimagined, devaluation would further overheat the US economy. A large Chinese revaluation, like the one being threatened by the US Congress, may switch around its relative components, but will reduce overall domestic spending in China. Worse, it would lead to deflation given China's near-zero inflation rate and enormous bad debts.

Exchange rates have a secondary part to play in this act. But Sadakazu Tanigaki, Japan's finance minister, got the right balance when he argued that it is dangerous to overemphasize exchange rate realignments before there is the will to initiate the necessary accompanying domestic policies. Exchange rate changes on their own could worsen global imbalances. If the political will is not there for the required macro-policy changes, let us at least press ahead with the longer-term micro-economic changes that would make us worry less about savings–investment imbalances in the future.

NOTES

1. Fred Bergsten suggests an import surcharge of 50 per cent on all Chinese imports.
2. Although the foreign exchange market attached much credence to the idea that President Clinton's first Treasury Secretary, Lloyd Bentsen, actively sought a weaker US dollar, after a few unguarded remarks over an open microphone, the US Treasury has always denied it.
3. For further description and analysis of the relationship between the dollar and Japanese deflation, see McKinnon (2005).
4. See www.nam.org.
5. See NAM Congressional Testimony on 'US–China Economic Relationship', 23 June 2005.
6. Source: IMF, International Financial Statistics.
7. For instance, the trade balance in the 12 months to March 205 was $108.1 billion vis-à-vis China, $128.1 billion in Russia, $84.6 billion in Saudi Arabia, $31.5 billion in Venezuela and $29.8 billion in Indonesia.
8. There were many calls for a yen devaluation by economic commentators. For a lucid example, see Nakamae (2003).
9. We would expect a developing country to have a higher target of say 4 per cent but this would be too kind to the direction of our argument.
10. I owe this realization to a discussion with Bob Mundell.

4. The Cost–Benefit Approach to Reserve Adequacy: The Case of Chile[1]

Esteban Jadresic

4.1 INTRODUCTION

Practical assessments of the level of foreign exchange reserves held by central banks are typically based on the examination of reserve adequacy indicators. The most popular indicators have changed through the years from the ratio of reserves to the money base, then to the number of months of imports that reserves can cover, and more recently to the ratio of reserves to short-term foreign debt (including contractual short-term foreign debt plus amortizations of medium and long-term debt). To assess the adequacy of reserves in a given country, these indicators are compared to those in others, especially countries with similar policy frameworks and structural conditions, or to simple rule-of-thumb benchmarks suggested by previous observers. The International Monetary Fund (IMF), with its need to provide concrete advice on individual countries, policies and vulnerabilities, has been a key driver of the use of the indicators approach to assess the adequacy of foreign exchange reserves[2].

While this has been a practical response to the need for advice and analysis, to any mind trained in economics, it is natural to think of the level of reserves in terms of rational optimizing decisions rather than an external benchmark. From this viewpoint, the adequate level of reserves, rather than corresponding to one defined by some simple benchmark, must be the one that equates the marginal benefit of holding reserves to its marginal cost. Although scant, the theoretical and empirical literature on reserves adequacy has indeed made efforts to analyse the issue in those terms[3].

This chapter presents part of the analysis on the appropriate level of reserves carried out at the Central Bank of Chile (CBC) between 2001 and 2003, which shows that it can indeed be very useful and practical to approach the issue of reserve adequacy by analysing the marginal cost and benefit of holding reserves. As shown below, such an approach provides a framework that can help to examine options more rationally, to organize thinking and discussions, and even to ponder quantitatively the importance of some of the consequences of changing the level of reserves. In addition, the evidence presented below downplays the usefulness of the indicators approach to offering guidance for making practical decisions regarding the level of reserves.

This information and analysis is interesting also because it helps to understand the late 2033 CBC's decision to start a program that, as expected at the time, would reduce its level of foreign exchange reserves significantly. Such a program is unusual on at least two counts. First, it was implemented at a time when the vast majority of central banks in emerging markets had been doing exactly the opposite. Second, unlike standard reductions of reserves motivated on a decision to intervene in the foreign exchange market, this program was designed to maintain constant the CBC's net supply of financial instruments denominated in foreign currency to the domestic market. Thus, the rationale for this program is purely related to a concern about the size of reserves, and not to a concern about the level of the foreign exchange rate.

The remainder of this chapter is organized as follows. The next section provides background information on the context in which Chile's reserve adequacy was examined during the first half of the 2000s. Section 3 reports and comments on some of the results we found at the CBC when using the indicators approach to assess reserve adequacy. Section 4 presents some key aspects of our use of a cost–benefit analysis for the same purpose. Section 5 presents the program to reduce reserves implemented by the CBC. The last section provides concluding remarks.

4.2   THE ECONOMIC CONTEXT

The analysis of reserve adequacy in Chile recent years was framed by at least three important developments.

First, during the 1990s and early 2000s, Chile developed significantly stronger economic fundamentals (see Table 4.1). On the monetary front, the country was able to rein in a history of over 100 years, persistent high inflation, establishing an autonomous central bank that gradually reduced inflation during the 1990s, and then succeeded in implementing a fully-fledged inflation targeting and floating exchange rate regime since 1999. On the fiscal front, significant and cumulative budget surpluses allowed substantial public debt reductions, to such an extent that recently the net public debt (debt minus foreign exchange reserves) became negative. Moreover, since 2000, fiscal policy has been organized around an innovative structural surplus framework, which requires transitory excess revenues to be saved, at the same time that it allows using part of those savings during downturns to smooth public expenditure. Advances in the macroeconomic arena were complemented with significant progress in other areas, most notably with signing free trade agreements with most of Chile's key trading partners, which consolidated a very open trade and economic policy regime. These developments, together with the actual delivery of strong and less volatile economic growth, the successful return to a democratic political system since 1990, a strong consensus regarding economy policies, and a solid and increasingly sophisticated financial system, provided the country with much stronger pillars to deal with adverse circumstances.

Second, during most of the 1990s, Chile's foreign exchange reserves built up substantially (see Table 4.1). The context was one in which the CBC was trying gradually to reduce severe and persistent inflation by maintaining high domestic interest rates, at the same time that it was trying to limit the upward pressures on the exchange rate stemming from very substantial capital inflows. While these inflows were contained partly by resorting to capital controls, which had been used in Chile almost continuously in one way or another since the 1930s, the CBC intervened heavily in order to reduce the supply of foreign currency in the economy[4]. The monetary effects of the reserves, build-up were sterilized by the issuance of debt. Since the interest rate differential between this debt and the return on international reserves was large, these operations involved a significant financial cost. One of the consequences was that the CBC, which began its operations as an autonomous institution with negative capital, was unable to reverse such situation.

Third, since adapting a floating exchange rate regime in 1999, the question whether Chile had built up excess reserves naturally intensified. If the CBC had chosen a regime where the normal rule was that it would not intervene in the foreign exchange market, then it was logical to wonder whether it would need to hold the same amount of reserves. Of course, this did not mean that the CBC had to consider getting rid of all of its reserves, as in practice even the most orthodox floaters hold reserves and maintain the right to intervene in the foreign exchange market under special circumstances. In particular, an adequate level of reserves would still be important to deal with potential liquidity shocks should access to international financial markets become difficult. However, the change in the exchange rate regime invited to reassess the level of reserves.

The Size of Central Bank Reserves

Table 4.1 Selected macroeconomic indicators: Chile 1970–2005

	Inflation (%)	Net central government debt (% of GDP)	Real GDP growth (%)	Sovereign spread (bp)	Country rating	Inter- national reserves ($ bln)
	(1)	(2)	(3)	(4)	(5)	(6)
Averages						
1970–1979	175.2	n.a	2.2	n.a	n.a	0.7
1980–1989	20.7	n.a	3.6	n.a	n.a	3.6
1990–1999	10.8	9.8	6.4	173	A –	13.1
2000–2005	2.9	4.6	4.4	140	A –	15.6
1990	27.3	30.3	3.7	n.a	n.a	7.1
1991	18.7	23.4	8.0	n.a	n.a	8.2
1992	12.7	15.4	12.3	n.a	BBB	10.4
1993	12.2	13.9	7.0	n.a	BBB+	10.7
1994	8.9	8.4	5.7	n.a	BBB+	14.2
1995	8.2	4.0	10.6	n.a	A –	15.2
1996	6.6	1.5	7.4	n.a	A –	15.8
1997	6.0	-0.4	6.6	n.a	A –	18.3
1998	4.7	-0.3	3.2	n.a	A –	16.3
1999	2.3	1.7	-0.8	173	A –	14.9
2000	4.5	3.2	4.5	197	A –	15.1
2001	2.6	5.8	3.4	192	A –	14.4
2002	2.8	7.9	2.2	177	A –	15.4
2003	1.1	6.7	3.9	126	A –	15.9
2004	2.4	4.2	6.2	82	A	16.0
2005	3.7	–0.1	6.3	65	A	17.0

Sources: (1) National Institute of Statistics of Chile, (2) Ministry of Finance of Chile, (3) Central Bank of Chile, (4) JP Morgan Bond Indices, (5) Standard and Poors, (6) Central Bank of Chile.

4.3 INDICATORS OF RESERVE ADEQUACY

The first approach used to assess reserve adequacy was computing a number of standard indicators, and comparing them with those in other countries. Table 4.2 presents the results of such analysis when using as reserve indicator the ratio between reserves and short-term foreign debt. As mentioned above, this is the preferred measure of the recent academic and public policy literature on reserve adequacy in emerging market economies with flexible exchange rates. The data include yearly observations for the period 1990–2002 from 148 countries.

Table 4.2 International reserves / short-term foreign debt ratio

| | Exchange rate regime | | | | |
	All	Fixed	Mixed	Floating	Unclassified
Chile					
2002	1.38	--	--	1.38	--
Average	1.69	--	1.75	1.50	--
Median	1.68	--	1.72	1.46	--
Standard deviation	0.19	--	0.17	0.14	--
# observations	13.00	--	10.00	3.00	--
All countries					
Average	11.17	7.87	10.11	2.63	16.12
Median	1.87	2.40	1.89	1.51	1.68
Standard deviation	94.80	24.46	43.15	3.75	148.81
# observations	1746.00	434.00	511.00	148.00	653.00
# countries	148.00	48.00	61.00	28.00	80.00
Emerging Markets					
Average	1.65	2.08	1.85	1.61	0.84
Median	1.30	1.14	1.63	1.57	0.70
Standard deviation	1.41	2.30	1.31	0.86	0.58
# observations	254.00	44.00	105.00	58.00	47.00
# countries	20.00	9.00	17.00	14.00	12.00

Source: Soto et al (2004).

Table 4.2 shows that, relative to short-term foreign debt, Chile's reserve level was consistent with the relevant average international practice. While the corresponding ratios computed for Chile (1.38 in 2002 and 1.69 on average during 1990–2002) were substantially below the average for the full sample of countries (11.17), they were much closer to the median of these countries (1.87). Most importantly, these ratios were in line with those observed in emerging market economies with floating exchange rate regimes (1.57 on average, and 1.61 for the median), a more relevant benchmark for the Chilean economy in recent years.

Under the presumption that the international liquidity that reserves provide in emerging market economies is best measured relative to short-term debt, these results appear to indicate that Chile's reserve level was adequate. As we discuss next, however, such a conclusion was unwarranted for at least two reasons.

A first and straightforward objection was that there is no a priori reason why one should compare Chile's ratios only with some average or median indicators. The truth is that there is huge dispersion on the ratios across countries. For the complete sample of countries, for instance, the standard deviation for the reserves to short-term debt ratio is of the order 100! Such measure includes the effects of some outliers, but even for the much more homogeneous group of emerging market economies with floating exchange rates, the dispersion on the measured ratios is very large. For this group, characterized by a mean ratio of 1.61, the measured standard deviation is 0.86, which implies that a 95 per cent confidence interval includes as acceptable values both a ratio equal to 0 and a ratio equal to twice the mean. Such a wide range provided no useful benchmark to guide the type of practical decisions considered by the CBC at the time.

In the absence of a useful international comparator, an alternative would have been to use as benchmark a simple rule-of-thumb such as the so-called Guidotti rule, according to which the level of reserves should be equal to short-term foreign debt. Unfortunately, there is no solid empirical (or theoretical) basis for such benchmark[5].

A second and most fundamental objection is that the ratio of reserves to short-term debt is unlikely to be the only relevant parameter to consider when assessing reserve adequacy. Using a rational optimizing approach suggests that idiosyncratic elements may be essential. In practice, it is revealing that in relative terms, advanced economies' reserves levels that are substantially smaller than those in emerging markets[6]. This suggests that development, particularly of institutions and markets, is very relevant.

To provide a perspective that recognizes that the ratio of reserves to short-term debt may not be the only relevant parameter Table 4.3 presents estimates, for Chile and other countries, of the ratio between reserves and GDP. In contrast with the conclusion suggested by the prior analysis, Chile's reserve level when using this indicator appears high. At 22 per cent, this ratio for Chile was above the average and median for all countries (18 per cent and 10 per cent), as well as for emerging market economies with floating exchange rates (15 per cent and 17 per cent). Most important, Chile's reserve level looks very high when comparing with the average and median reserves to GDP ratios in developed countries (5 per cent and 4 per cent)[7]. In this comparison, unlike others, the differences are statistically significant.

Table 4.3 International reserves / GDP ratio

		Exchange rate regime			
	All	Fixed	Mixed	Floating	Unclassified
Chile					
2001	0.22	--	--	0.22	--
Average	0.22	--	0.22	0.22	--
Median	0.22	--	0.22	0.22	--
Standard deviation	0.01	--	0.01	0.01	--
# observation	12.00	--	10.00	2.00	--
All countries					
Average	0.18	0.13	0.17	0.10	0.30
Median	0.10	0.11	0.11	0.06	0.08
Standard deviation	1.47	0.11	0.21	0.12	2.80
# observation	1.571.00	445.00	499.00	200.00	427.00
# countries	146.00	57.00	64.00	31.00	61.00
Emerging Markets					
Average	0.13	0.13	0.14	0.15	0.09
Median	0.12	0.12	0.12	0.17	0.07
Standard deviation	0.08	0.08	0.08	0.08	0.07
# observation	226.00	40.00	99.00	48.00	39.00
# countries	20.00	9.00	17.00	14.00	12.00
Developed countries					
Average	0.07	0.07	0.08	0.05	--
Median	0.06	0.07	0.07	0.04	--
Standard deviation	0.05	0.04	0.05	0.04	--
# observation	245.00	78.00	79.00	88.00	--
# countries	23.00	15.00	11.00	9.00	--

In short, the use of an indicator's approach provided little guidance regarding the adequacy of Chile's reserves. The ratio between reserves and short-term foreign debt in Chile appeared to be in line with the average one observed in emerging market economies with floating exchange rates, but the dispersion among the ratios measured within this group of countries was so large that this comparison does not help much. More fundamentally, it is unlikely that using any single indicator will permit a clear-cut assessment of reserve adequacy. If other variables are also important, the examination of alternative indicators can lead to very different conclusions.

4.4   COST–BENEFIT APPROACH

In addition to examining alternative indicators of reserve adequacy, we developed a cost–benefit analysis of the level of reserves. The use of such an approach was appealing because it was consistent with an optimizing criterion, and because it was better suited for the type of analysis required by policy makers to support their decisions. Moreover, it was clear that this approach could take into account more explicitly idiosyncratic characteristics of each country. We focused on marginal rather than total costs and benefits, since any practical decision of reducing the level of reserves was likely to be on the margin rather than absolute.

Identifying and measuring the marginal cost of reserves was the simplest part. We estimated it as the difference between the expected return on reserves and the cost of financing them, as seen from the perspective of the Central Bank of Chile. We found that a broad approximation to this number was provided by Chile's sovereign spread, i.e. the difference between the yield of US Treasury bills and the yield of the international bonds issued by the Chilean government. Although the return on foreign exchange reserves is higher than the return on US Treasury bills, it had to be considered that, at the time, the marginal cost of financing reserves was larger than the cost of issuing sovereign debt. Indeed, the relevant source of financing of reserves was the issuance of dollar-denominated CBC debt in the domestic market, which carried a premium relative to internationally issued debt.

To assess the marginal benefit of reserves, and given the floating exchange rate regime adopted by the CBC, we focused on the precautionary argument for holding reserves; i.e. the argument that reserves are held as an insurance against a liquidity crisis. Accordingly, we attempted to estimate the effect of a change in the level of reserves on the probability and cost of a crisis. Also, we examined the extent to which a change in the level of reserves could affect financing costs. Interestingly, we found a number of papers that have estimated these types of effects empirically, with statistically significant results. In addition, some of my colleagues at the bank produced their own estimates.

Table 4.4 summarizes a number of empirical studies on the relationship between crisis probability and foreign exchange reserves. The studies focus on data for emerging market or developing economies covering the period

1970–2001. The crisis indicators used in these studies typically involve some measure indicating a large real or nominal devaluation of the domestic currency. They could also include some other indicators such as a large loss in international reserves, or change in capital flows, on the current account balance, or in the terms of trade. The liquidity indicators, in turn, correspond to the ratio of reserves to short-term foreign debt, M2, or imports.

Table 4.4   Empirical studies on crisis probability, and derived implications for Chile

Study	Econometric method	Sample	Crisis indicator	Liquidity indicator (X)	Implied effect on Chile's crisis probability of a $1 billion reduction on its reserves
Bussiere and Fratzscher (2002)	Logit	20 emerging economies for 1993–2001, with monthly data	Weighted Average between Δ real exchange rate (RER), Δ international reserves (IR) and Δ terms of trade (TT) higher than average plus two Standard Deviations (SD)	Short-term foreign debt (STFD)/ IR	10 bp (from 6.5%–6.2%)* (e)
Kamin and Babson (1999)	Probit	Argentina, Brazil, Chile, Colombia, Venezuela and Mexico (1980–98)	Weighted average between Δ RER, Δ IR and Δ TT higher than average plus three SD	IR / STFD (a), (b)	9 bp**
			Weighted average between Δ RER, Δ IR and Δ TT higher than average plus two SD	M2 / IR (3-year change) (b), (c)	9 bp**
			Imports drop higher than 75% of one SD	M2 / IR (3-year change) (b), (c)	8 bp**
Krueger, Oskwe and Page (1998)	Probit	19 developing countries from 1977 to 1993	Weighted average between Δ RER, Δ IR and Δ TT higher than average plus one and a half SD	M2 / IR	4 bp**

Radelet and Sachs (1998)	Probit	22 emerging economies from 1994 to 1997	Sharp change on capital flow	STFD / IR (d)	40 bp (from 7%)*
Berg and Patrillo (1999)***	Probit	100 developing countries (1970–96)	Nominal devaluation (ND) higher than 25% and 10% higher than last year nominal devaluation	IR / Imports	6 bp**
				IR / M2	69 bp**
Milesi-Ferretti and Razin (1998)	Probit	105 developing countries to 1973–94	Current account balance change higher than 3% of GDP in a 3–year term.	IR as import months	44 bp**
			ND higher than 25% and 10% higher than last year ND	Idem	101 bp**
			ND higher than 15%, 10% higher than previous period, which must be lower than 10%	IR / M2	51 bp**
			ND higher than 15% and fixed exchange rate before crisis	Idem	24 bp**
Garcia and Soto (2004)	Logit	Yearly observations from 1975 to 2003 for countries in World Bank and BIS debt data bases	Weighted average between Δ RER and Δ IR higher than average plus two SD	IR/STFD	20 bp

* Calculations applied to Chile, assuming a value for the explaining variable equal to that observed in 2002, and a real exchange rate (RER) value equal to that of equilibrium.
** Calculation applied to the sample mean.

*** Frankel and Rose (1996) revised estimations. The authors found that the reserves level / imports ratio is not significant to explain the probability of a crisis.
(a) M2 / IR not significant (b) IR / Imports not significant (c) IR / SD not significant (d) TD / IR not significant (e) with data for the average country in the sample, a $4,200 billion reserves drop means 80 basis points (bp) of higher crisis probability.
Source: Soto et al (2004) and own elaboration.

Although these studies did not intend specifically to provide estimates for Chile, we found we could use them for such purpose. Since the models are non linear, this was done by obtaining point estimates for conditions similar to those observed in Chile in 2002, or by using the sample mean when that was not possible. The specific question we asked was: what would be, for the case of Chile, the implied effects on the probability of a crisis of a $1 billion reduction of reserves. The point estimates we obtained indicated that the probability of a crisis would increase between 4 and 100 basis points per year, with the more typical estimates implying that it would increase between 10 and 40 basis points per year approximately (see Table 4.4).

Table 4.5, in turn, summarizes a number of studies on the relationship between sovereign spreads and foreign exchange reserves. These studies focus on data for emerging market economies during the 1990s. In most models, the relationship between spreads and the level of reserves is nonlinear, with reserves measured relative to months of imports, short-term foreign debt, or GDP. As in the case of crisis probability, we used these models to obtain implied estimates of the effects of a $1 billion reduction of reserves in Chile's sovereign spreads. The point estimates indicated an increase in the sovereign spread between 0.04 and 10 basis points.

While the ranges for these estimates were too wide to sustain by themselves any definite assessment, they were useful to explore the consequences of a reduction in reserves under alternative assumptions. For such purpose, an additional ingredient was required: the cost of a crisis. Conveniently, the IMF has estimated GDP lost during actual crises, providing orders of magnitude of such cost (see IMF 1998). Its analysis suggested the need to distinguish between three cases: currency crash, currency crisis and banking crisis, with costs roughly equivalent to 5, 10 and 15 per cent of GDP, respectively.

The following simple example illustrates how these estimates can be used to explore reserve adequacy. Suppose that the central bank reduces reserves by $1 billion. Assume that this increases the probability of a currency crisis by 20 basis points, and the cost of the crisis is 5 per cent of GDP, which, in the case of Chile in 2003 amounts to approximately $4 billion. Also assume that the marginal cost of reserves is 100 basis points, which was more or less Chile's sovereign spread in 2003, and that the reduction in reserves has no effect on the sovereign spread and the cost of financing reserves. In this case, it is easy to check that:

– the cost of reserves falls by 100 bp x $1 billion = $10 million per year,
– the benefit of reserves falls by 20 bp x $4billion = $8 million per year;

therefore, the drop in the cost of reserves due to the reduction in the level of reserves more than compensates the drop in the benefits from reserves.

Table 4.5 Empirical studies on sovereign spreads, and derived implications for Chile

	Arora and Cerisola (2001)	Cline and Barnes (1997)	Eichengreen and Mody (1998)	Min (1998)	Soto, Naudon, López and Aguirre (2004)
Sample period	Monthly data in 1994–99	1992–96	1991–97	1991–95	1998–2002
Sample of countries	Argentina, Brazil, Bulgaria, Colombia, South Korea, Philippines, Indonesia, Mexico, Panama, Poland and Thailand	12 emerging economies and 6 European countries	1,488 bond emissions by 82 emerging economies, in the period	482 debt issues for Argentina, Brazil, Chile, China, Colombia, South Korea, Philippines, Mexico and Venezuela	15 emerging economies
Functional specification	Log(spread) = $\partial + \beta X$	Spread=?+ βX	Log(spread)= $\partial + \beta X$	Log(spread) = $\partial + \beta X$	Log(spread)= $\partial + \beta X$
Reserves functional specification	Reserves over goods and services import	Reserves over goods import	Reserves over short-term foreign debt	Reserves over GDP	Reserves over short-term foreign debt
Reserves parameter	Estimate for each country. Results report for three countries: Mexico (−0.39), Poland (−2.25) and Philippines (-3.71)	−88.3 with t test at 2.9	Report of four specifications, whose values fluctuate between −0.052 and −0.04	Three specifications whose values fluctuate between −0.026 and −0.024	−0.085 for the authors' preferred specification
Implied effect on Chile's spread of a $1 billion reduction of its reserves	Spread increases by 2 bp, (using Mexico estimate)	Spread increases in 10 bp	Spread increases between 0.5 bp and 0.4 bp	0.04 bp spread increase	Spread increases by 1 bp

Source: Soto et al (2004) and own elaboration.

This was merely an example, and one could think of many extensions. For instance, the decision of reducing reserves could increase the cost of a crisis and/or it could increase the sovereign spread and the cost of financing reserves. If extended along those lines, these considerations could reverse the conclusions of the above analysis. On the other hand, if the reduction in reserves reduces short-term external debt, then the increase in the probability of a crisis implied by some of the models would be smaller than estimated.

Another complication would be to take explicitly into account the effects of the level of reserves on the cost of financing of the private sector, and of the rest of the public sector. Owing to these effects, the social cost of an increase in the sovereign spread could be larger than the cost perceived by the central bank. On the other hand, it could also be taken into account that, to the extent that the increase in these financing costs reflects a higher probability of default on the country's external debt, then this effect might be compensated by lower contingent payments under a crisis scenario.

Some of these complications are easy to analyse with simple extensions of the above framework. Others are more difficult. The cost benefit approach, however, provides a useful general framework to analyze and discuss them.

4.5 THE CBC's PROGRAM TO REDUCE RESERVES

The practical conclusion of the CBC's analysis of reserve adequacy was that in November 2003 its board announced a new financial program. The holders of the CBC's debt denominated in US dollars but paid in Chilean pesos (the so called 'BCD' and 'PRD' bonds), were offered to exchange it with debt both denominated and paid in US dollars ('BCX' bonds). Subsequently, this new debt was redeemed at maturity by paying with foreign reserves, thus reducing both the level of reserves and the level of liabilities held by the CBC.

In practice, the (voluntary) exchange of BCD debt for BCX debt was not very significant, and the CBC thus decided to complement this program with the policy not to renew the US-dollar denominated bonds (BCDs) at their maturity, and to offer as their replacement during 2004 and 2005, one-year BCXs. These BCXs, in turn, are being redeemed at maturity making use of reserves. Therefore, the downsizing of liabilities and reserves has been occurring as expected, but with a one-year lag. Because of this program, by the end of 2006, the cumulative implied drain of reserves is expected to reach about $3.7 billion, most of which has already occurred[8].

It is important to note that, unlike standard central banks' initiatives to change their levels of reserves, this reserves-reduction program did not originate in a desire to intervene in the foreign exchange market, in the sense that it did not intend to affect the net supply of instruments denominated in foreign currency offered by the CBC to the private sector. The CBC rather designed this program with the purpose of reducing simultaneously its assets and liabilities denominated in foreign currency, without affecting the net foreign exchange position of the central bank vis-à-vis the private sector.

Consistently with the cost–benefit approach to reserve adequacy, the actual justification for this program was rather the decision to reduce the cost of holding foreign exchange reserves, in a context in which the stronger fundamentals of the Chilean economy had reduced the benefits of holding a high level of reserves. While also the cost of holding reserves had diminished, partly due to the same improvement in fundamentals that contributed to reducing the sovereign spread, the Board of the CBC nevertheless assessed that the marginal benefit of reserves had fallen below their marginal cost.

4.6   CONCLUDING REMARKS

There has been a substantial increase in the foreign exchange reserves held by many emerging market economies in recent years. While the source of this increase has had much to do with the sterilization of capital inflows in order to avoid an appreciation of domestic currencies, this development also has prompted increased concern, and welcomed debate, about what should be an adequate level of reserves in these countries.

To assess reserve adequacy, the standard approach to examine certain indicators can be helpful for some purposes, but its limitations need to be recognized. As shown by the use of this approach in the Chilean case, the wide cross-country dispersion of the distribution of the indicators appears to preclude statistically significant comparisons that are of practical relevance. Most importantly, it is highly unlikely that simple reserve adequacy indicators such as those currently used can capture properly the idiosyncratic characteristics relevant to determine an adequate reserves level.

In the CBC's recent assessment of its level of reserves, the use of a cost–benefit approach proved useful in practice. Examining the marginal costs and benefits of changing the level of reserves provided a framework consistent with rational optimization, and helped to organize and present the information and analysis in a way that is more in touch with the type of technical support and advice required by policymakers. Although available models and estimates are insufficient to deliver precise recommendations, using this approach also permitted them to explore quantitatively the relative importance of alternative effects, while explicitly recognizing that one size does not fit all.

While the type of marginal costs and benefits considered in the CBC's recent assessment are likely to be relevant also in many other cases, they do not provide a general taxonomy of costs and benefits that need to be considered when analysing reserve adequacy. Moreover, even in the particular context of an assessment based on a precautionary argument for holding reserves, many complications and extensions may be considered, some of which were mentioned above. Regardless of the specific arguments and effects considered relevant, however, the cost–benefit approach offers a promising methodology for analysing reserve adequacy.

NOTES

1. I am grateful to Age Bakker, whom encouraged me to write this article, as well as colleagues at the Central Bank of Chile with whom I examined and discussed during 2001–3 the issues summarized in this chapter, including initially Alvaro Rojas and Alfredo Pistelli and later Claudio Soto, Alberto Naudon, Alvaro Aguirre, Eduardo López, Rodrigo Valdés and Pablo García, among others. I also thank Ricardo Consiglio, Sergio Godoy and Nancy Silva for their more recent collaboration on the same topic. The views expressed herein are my own and are not necessarily shared by the Central Bank of Chile.
2. De Beaufort Wijnholds and Kapteyn (2001) provide a useful review of the literature on Reserve Adequacy as of the early 2000s.
3. For instance, see Heller (1966), Ben-Bassat and Gottlieb (1992) and, more recently, Garcia and Soto (2004).
4. The Central Bank of Chile fully eliminated capital controls in April 2001.
5. A valuable attempt to provide such an empirical basis can be found in Bussière and Mulder (1999).
6. Data for advanced economies on short-term foreign debt including amortization of medium and long-term debt is not available. As shown in Table 4.3, however, the amounts of reserves relative to GDP observed in advanced economies are substantially smaller than those observed in emerging market economies.
7. Although not shown in Table 4.3, a comparison of the rations between reserves and broad money in Chile with those in other countries delivers similar results.
8. By May 2006 this program had not led to a significant reduction in the level of reserves held by the CBC. This is because the drain in reserves due to the program was offset by an increase in reserves due to the accumulation of foreign currency deposits and swap operations made by the banking system and the government with the Central Bank of Chile. The increase in reserves due to these operations, however, was mirrored by an increase in the CBC's short-term liabilities.

5. Foreign Reserve Adequacy from the Asian Perspective

Hidehiko Sogano

5.1 INTRODUCTION

Following the currency crises in the late 1990s, Asian emerging economies have substantially increased their foreign reserves. As of the end of 2005, the world's four largest reserve-holding countries – Japan, China, Taiwan and Korea – held more than $2,000 billion reserves combined, roughly 50 per cent of the global total and nearly four times more than the corresponding figure for 1996.

There are pros and cons regarding this massive reserve accumulation by Asian countries. Some argue that the current reserve levels are too high, forcing countries in this region to bear unnecessary costs. An opposing view is that reserve accumulation on this scale is justifiable given the need to prevent the kind of currency crises as we saw occurring in the late 1990s.

This chapter sets out by reviewing conventional indicators for reserve adequacy and discussing possible rationales for recent reserve accumulation by Asian central banks. It then proceeds to survey the foreign exchange policies of the two biggest reserve holders in Asia: Japan and China. Finally, some tentative perspectives on the future direction of reserve management policy will be given.

5.2 INDICATORS FOR RESERVE ADEQUACY

Conventional indicators

Reserve adequacy is not a static concept but depends on a range of factors. Thus, empirical researchers have analysed reserve adequacy by using multiple indicators. The most popular among them are as follows.

The Size of Central Bank Reserves

Reserves-to-nominal GDP ratio

Since foreign reserve requirements should vary depending on a country's economic size, it makes sense to compare foreign reserves with nominal GDP. In Asia, Singapore and Taiwan have quite high reserves-to-nominal GDP ratios, while Japan's ratio is much lower (see Figure 5.1).

Figure 5.1 Reserves to nominal GDP

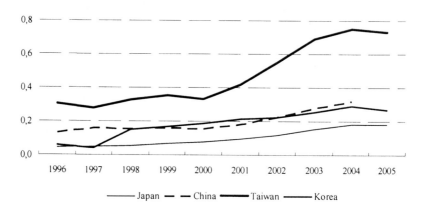

Sources: IMF, IFS Database; for Taiwan: Foreign Exchange Reserves, Department of Investment Services, MOEA.

Reserves-to-imports ratio

Conventional wisdom requires that the ratio of reserves to monthly imports be three at the minimum. When hit by the Asian currency crisis in 1997, foreign reserves of Korea and the Philippines were significantly below this minimum level. In Thailand's case, the reserves-to-imports ratio was also below 3 if off-balance sheet items such as the forward obligations borne by the central bank were included. In recent years, however, the reserves-to-imports ratio for major Asian economies has been on a sharp rise. At the end of 2005, it stood at 19 for Japan, 17 for Taiwan, 14 for China, and 10 for Korea (see Figure 5.2).

Reserves-to-short-term external debt ratio

The reserves-to-short-term external debt ratio is a good proxy for the country's liquidity capacity. At present, the ratios for China, Taiwan and Thailand are high, while those for Indonesia, Singapore and the Philippines are on the lower end (see Figure 5.3).

Figure 5.2 Reserves in terms of months import

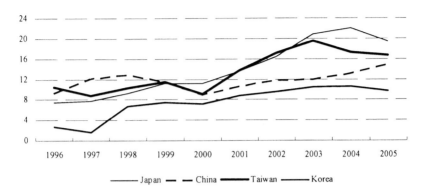

Sources: IMF, IFS Database; for Taiwan: Foreign Exchange Reserves, Department of Investment Services, MOEA.

Figure 5.3 Reserves to external debt

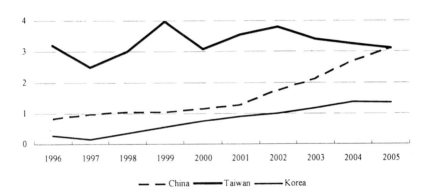

Sources: IMF, IFS Database; for Taiwan: Foreign Exchange Reserves, Department of Investment Services, MOEA.

Reserves-to-money supply ratio

Reserve adequacy measured against money supply is also informative as some components of the money supply may quickly leave the country once a financial crisis occurs. The reserves-to-M2 ratio is particularly worth monitoring when the country's banking sector is under pressure as a consequence of speculative attacks on its fixed exchanged rate regime (see Figure 5.4).

Figure 5.4 Reserves to M2 ratio

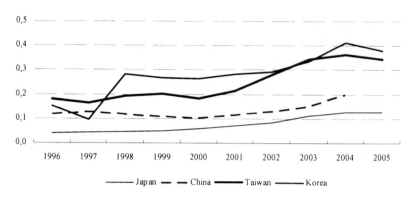

Sources: IMF, IFS Database; for Taiwan: Foreign Exchange Reserves, Department of Investment
Services, MOEA.

Buffer-stock model

Charts show that reserve adequacy of Asian countries, as measured against
nominal GDP, imports, and short-term external debt, have visibly improved
in recent years, although an improvement for the reserves-to-money supply
ratio is less clear. Given the sizable dispersions of these ratios across
countries, it seems sensible to avoid focusing on just one particular indicator.

To analyse reserve adequacy on a somewhat more theoretical plane, a
classical approach like the buffer-stock model could be applied. This model
explains reserve adequacy in terms of opportunity costs versus benefits.
Opportunity costs of holding reserves are equivalent to the gains that would
accrue without reserve accumulation. On the other hand, benefits of reserve
accumulation as a buffer stock become apparent when the country faces
external payment difficulties. In the buffer-stock model, adequate reserve
levels are determined by two major factors: interest rate differentials between
currencies and the country's external vulnerabilities. Aizenman and Marion
(2003) present a well-known result along this line. In their model, reserve
adequacy depends on such scaling factors as population and per capita GDP
plus a country's sensitivity to external shocks as captured by the volatility of
net exports and nominal effective exchange rates as well as the degree of
openness as defined by the import-to-GDP ratio. According to this analysis,
foreign reserves of several Asian countries, including Japan, China, Korea,
Thailand, and the Philippines exceed these countries' needs.

Reserves as a shock absorber

Yet, we should not jump to the conclusion that Asian countries should reduce their 'excessive' foreign reserves. As can be easily seen, the buffer-stock model does not take into account the possibility that monetary authorities have an incentive to hold precautionary reserves against future external difficulties. If monetary authorities are 'loss averters' they are more averse to downside risk than to upside risk. Such conservatism leads them to hold precautionary reserves against potential financial contingencies. The fear of contagion effects associated with a currency crisis has also prompted monetary authorities to increase reserve holdings. As foreign reserves can serve as a shock absorber in times of external difficulties, it is understandable that the desired reserve levels for emerging Asian economies have shifted upward after the 1997–8 crises.

Relationship with the exchange rate mechanism

Viewed from a different perspective, Asia's reserve accumulation is taking place at the same time as the monetary authorities in this region attempt to stabilize exchange rates in an environment of global capital mobility. After the currency crises, some Asian economies reverted to a de facto US dollar-peg, and their reserves subsequently began growing. In July 2005, China and Malaysia announced the adoption of managed float exchange rate systems. However, judging from the daily movements, their currencies are still virtually tied to the US dollar. Under such quasi-fixed or strictly managed exchange rate regimes, central banks tend to hold larger reserves to maintain exchange rate stability.

Therefore, to have a better understanding of Asia's large-scale reserve pile-ups, it is useful to look at the background of exchange rate policies in this region.

First, most Asian countries base their economic success on strong exports as well as massive inflows of foreign direct investment (FDI). Empirical studies confirm that exchange rate volatility could have adverse effects on cross-border trade and FDI. This is the primary reason for Asian countries to try to keep exchange rates within narrow ranges.

Second, cross-border transactions in and out of Asia are still invoiced in the US dollar. This creates a strong preference for stable exchange rates vis-à-vis the US dollar. Also, for relatively small open economies such as most countries in Asia, stable exchange rates contribute to domestic price stability as well.

Third, a large foreign reserve buffer reduces the dependency on the international funding environment. The funding costs for emerging economies can be highly volatile and sensitive to the international interest rate environment. Adequate foreign reserves may be helpful in bridging a temporary funding gap during times of unfavourable external funding conditions.

Moreover, even if a country can borrow on the international financial markets, it cannot necessarily borrow in its own currency. In the pre-crisis period, many Asian countries had to rely on short-term external debt denominated in the US dollar. This funding constraint is sometimes referred to as the 'double mismatch (of maturity and currency)' or the 'original sin', which ended up triggering an abrupt reversal of capital inflows once the economic conditions of Asian countries worsened in the late 1990s. In Asia's case, the 'original sin' problem was amplified by the weak banking sector being badly damaged by the sharp fall in exchange rates. Emerging economies tend to have an aversion against floating when they are subject to 'original sin' constraints. Under such circumstances, they are likely to hold large reserves to limit currency volatility.

5.3　COUNTRY EXPERIENCES: JAPAN AND CHINA

Asia is an area of immense diversity in culture, religion, language, and political and economic systems. This also holds for foreign exchange policy in this region, though. This paragraph discusses the experiences of Japan and China in this regard.

Japan

Since the early 1970s, the yen has followed an appreciation trend. In this process, Japan's monetary authorities intervened occasionally in the foreign exchange market to stop the yen's sharp rise, which led to the accumulation of the world's largest foreign reserve holdings. It is fair to say that this pro-intervention stance was prompted, to some degree, by the alleged vulnerability of Japan's growth performance to exchange rate swings.

In 2003 and 2004, Japan conducted yen-selling interventions on an unprecedented scale. This was done in order to contain the deflationary spiral when business confidence was still weak. Coupled with the Bank of Japan's monetary easing, this massive intervention proved to be effective. Besides, when the Ministry of Finance was short of necessary funds for intervention, the Bank provided the Ministry with additional funding through a special swap arrangement. But currency intervention, including such large-scale operations as the one in 2003–4, is more of an exception than a norm.

Yen-selling operations are financed by the issuance of Financing Bills (FB). FBs are registered on the credit side of the balance sheet of the government Foreign Exchange Fund Special Account, while foreign reserve assets are posted on its debit side. Due to the accounting standards used by the Japanese government, valuation losses arising from exchange rate fluctuations do not materialize on the balance sheet of this special account at the end of each fiscal year. However, it could be debated whether such treatment is really appropriate from a risk management viewpoint. Part of the profits of the Foreign Exchange Fund Special Account has been transferred to the government General Account. From the 1990s onwards, this profit transfer has amounted to a significant sum while Japan's tax revenues have remained stagnant in the economic downturn.

Because the liability side of the Fund currently carries extremely low interest rates, Japan's foreign reserves, a substantial portion of which is invested in US Treasury securities, earn high net returns. If and when domestic market rates go up, the spread will of course narrow.

Japan's reserve management practices

Japan's foreign reserves totalled almost $846 billion at the end of August 2005. About 5 per cent of this is held by the Bank of Japan (BOJ) and the rest by the Ministry of Finance (MOF). Both institutions manage their reserves separately. Although the Ministry has a front office for its reserve operations, all the back office functions (including those for the Ministry) are executed by the BOJ. As for information disclosure of foreign reserves, the BOJ compiles monthly data on an aggregated basis, and the MOF publishes them in line with the IMF SDDS template[1].

Japan had been a 'dormant investor', because it had kept investing large portions of its foreign reserves in bank deposits and US Treasury Bills, which required little sophistication in investment strategy. In 2000, the BOJ introduced a new reserve management strategy, making the maintenance of safety and liquidity of the portfolio a top priority. Within this constraint, the BOJ pursues return enhancement as a secondary objective. Due to its large-scale dollar-buying intervention in 2003–4, Japan is facing a new challenge of reorganizing the management of its huge foreign reserves. Japan is changing the maturity profile of its foreign reserves to replicate pre-defined benchmarks. The MOF has also publicized similar principles of its reserve management in 2005.

Bank of Japan's reserve management policy

Like many other central banks, the Bank of Japan subdivides its reserve portfolio into two distinct tranches: a liquidity portfolio and an investment portfolio. The tranche structure allows the BOJ to define separate objectives and benchmarks for each portfolio, depending on the potential liquidity needs estimated over different time horizons.

The liquidity portfolio comprises assets with the highest level of liquidity. Its maturity does not exceed one year. The size of the liquidity portfolio is adjustable in accordance with the Bank of Japan's liquidity considerations. Two issues are of particular relevance with regard to the importance of liquidity management for the reserve portfolio.

First, as in many other countries, Japan's monetary authorities need to remain capable of conducting currency intervention in times of market disturbances. Such intervention is aimed at ensuring an orderly functioning of the foreign exchange market. Thus, the BOJ needs to preserve sufficient foreign reserves.

Second, it is also vital for monetary authorities to retain the capacity to meet emergency liquidity needs whenever they arise. Sharp drains on foreign reserves could happen when the country is hit by external payment difficulties. When determining the foreign reserve structure in terms of total amount, asset composition, maturity configuration, etc, the BOJ needs to simulate various scenarios that could trigger sudden drains on reserves. Of course, it is extremely difficult to quantify the magnitude of such drains in advance.

Each external crisis is different. From the early 1980s through the 1990s, foreign reserves were often mobilized for international financial assistance on a bilateral basis. When a country was hit by balance-of-payment difficulties, temporary liquidity assistance was extended in the form of bridging loans in order to give the country sufficient breathing space until an IMF loan was disbursed.

Another example in this connection are the 9/11 terrorist attacks in the US. Almost all the financial institutions and major clearing houses based in New York were thrown into confusion for a certain period of time. Central banks were gravely concerned about whether the financial institutions could settle dollar transactions and the possible impact of payment disruptions on the functioning of financial markets. In order to respond properly to financial contingencies like these, reserve managers should simulate potential drains on their portfolios even in normal times. Worst-case scenario analysis may provide useful insights into this forward-looking exercise.

The investment portfolio, in contrast, consists of securities and deposits with longer maturities and somewhat less liquidity. Interest rate risk of the investment portfolio is managed within the framework of passive index tracking, with the target maturity falling within the 1–5 year range. The investment portfolio contains a diversified set of currencies, including the US dollar, euro, and pound sterling. In terms of currency composition, durations and other key elements, the Bank of Japan considers market neutrality, in the sense of not sending disturbing signals to financial markets, to be very important.

Because of a high aversion to credit risk, the BOJ puts the bulk of its investment portfolio in securities and deposits issued by entities with the highest credit standings, meaning sovereigns and international financial institutions. While the Bank of Japan conducts its asset management entirely in-house, it is now exploring the possibility of using external reserve managers. The motivation behind this is to broaden the asset universe to buy structured debt, whose risk profile is too complex to manage in-house. The BOJ is also conducting securities lending, by which US Treasuries are lent out of the investment portfolio. Profits earned from securities lending accrue to the investment portfolio.

China

Under the quasi dollar-peg system, China enjoyed solid growth driven by strong exports and FDI inflows. This trend was further accelerated by China's admission to the WTO in 2001. Growth in exports and FDI has resulted in China's large external surplus as well as its enormous stockpile of foreign reserves. But this situation is posing a new policy dilemma: how should China reconcile rapid reserve accumulation under the mounting upward pressure on its currency (RMB) with the smooth monetary management in a domestic context?

In order to maintain a quasi US dollar-peg, the Chinese central bank has purchased virtually all foreign currencies flowing into the country. Over the three years to June 2005, the central bank's foreign currency assets had almost tripled in size to RMB5.5 trillion ($686 billion), pushing up their share of the total central bank assets from 42 per cent to 59 per cent. As of end January 2006 China's foreign exchange reserves reached $845 billion, making China for the first time the largest reserve holder. This centralized buy-up of foreign currencies has been boosting China's monetary base, which has been sterilized by sales of central bank bills. In April 2003, the central bank began to sell bills to absorb liquidity from the domestic money market. Throughout 2004, the bank issued these liquidity-draining bills 105 times, with their total balance reaching RMB1.5 trillion ($187 billion).

Yet, sterilization operations have their limitations. First of all, the central bank is exposed to potential valuation losses on its foreign reserves as the RMB inches toward appreciation. Valuation losses of this magnitude could erode the central bank's financial soundness. Second, profitability of China's foreign reserve is affected by the interest differentials between China and the US, because a sizable portion of its foreign reserves is held in US sovereign securities. In February 2004, for example, the Chinese central bank earned roughly 1 per cent on its three-month US Treasury holdings while paying 2.3 per cent for its sterilizing (liquidity-absorbing) operations. By now this negative spread (−1.3 per cent) has disappeared, but the large outstanding volume of the bills sold (worth RMB1.6 trillion at end-June 2005) makes the central bank susceptible to global interest rate dynamics.

Another question to be asked is how China can achieve a domestic economic equilibrium. Even though its export sector is highly competitive, China's agriculture sector is believed to be vulnerable to the strong RMB. In order to create sufficient jobs for keeping poverty and unemployment in check, China may be reluctant to see a rapid appreciation of the RMB exchange rate.

The Chinese private sector possesses only a limited amount of foreign assets. Due to capital controls, it is very difficult for the Chinese private sector to hold overseas assets, while the US private sector holds foreign assets almost equal in value to nominal GDP. If capital account liberalization proceeds in the near future, the Chinese private sector will considerably increase its foreign asset holdings. In this process, the Chinese government could transfer some of its huge foreign reserves to the private sector in order to avoid exchange rate disturbances.

5.4. FUTURE DIRECTION OF FOREIGN RESERVE MANAGEMENT

In the medium- to long term, we may find various elements that decrease the need for reserve accumulation. Looking at Asian foreign exchange rate policy, many central banks in the region put primary emphasis on domestic price stability, rather than fixing the exchange rate at a certain level. Supported by strong capital inflows, many countries in the region are able to maintain lower interest rates and enjoy rising domestic demand, which may create more room for accepting some currency appreciation.

In the long run, it may seem plausible that Asian emerging economies will become less dependent on exports as a growth engine. As more Asian countries become aware of the downside of the dollar peg policy, a flexible exchange rate regime may gain further prevalence in this region, which will eventually affect their reserve accumulation policies, too.

Asian countries are trying to establish a new safety net to counter future financial crises. Under the Chiang Mai Initiative (CMI), bilateral swap agreements among the ASEAN+3 nations (ten ASEAN countries plus Japan, China and Korea) are being expanded, with their overall funds exceeding $80 billion. In view of the rescue packages offered to the Asian countries in the 1997–8 crises, this total amount of $80 billion should not be taken lightly. Logically speaking, the larger the aggregate funds of the swap arrangements become, the smaller the need for each country to hold precautionary foreign reserves. Asia's network of bilateral swap agreements could be developed into a regional pooling of reserves, though only in the long run.

Along with the CMI, Asian countries are working together towards the development of Asian bond markets. For instance, a group of central banks in the Asia-Pacific, known as EMEAP, Executives' Meeting of East Asia and Pacific, is pursuing the so-termed Asian Bond Fund (ABF) project. The ABF invests in sovereign and quasi-sovereign bonds issued by EMEAP economies excluding Australia, New Zealand and Japan. The first stage (ABF1) launched in 2003 invested in US dollar-denominated bonds, while the second one (ABF2) of 2005 invested in local currency denominated bonds[2].

The ABF projects are expected to raise investor awareness and interest in Asian bonds by providing innovative, low-cost and efficient products in the form of passive-style investment funds. It is also believed that the ABF serves to further broaden and deepen the regional bond markets and hence contribute to more efficient financial intermediation in Asia, specifically through promoting new products, improving market infrastructure, and accelerating developments in EMEAP markets.

The ASEAN+3 group, comprised of both finance ministries and central banks in this region, is working on the sophistication of the local bond market infrastructure. By resolving 'original sin' problems, regional bond market development will contribute to reducing the frequency of financial crises, and therefore obviate the need for massive reserve accumulation.

NOTES

1. See for an overview of the SDDS template http://dsbb.imf.org/Applications/web/overview.
2. See also http://www.bis.org/press/p030602.htm.

6. Dealing with Reserve Accumulation: The Case of Korea

Heung Sik Choo

6.1 INTRODUCTION

Since the Asian currency crisis broke out in 1997, the foreign reserves of the Bank of Korea have increased dramatically from $9 billion to more than $210 billion at the end of 2005. This build up of reserves reflects the resilience of the Korean economy, but it also places policy makers under greater pressure to improve returns on reserves and to address other issues related to reserve management.

This chapter will discuss recent changes in portfolio management at the Bank of Korea, which are largely due to the dramatic increase in its reserves. Before taking up this theme, this chapter will first briefly review the history of the Bank of Korea's foreign reserve management.

6.2 TOWARD A NEW FRAMEWORK FOR RESERVE MANAGEMENT

The foreign reserves held by the Bank of Korea started to increase from 1988 and grew to over $10 billion in 1990. This accumulation of reserves generated increased interest in efficient asset management, and gave rise to more attention being given to profitability. Reflecting these changes in environment, the Bank of Korea fundamentally reformed its system of reserve management, beginning from 1996, shortly before the Asian currency crisis broke out.

Firstly, the Bank of Korea transformed its reserve management system from deposit-based cash management to fixed-income portfolio management. At the same time, the Bank extended its asset duration to beyond two years, from the previous short-term duration of only several months. With government bond liquidity being much higher than that of time deposits, this change actually strengthened the liquidity of the assets. Also, returns could be returns could be enhanced by extending the asset duration at periods of globally lower interest rates.

Secondly, the reserve assets were split into two tranches in accordance with their purposes and each with their own different benchmarks. With the continuous increase in foreign reserve holdings, the Bank of Korea was able to seek higher returns than before despite some sacrifices in terms of liquidity and safety. This was considered to be a more efficient style of management. The liquidity portfolio was mainly composed of US dollar-denominated money market instruments such as Treasury bills, agency discount notes and short-term time deposits, in order to be prepared for any possible short-term demand for foreign payments. The optimal size of the liquidity portfolio was based upon the supply and demand outlook for foreign currencies. When the size of the liquidity portfolio deviated from the appropriate range, it was adjusted by shifting funds to or from the investment portfolio. Such adjustments might take place every quarter. In this context, the liquidity tranche played the role of a buffer portfolio, which prevented any sudden inflow or outflow of foreign reserves from affecting the exposure of the investment tranche with respect to interest and exchange rate risks.

With the continuous increase in Korea's foreign exchange reserves in the aftermath of the 1997 currency crisis, the short-term demand for foreign currency has generally remained at a very low level, as a result of which the size of the liquidity portfolio could be kept at a relatively low level.

The investment portfolio takes the greatest weight among the reserve tranches and its management focus is on satisfying the needs for liquidity and safety as well as on the maximization of returns on assets. It is mainly concentrated in medium to long-term government bonds and government agency bonds, and also includes supranational bonds. In setting up the investment portfolio's benchmark, currency allocation is determined first and then comes asset allocation. The currency benchmark is decided in consideration of economic factors such as the currency composition of Korea's foreign payments, foreign liabilities, and the size of the various major bond markets.

Meanwhile, the asset composition for products is customized using the Lehman Global Aggregate Index, and a portfolio is selected with the highest expected return given a maximum loss probability of 5 per cent. The benchmark portfolio can serve as a standard for the investment guidelines as well as the performance of asset managers. The appropriateness of the benchmark portfolio is regularly checked. Along with these changes, the Bank of Korea initiated mark-to-market analysis of its reserve management, and at the same time put in place the necessary IT support systems.

These changes did not initially see the light of day, however, due to the outbreak of the 1997 currency crisis, at which time the Bank was forced to liquidate all portfolios. However, the foreign reserves have increased remarkably since then, which gave an opportunity to put the changes at work effectively.

6.3 ADEQUATE LEVELS OF RESERVES

The foreign reserves of the Bank of Korea increased dramatically after the 1997 currency crisis and quickly passed the $100 billion level. Now they are over $200 billion and rank fourth in size worldwide. This substantial increase in the country's foreign exchange reserve holdings has resulted in more attention being given to the issue of what represents an adequate level for foreign reserves.

Controversy concerning the adequate level of foreign reserve holdings is mainly focused on the costs and benefits of holding reserves. Having ample foreign reserves provides intangible benefits, such as a positive impact on the sovereign credit ratings and guarding against vulnerability in the economy, with the securing of foreign exchange market stability being considered the priority task.

Meanwhile, the opportunity cost of holding reserves can be directly explained as the gap between the costs in financing them and the returns on the portfolio. In particular, monetary policy considerations call for stabilizing interventions in domestic markets and, therefore, Korea has to bear the heavy burden of greatly increased costs of monetary operations. Specifically, monetary stabilization bonds are issued to absorb the expanding domestic money supply that comes with the accumulation of foreign reserves.

The Bank of Korea belongs to the group of those central banks that have actually experienced and come to understand fully the meaning of being lenders of last resort. The Bank of Korea is painfully aware of the importance of liquidity and safety in managing reserves, although people tend to forget these things rather easily. Foreign reserves of the Bank of Korea amounted to over $60 billion in the mid-1990s. However, over half of this amount was used as government funding for private financial institutions in the wake of the severe banking crisis and, hence, was not available as truly worthy foreign reserves. In 1997 Korea's reserves declined from $30 billion to $5 billion in a period of 30 days.

At the moment, the foreign exchange reserves of the Bank of Korea amount to more than $200 billion. The current level of reserves is estimated to be sufficient to cover any sudden outflows of foreign exchange from the country. It is very difficult, however, to evaluate whether this current level of reserves is adequate or not. There is no standard for an adequate level of reserves that can be uniformly applied to all countries. Indicators that are frequently used, such as reserves-to-GDP, reserves-to-imports, reserves-to-money supply indicate that the Bank of Korea has an above-sufficient level of foreign reserves. These figures, however, do not take into account the unique situation of Korea.

The Republic of Korea (South Korea) has to pay particular attention to the political tensions in its relation with North Korea, as well as the enormous potential costs in the case of unification. Considering this special factor together with the experience of the currency crisis in 1997, it is deemed desirable by the Bank of Korea to take a relatively conservative approach towards judging the adequate level for its foreign reserves.

Figure 6.1 Growth of foreign exchange reserves, Bank of Korea

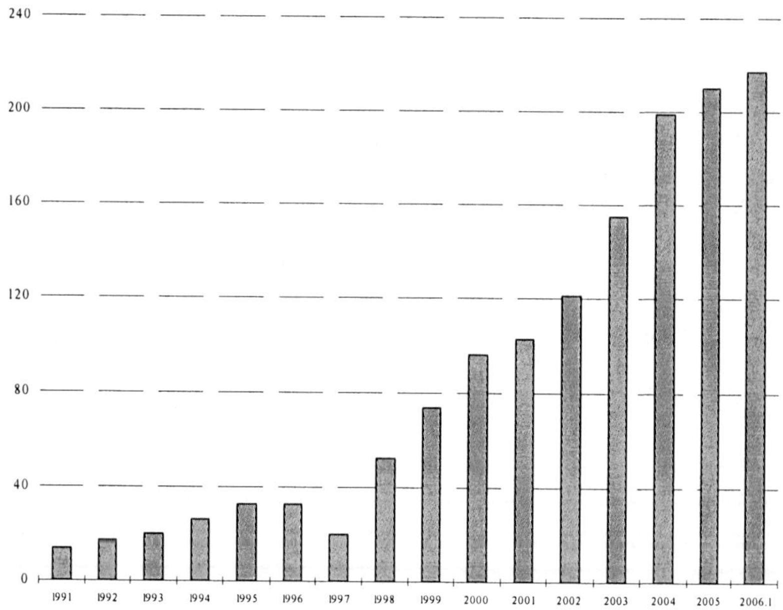

6.4   ENHANCING RETURNS ON INCREASING RESERVES

In recent years, the profitability of central bank reserves has been watched with greater interest than before. This is the situation for the Bank of Korea as well. This phenomenon has come about for three main reasons.

Rapid increase in reserves

The total volume of global reserves has increased rapidly over the past decade, principally in order to combat financial market turbulence. The sheer size of foreign reserves, which stood $217 billion at the end of the first quarter of 2006, reduced the need to hold all reserves in highly liquid assets. This has fed through to affect foreign exchange reserve management policies and operations at the Bank of Korea.

Shortage of traditional central bank investment products

It is worth pointing out that in recent years the growth of advanced countries' government bond markets has fallen behind the growth of central bank reserves. In the early 1990s, for example, the outstanding amount of US Treasuries totalled about $3.3 trillion, while the amount of reserves held by central banks globally amounted to just around $1 trillion. By the end of 2004, however, while the amount of reserves worldwide had risen dramatically to over $3.9 trillion, the outstanding amount of US Treasuries had grown by only a relatively small amount, to $4 trillion. In response, central banks have expanded their investment universe to include government agency bonds. However, the scale of the agency bond market is not large enough to match the pace of the increases in central bank reserves. Furthermore, these instruments are not completely free of credit risk.

Therefore, central banks face some very critical decisions with respect to their foreign reserve management policies and operations. One of the questions that central banks ask themselves is whether they want to extend their investment universe to products such as mortgage-backed securities (MBS), corporate bonds or equities. Some of these products would involve lowering their minimum credit rating requirements further to single A or even BBB. Another key issue is how far and how fast they will carry out such portfolio changes.

Strengthened capability for reserve management

Central bank reserve management capabilities have also made rapid progress. In order to diversify their investment universes successfully, central banks must be able to control and analyse the related risks effectively. They must be equipped with quality IT support systems and experienced staff with specialized expertise. It is generally agreed that central banks were in the past unable to fulfil these requirements. Recently, however, realizing the importance of reserve management, central banks have invested heavily in IT support systems, while attracting specialists in the field of asset and risk management. Accordingly, this has increased the capabilities for diversification into new products.

6.5 THE BANK OF KOREA'S POLICY RESPONSES

It is against this background of a changing reserve management environment that changes in the reserve management of the Bank of Korea have taken place.

Diversification of the investment universe

As of 2005, the Bank of Korea has invested directly in agency bonds, supranational bonds and top quality financial sector bonds, as well as government bonds issued by major developed countries. It has also invested indirectly, through external managers, in MBS, ABS and corporate bonds.

Certainly, additional diversification of the investment universe will be the only option available as the level of reserves continues to grow. The Bank of Korea began investing in MBS early 2006, using a small proportion of its reserves. MBS can produce higher long-term returns than Treasuries, while allowing maintenance of very similar liquidity and security. On the other hand, specific back office and middle office expertise is necessary for settling the instruments and managing the prepayment risk that is a distinctive feature of MBS. That is why it took almost a year for the Bank of Korea to prepare for MBS investment.

The next step will be investment in corporate bonds. However, successful investment in corporate bonds requires analysing and monitoring information on individual issuers in terms of their credit risk, which requires staff that is skilled in this area. Moreover, some sectors of the corporate bond market do not have sufficient breadth to enable a central bank to invest in them on a large scale. It will probably take time to explore corporate bonds as vehicles for direct investment.

In line with its increased tolerance of risk within the overall portfolio, the Bank of Korea has classified its reserves into three tranches, setting up a new 'long-term investment tranche' in addition to the already existing liquidity and investment tranches. The purpose of the long-term investment tranche is to achieve high returns on a long-term basis. Thus, the investment horizon of the long-term investment tranche is twice as long as that of the investment tranche.

Investment of the long-term investment tranche can ultimately be extended into equity-linked notes and emerging market bonds, and it may also involve relaxing the credit rate requirement from the current AA level to a somewhat lower level.

Strengthening of organizational structure and personnel management

The objectives of reserve management must include enhancing profitability as well as securing liquidity and safety, by extending the investment universe. Consequently, it is essential that the Bank of Korea's organizational set-up, including our governance structure and human resource management, be more closely aligned to these objectives.

In August 2005, the reserve management units at the Bank of Korea were divided into three parts: front office, middle office and back office. The responsibilities of each function are very clear and independent of each other, and strict Chinese walls are established between our front and back offices. Moreover, several teams were created to focus more on quantitative analysis in developing advanced asset allocation frameworks and investment strategies. Among these new teams are the MBS Team, the Quant Analysis Section and the Investment Strategy Team.

Figure 6.2 Organizational chart

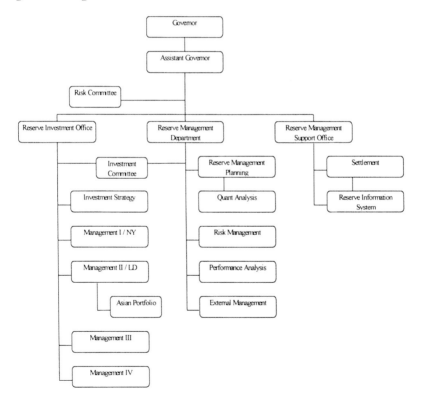

In terms of expanding the workforce and to attract the necessary skills, in addition to the mainstream human resources system, which usually hires and trains recruits straight from college, the Bank of Korea has now begun hiring outside specialists. In the last quarter of 2005, the Bank recruited five investment professionals from the private sector in areas such as MBS investment, quantitative analysis, and investment strategy. As a separate development, on 1 July 2005 the Korean government launched the Korea Investment Corporation (KIC). The KIC will manage part of the foreign exchange reserves, initially $20 billion, to achieve a sustainable return on foreign-currency assets through a diversified investment strategy.

6.6 CONCLUSION

This chapter has focused on the changes affecting central bank reserve management, and on the Bank of Korea's responses to them. Central banks are faced with ever increasing calls for enhanced returns, and therefore need to put greater efforts into professionalizing their reserve management. As the demand for higher returns on investment increases, the effective management of risks arising from reserves management also becomes more critical. Above all, since any failure in risk management on the part of a central bank would severely affect its credibility, efforts to raise profitability are meaningless unless there is a firm risk-management system in place.

7. Reserve Accumulation: A View from the United States

Matthew Higgins[1]

7.1 INTRODUCTION

The period since 2002 has seen an unprecedented build-up in foreign exchange reserves, mostly by Pacific Rim countries and, more recently, major oil exporters. This fact is undoubtedly one of the key reasons for the growing interest in reserve management. Simply put, for many countries, potential gains and losses on the reserve portfolio have grown too big to be ignored.

The other chapters in this volume provide an illuminating survey of the challenges of reserve management. My aim is to provide background. In particular, I will review trends in overall and dollar reserve accumulation. I will then turn to the role of foreign reserve accumulation in financing the US current account deficit, and the potential impact of reserve accumulation on US and global financial markets. I will close with some comments on reserve accumulation and the domestic policy mix.

7.2 TRENDS IN GLOBAL RESERVE ACCUMULATION

Global reserve holdings have swelled in recent years. All told, central bank foreign exchange holdings came to $4.2 trillion at the end of 2005, more than double the holdings at the end of 2001[2]. Of that sum, $2.9 trillion, or almost 70 per cent, was held by central banks in the developing world. Just $1.3 trillion was held by industrial economy (or more accurately, post-industrial economy) central banks.

Of course, economies have been growing along with reserve stocks. Scaling reserve holdings relative to GDP reveals a marked contrast.

Reserve holdings by industrial countries have edged up only slightly in recent years, from just over 3 per cent of GDP at end-2001 to just under 4 per cent at end-2005 (see Figure 7.1). Reserve holdings by developing countries have mushroomed, rising past 24 per cent of GDP, an increase of roughly 7.5

percentage points over the period. Looking farther back, developing country reserve holdings as share of GDP have maintained a clear upward trend since about 1990.

Figure 7.1 Reserve gains outpace developing country GDP
            foreign exchange reserves, % GDP

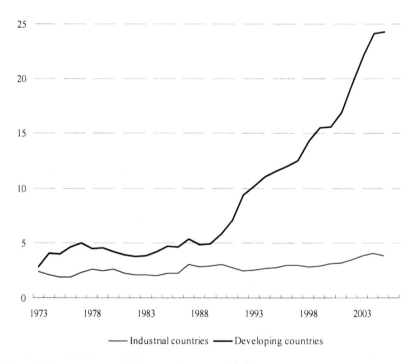

Industrial countries ——— Developing countries

Source: IMF.

Which countries are responsible for the surge in global reserve holdings? In the developed world, Japan has accounted for the bulk of reserve purchases in recent years; but Japan has been essentially absent from the market since the spring of 2004 (see Table 7.1)[3]. In the developing world, China and other Asian economies have been making the largest reserve purchases. More recently, however, reserve purchases by oil exporters have risen to become roughly equal in scale, reflecting central bank recycling of growing petrodollar receipts.

Table 7.1 Reserve accumulation ($ billion)

	2003	2004	2005
Japan	187	161	22
China	153	207	233
Other Asia	123	133	86
Fuel Exporters	89	153	275
Total	552	654	616

Sources: IMF, national sources. Data for China adjusted to include reserves used for bank recapitalizations. Under *Fuel Exporters*, data for Saudi Arabia include all central bank foreign currency assets, not just those labeled by the Saudi authorities as reserves.

The US dollar has remained the main global reserve currency. Estimates from the BIS place dollar reserve holdings at almost $2.6 trillion at the end of 2004, roughly 70 per cent of the total (see Figure 7.2)[4]. The estimated dollar share is down from 76 per cent as recently as 2001, but is up several percentage points from the share a decade ago[5].

Unfortunately, it will be harder to track the fraction of reserves held in dollar assets going forward. The BIS no longer estimates the fraction of total reserves held in dollars. And while the IMF continues to construct estimates of dollar reserve holdings, it classifies a large and growing fraction of total reserves as held in unspecified currencies.

Of note, however, there has been a sizeable gap between total dollar reserve assets as estimated by the BIS, and US reserve liabilities as reported by the Bureau of Economic Advisers (BEA). At end-2004, for example, the BEA reported US reserve liabilities of just under $2 trillion, roughly $600 billion below dollar reserve assets as estimated by the BIS (see Figure 7.3). What explains this gap?

The explanation has several parts. First, US securities are often purchased by foreign private brokers and dealers acting on behalf of foreign central banks. Similarly, foreign private custodians hold US securities on behalf of foreign central banks. The US reporting system would correctly show such securities as held by foreign investors. But the US reporting system would incorrectly show the ultimate beneficial owner as private rather than official.

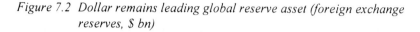

*Figure 7.2 Dollar remains leading global reserve asset (foreign exchange
           reserves, $ bn)*

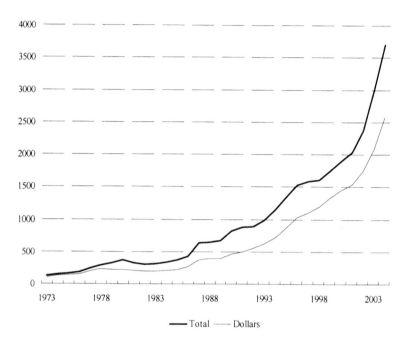

Sources: IMF, BIS.

Third, central banks hold some dollar-denominated claims on non-US
sovereigns and international institutions. We have no reliable data on the
scale of such holdings.

Should we consider such central bank dollar holdings as part of US
reserve liabilities? There is no ambiguity concerning dollar securities
purchased for, or held on behalf of, central banks by non-US private brokers
or custodians. Such central bank holdings would be counted as US reserve
liabilities under a globally comprehensive reporting system. (Limited
regulatory sway over foreign financial institutions may mean that there is little
the US authorities can do to address the issue.) What about dollar deposits
and dollar securities created outside the US?

Consider the case of deposits. Foreign central banks would of course
count those claims as dollar reserve assets. But because foreign monetary
authorities have no direct claim on a US bank, standard reserve accounting
would not treat the deposits as constituting US reserve liabilities[6]. However, a
foreign central bank buying a US dollar deposit makes the same contribution

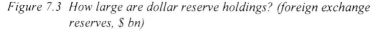

Figure 7.3 How large are dollar reserve holdings? (foreign exchange reserves, $ bn)

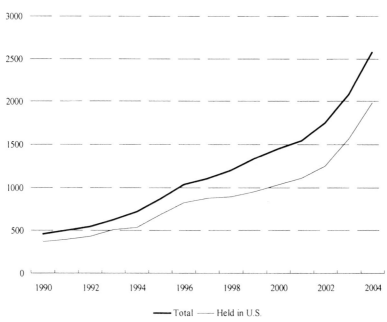

Sources: BEA, BIS estimates

to global demand for dollar assets regardless of where the deposit is held. In my view, such deposits should be considered along with standard US reserve liabilities from an economic perspective. That includes analysis of the role of foreign authorities in financing the US current account deficit, and in determining the exchange value of the dollar.

Much the same holds true for dollar denominated securities issued by non-US entities. To buy such a security, a foreign central bank must first acquire US dollar liquidity. Equally, the issuer must acquire US dollar liquidity in order to make payment. While transactions in offshore dollar securities don't generate a claim on a US entity, they are matched by a transaction elsewhere that does generate such a claim. For this reason, offshore dollar bonds should be considered along with standard US reserve liabilities for purposes of economic analysis.

To be sure, the argument is not that offshore dollar deposits and securities are economically identical to their on-shore counterparts. Offshore and on-shore dollar assets are close but not perfect substitutes. Rather, the argument is limited to the first-order impact on the dollar exchange rate, and to identifying the ultimate source of demand for dollar assets.

Figure 7.4 Balance of payments flows in emerging Asia ($ billion)

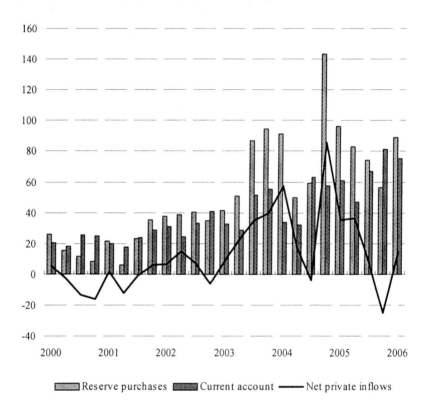

Sources: CEIC, national sources. Private inflows calculated as a residual.

7.3 RESERVE ACCUMULATION, THE US CURRENT ACCOUNT DEFICIT AND GLOBAL FINANCIAL MARKETS

How important a role have foreign central banks recently played in financing the US current account deficit? In a simple accounting sense, a very important role. The US current account deficit is linked to reserve purchases via the following identity:

Current Account Deficit = *Net Private Financial Inflows + Net Official Financial Inflows*

During 2003 through 2005, according to BEA data, the net flow of official capital to the US totalled $857 billion, enough to finance 44 per cent of the US current account deficit. Private investors, according to these data, financed the remaining 56 per cent of the US deficit.

However, the BEA data largely miss inflows by private investors made on behalf of central banks. Some fraction of recorded private inflows, especially from London and Caribbean financial centres, represent official inflows at one remove.

The BEA data also do not capture central bank purchases of dollar deposits and dollar-denominated, non-US securities. As an accounting matter, this is as it should be, as such assets do not involve a claim on a US resident. However, they do add to global demand for dollar assets. As a result, such purchases allow the US current account deficit to be financed on more favourable terms, even if they do not directly finance it.

The impact of central bank purchases of dollar assets on US and global financial markets has generated much discussion, but little consensus. On the face of it, the figures involved sound large. Absent inflows of foreign official capital (and holding constant the current account deficit), expected relative returns on US assets would have had to rise by enough to attract at least $857 billion in additional foreign private capital during 2003–5[7]. Since this BEA figure represents a lower bound, expected relative returns on US assets might have had to rise by many billions more than that.

However, the figures involved sound less large when scaled against the global and US financial markets. According to the BIS, debt securities outstanding totalled $59 trillion worldwide at end-2005[8]. Debt securities issued in the US totalled $24 trillion. Cross-border banking claims totalled another $21.1 trillion, of which $2.4 trillion involved claims on US residents. Given the size of the financial markets, it's at least not immediately obvious that a switch to purely private financing of the US current account deficit would have a large impact on dollar interest rates or other dollar asset prices.

Greenspan (2004) offers a cogent presentation of the view that the impact would be relatively small. He notes that official foreign holdings of US securities tend to be concentrated in shorter maturities, where rates are closely tied to the Federal funds rate. He also points to the large size of dollar fixed income markets, the efficiency of arbitrage and global fixed income markets, and the declining home bias in global investment allocation.

Other authors have argued that the impact of dollar reserve accumulation on US interest rates has been sizeable (see ECB 2006 for a survey of the empirical literature). Warnock and Warnock (2006), for example, estimate that foreign official purchases of US Treasuries have lowered Treasury yields by as much as 90 basis points during certain periods.

On the exchange rate side, empirical studies frequently find a link between foreign exchange intervention and short-term exchange rate movements (see Humpage (2003) for a survey). However, results are typically not robust across countries, time periods or statistical techniques. Equally important, there are no studies that find an economically significant and lasting impact of intervention on exchange rates[9]. There is, at least, room to doubt what appears to be the popular presumption that the dollar would now be substantially and broadly weaker absent the large official purchases of dollar assets of recent years.

The fact that the value of the dollar versus the yen changed little in the weeks after the Japanese authorities moved from massive intervention to zero intervention lends support to this sceptical view.

That said, in my view, identification difficulties place strong limits on how much we can know about the effects of reserve accumulation on asset prices and exchange rates. In Asia, pressures for local currency strength have generally occurred alongside heavy inflows into local markets, often speculative in character (see Figures 7.4 and 7.5). Reserve accumulation to mop up those inflows might be very large relative to any underlying market disequilibrium. For this reason, it is a mistake to equate the scale of reserve purchases with the degree of official support for US financial markets and asset prices.

To restate the point, reserve accumulation that recycles speculative inflows back into global dollar markets might have more modest asset price and exchange rate impacts than accumulation that affects an exogenous increase in demand for dollar assets.

There is a counterargument, one that also turns on the endogeneity of reserve purchases. Reserve purchases, after all, tend to 'lean against the wind'. If they systematically occur when the local currency would otherwise tend to be rising versus the dollar, statistical estimates of their impact would tend to be biased downward. The same holds for the impact of reserve purchases on local and dollar interest rates. If purchases systematically tend to occur when local interest rates would otherwise tend to be falling relative to dollar interest rates, estimates of their impact on rate differentials would tend to be biased downward.

The most general point, though, is as follows. To ask what economic and market outcomes would look like absent recent heavy reserve accumulation, in Asia and elsewhere, is to ask what outcomes would be if reserve purchasers were to adopt a very different set of monetary and exchange rate policies. This is not a counterfactual we can describe with any high degree of confidence.

Figure 7.5 Balance of payments flows in Japan ($ bn)

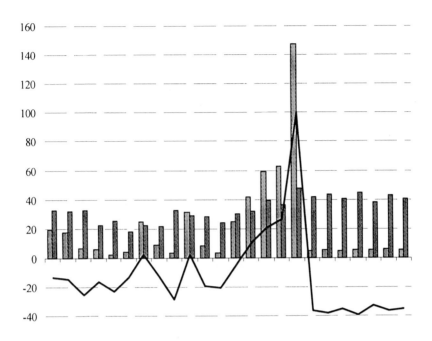

Reserve purchases ▨ Current account ━━━ Net private inflows

Source: Bank of Japan. Private inflows calculated as a residual.

7.4 RESERVE ACCUMULATION AND THE DOMESTIC POLICY MIX

As observed earlier, growing reserve holdings naturally lead to growing interest in issues related to reserve management. But the core mission of central banks is to conduct monetary policy: how reserve policy interacts with larger monetary policy goals is more important than how reserves are managed. For some countries, growing reserve holdings are a symptom of monetary policies that leave the central bank with an ever-expanding balance sheet, and that expose it to ever-growing foreign exchange risk.

Foreign exchange reserves should be trendless for countries with a floating exchange rate, assuming open capital markets. The monetary policy rate is set with an eye to domestic growth and inflation objectives, and the market exchange rate adjusts accordingly. The US and the euro zone are good examples.

Foreign exchange reserves should also be trendless for economies with a fixed exchange rate, again assuming open capital markets. Given the chosen parity, the monetary base and market interest rates adjust endogenously. Hong Kong is a canonical example. Singapore, with its currency basket target, represents a closely related case. The central bank adds or drains liquidity to keep the exchange rate in the target range; market interest rates, in effect, 'float'.

Ongoing reserve accumulation is a symptom of domestic monetary policies that are 'too tight' relative to an exchange rate target (hard or soft), or equivalently, an exchange rate target that is 'too weak' relative to domestic monetary policies. To see why, consider what happens when monetary authorities aim at the opposite combination: liquidity conditions that are 'too loose' relative to an exchange rate target. In such a case, the authorities will see a continuing drain on their foreign exchange reserves. The policy regime breaks down when reserves fall too low.

Similarly, authorities aiming at liquidity conditions that are 'too tight' relative to their exchange rate target will face a continuing drain on their *net* domestic assets (matched, of course, by rising foreign exchange reserves). But the authorities face no hard limit on their ability to issue additional domestic liabilities: net domestic assets can be allowed to fall below zero. Instead, the authorities' ability to issue additional domestic liabilities is limited only by the terms on which the market is willing to continue absorbing them.

In this connection, it is notable that every major central bank in Emerging Asia except China's now has negative net domestic assets[10]. In China, heavy issuance of sterilization liabilities has reduced net domestic assets from more than 20 per cent of GDP at the end of 2003 to less than 1 per cent of GDP at the end of 2005.

In effect, the monetary policy mix in parts of Emerging Asia has left central banks with ever-expanding balance sheets: growing foreign exchange reserves on the asset side, and growing sterilization debt on the liability side.

The constraints on central bank sterilization capacity ultimately derive from sterilization's quasi-fiscal cost. After all, sterilization typically involves purchasing relatively low-yield foreign assets via issuance of relatively high-yield domestic liabilities (or via sales of relatively high-yield domestic assets). The result is reduced earnings for the central bank, and thus, reduced remittances to the Treasury. As sterilization continues, these quasi-fiscal costs rise. Moreover, the authorities may have to offer ever-higher interest rates in order to induce domestic investors to continue adding central bank liabilities to their portfolios.

Sterilized reserve purchases also expose the central bank to foreign exchange risk. If the local currency eventually appreciates against the dollar and other reserve currencies, the central bank's foreign assets lose value in local currency terms. The capital loss is then passed on to the Treasury, in the form of reduced local currency payments of interest and principal. Alternatively, the capital loss could be monetized, at the cost of higher inflation.

The desire to limit foreign exchange risk exposure, not interest rate carrying cost, is the main obstacle to continued rapid reserve accumulation in Asia. For Emerging Asia as a whole, foreign exchange reserves already stand at 36 per cent of GDP. As a result, a 10 per cent appreciation of the local currency versus the dollar and other reserve currencies bring a capital loss equivalent to 3.6 per cent of GDP. The risk exposure for some individual countries is considerably higher.

Partly for this reason, there now appears to be a widespread consensus that economies in Emerging Asia should move toward greater currency flexibility and scaled back foreign exchange intervention over the long run. There is a considerable diversity of views, though, on how best to manage the transition to the long run.

Oil exporters are the second group of countries that have recently engaged in heavy reserve accumulation. However, the exchange rate and monetary policy backdrop has generally been quite different from those in Emerging Asia. In particular, reserve purchases by oil exporters have generally not occurred alongside market pressures for domestic currency appreciation. A key reason is that they have generally amounted to a transfer of foreign exchange from one branch of the official sector to another: from the central government to the central bank.

Most oil export revenues in oil exporting countries flow to the central government; either directly, when the oil industry is state owned; or indirectly, through often heavy taxes on oil production. When government oil export revenues are deposited at the central bank, the central bank makes payment by crediting the government's account at the central bank. As long as the government deposit goes unspent domestically, however, there is no increase in demand for the domestic currency, and no new domestic currency liquidity is injected into the economy.

Instead, the central bank simply recycles the government foreign exchange deposit back out of the country, into foreign exchange reserves, in the form of foreign securities or foreign bank deposits. In effect, reserve accumulation occurs *faute de mieux* – lack of better investment alternatives for the petrodollar windfall – rather than as a deliberate instrument of exchange rate policy.

Saudi Arabia is a good example of a country where reserve purchases follow this pattern. Higher government deposits have offset the bulk of the increase in foreign exchange reserves, leaving little imprint on the monetary base.

When reserve purchases do not affect monetary base, they exert little material pressure on domestic interest rates or the exchange rate. Indeed, Saudi Arabia and many other oil exporters have long maintained fixed exchange rates with little difficulty.

Some other major oil exporters insulate monetary and exchange rate management from petrodollar recycling by keeping it outside the central bank, in a non-monetary, government-run investment agency. Examples include Norway, Kuwait and the United Arab Emirates.

7.5 CONCLUSION

The US data on US reserve liabilities understate the pace of dollar reserve accumulation in recent years. These data do not include official dollar deposits held offshore or most dollar securities purchased from private brokers outside the US. Official purchases of such dollar assets should have essentially the same economic impact as dollar reserve purchases conducted in the US

Reserve accumulation by central banks has played an important role in financing the US current account deficit, at least from an accounting perspective. However, in an economic sense the impact may again be more substantial as for example dollar-denominated non-US securities do not involve claims on US residents but add to the global demand for dollar assets which allowed the US current account deficit to be financed on more favourable terms.

The impact of central bank purchases of dollar assets on US and global financial markets may seem large when measured in terms of the cumulative inflow of foreign official capital into the US over the period 2003–5. However, when scaled against the global and US financial markets, it is not immediately obvious that they would have a large impact on dollar asset prices or the exchange rate. The continuous accumulation of reserves, particularly in emerging Asian countries, generally points at domestic monetary policies that are too tight relative to the exchange rate target. The desire to limit foreign exchange risk exposure by the central banks involved will likely render this policy ultimately unsustainable over the long run, and should trigger an eventual move toward greater currency flexibility.

NOTES

1. The views expressed in this chapter are those of the author, and should not be interpreted as representing the views of the Federal Reserve Bank of New York or the Federal Reserve System.
2. Throughout, I refer to 'central banks' as a convenient shorthand for the more accurate term 'monetary authorities'.
3. Reserve accumulation since then has come entirely or almost entirely from interest receipts on the existing reserve stock.
4. See BIS Annual Report, various issues, and McCauley (2005).
5. The creation of the EMU is one factor that has helped to push the dollar share higher. National central bank claims on other sovereigns in the region no longer count as foreign currency assets.
6. At the same time, standard reserve accounting would treat the deposits as constituting foreign authorities' reserve assets. See the IMF's Manual 5th Edition (1993), pp. 97–8.
7. A rise in expected relative returns on US assets could come from higher US interest rates, an initial decline in the value of the dollar followed by expected dollar appreciation at unchanged interest rates or some combination of the two.
8. See BIS tables 12A, 16A and 2A.
9. This statement applies, of course, to sterilized intervention. The issue is whether sterilized intervention has a large and lasting impact on exchange rates.
10. As I use the term here 'Emerging Asia' refers to China, Hong Kong, India, Indonesia, Malaysia, the Philippines, Singapore, South Korea, Taiwan and Thailand.

PART TWO

Reserve Management: Return versus Liquidity

8. Trends in Reserve Management by Central Banks

Jennifer Johnson-Calari, Roberts Grava and Adam Kobor

8.1 INTRODUCTION

Since the gold standard, foreign currency reserves have provided confidence or backing to fiat money and foreign debt, supported the exchange rate system and provided self-insurance against short-term balance of payments crises. In seeking to understand current trends, it is important to take a historical perspective to understand both the drivers of changes and legacies from earlier regimes. Certain exogenous trends are likely to continue and will fundamentally influence the management of foreign currency reserves. International capital markets are bound to continue widening and deepening with globalization and the relatively higher growth rates of emerging market countries. Non-US dollar currencies will become increasingly acceptable as reserve assets and diversification a more important investment criteria. The prevailing exchange rate regime is likely to remain a managed float with fixed rate regimes existing only within small regions or perhaps replaced with common currency blocks. Finally, the large build-up in reserves due to global financial imbalances is likely to persist in the near term and commodity exporters, in particular, will be the long-term recipients of windfall profits from the extraction and sale of natural resources. It is against this backdrop that one needs to view central banks' traditional investment objectives of liquidity and capital preservation and the catalysts for change.

Under the gold standard, countries backed their currency with gold held in central bank vaults to finance trade and capital account imbalances. In 1968, the French Government demanded reimbursement of their US Treasury debt in gold causing the gold standard to collapse. Subsequently, countries pegged their currencies to the US dollar, which increasingly replaced gold as a reserve asset. The US Government dismantled the so-called dollar system in

1973 when it unilaterally devalued and this system was then replaced by a fixed exchange rate system, whereby countries were free to choose the currency or basket of the peg. Given the global importance of the US economy, however, the US dollar was the still favoured as a currency peg and, until recently, reserves were held overwhelmingly in US dollar short duration assets.

As international capital flows were liberalized in the 1990s, a global fixed exchange rate regime proved untenable in the face of fundamentally misaligned exchange rates. As central banks attempted to defend the fixed exchange rate system, the volatility in the level of reserves was spectacular. In 1992–3, both France and the UK were forced to sell all of their own and borrowed reserves in a vain attempt to defend the peg against short-selling. After the forced realignment of exchange rates, the international investment community then focused its sights on emerging market countries. First the Asian countries (South Korea, Thailand, Indonesia) ran through their reserves before floating followed a few years later by Brazil, Argentina and Turkey. In the speculation against the Brazilian Real, the Central Bank of Brazil was selling up to US$1 billion of reserves in a single day to cover the domestic banks' open foreign currency positions. Given this inherent instability, short-term capital preservation and liquidity were paramount. While important to government budgets, portfolio return was merely a by-product of holding financial assets for liquidity.

By 2001, most exchange rate regimes were characterized by a 'managed float'. Alan Greenspan, Chairman of the Federal Reserve System and Pablo Guidotti, Minister of Finance of Argentina, all espoused building reserves not to defend fixed exchange rates but rather, again, as backing against countries' external debt. Statistical studies done by the IMF[1] validated the fact that countries were less vulnerable to external crises if reserves covered at least 12 months of all debt to non-residents.

Over the last five years, an intertwined skein of factors have contributed to a dramatic build-up in government wealth, mainly in the form of foreign currency reserves. This build-up was particularly concentrated amongst emerging market countries, in which reserves more than doubled to $2.9 trillion in the period 2001–6. Some governments, such as South Korea, heeded the advice of international financial institutions and deliberately ran large current account surpluses to rebuild reserves. More broadly speaking, however, export-driven growth in emerging market countries and corresponding balance of payments deficits in the US led to unprecedented global imbalances, with US current account deficits in large part financed by the increase in emerging market holdings of US Treasury debt. In most emerging market countries, reserves today are thus substantially in excess of what was needed for traditional purposes. The boom in commodity prices furthered this trend, particularly in the case of oil exporters where revenues exceeded the countries' absorptive capacity and ended up either as part of the central bank reserves portfolio or were ring-fenced in a separate government oil fund. During the same period, the European Central Bank was established and the national banks were left with legacy reserves not needed for day-to-day interventions but rather as a war chest of financial assets and gold.

Table 8.1 Reserves relative to short-term debt (STD) and GDP
2001–5

	Dec. 2001		Dec. 2005	
	Reserves/ STD	Reserves/ GDP (%)	Reserves/ STD	Reserves/ GDP (%)
Algeria	3.8	33	11.0	67
Angola	0.5	8	4.0	19
India	3.3	10	7.6	18
Romania	1.0	10	3.0	24
Russia	0.8	11	4.1	28
Ukraine	0.8	8	11.3	22

Sources: IMF, World Economic Outlook Database

This accumulation of national wealth threw down the gauntlet of profitability.

While part of the build-up may prove temporary, with the inevitable unwinding of global imbalances, a substantial part can be considered stable over the medium term – or longer in commodity exporting countries contemplating setting up permanent endowment funds. With a few important exceptions, most countries currently operate under floating rate currency regimes, whereby exchange rate adjustments would take the brunt of adjustment to external imbalances rather than abrupt changes in the level of reserves. Other things being equal, reserves in these countries would tend to be more stable and can be invested over longer investment horizons with more emphasis on return. While many governments have urged central banks to seek higher returns, however, few countries have been able to realize more optimal investment strategies. Misalignment of incentives, legacy investment policies, fragmented institutional decision-making and gaps in financial know-how have all impeded the adoption of more rational policies. Governments and central banks, however, are responding – some in incremental ways, and a few by breaking out of the box. The remainder of this chapter explores the pursuit of return, alongside continued liquidity and capital preservation constraints, and how central banks are responding to these pressures.

8.2 INSTITUTIONAL CHALLENGES: IMPETUS AND IMPEDIMENTS TO CHANGE

Before discussing central bank trends, it is worthwhile investigating the opportunity cost of sub-optimal investment policies and the institutional impediments to change. One of the most important of such impediments is the asymmetrical treatment of opportunity cost – or foregone national wealth – versus reported market value losses. The opportunity cost of a sub-optimal investment policy is rarely measured or reported. Foregone income from adopting a low risk–return strategy is reported neither to the Board nor is it disclosed in the annual report. Any market value losses, however, are required to be disclosed under the market valuation standards of International Financial Reporting Standards (IRFS). This asymmetrical treatment and central banks' natural aversion to risk make it inherently difficult for these public policy institutions to pursue higher risk–return strategies.

Opportunity cost

The opportunity cost of constraining investment strategies to a short-term investment horizon can be enormous. No matter how stable the funds, however, traditional liquidity and capital preservation constraints have continued to prevail. Using a set of simulations based on historical return data, Figure 8.1 seeks to measure the opportunity cost of investing in a short-term government bond portfolio versus a broad investment grade fixed income portfolio. The top graph shows the expected cumulative wealth of a portfolio invested in the Lehman Aggregate Index over a period of 50 years. The bottom graph shows the opportunity cost of investing in a 1–3 year government-only US dollar portfolio, measured as the difference between the wealth of the Lehman Aggregate portfolio and the government-only portfolio at each year. Under normal market conditions, both strategies are quite liquid, although bid-ask spreads on non-governments do widen relative to government bonds during periods of market stress. A broad fixed income mandate could be appropriate for reserves that are likely to be stable, recognizing that such investments can be easily liquidated if necessary. Interim market value volatility and additional liquidation costs are generally more than compensated by additional investment income over time, as can be seen in the following graphs.

Figure 8.1   Opportunity cost of investing in a US$ 1–3 year government
bond portfolio. Lehman Agg portfolio

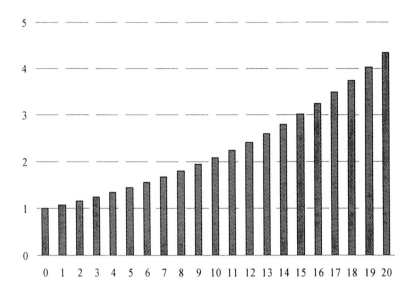

Bond portfolio; government vs Lehman Agg

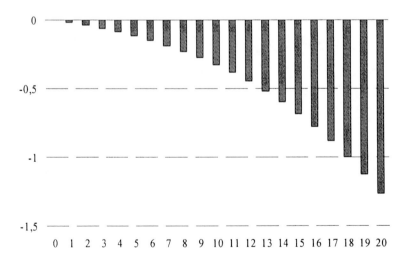

*Figure 8.2 Opportunity cost of investing in a US$ 1–3 year government
            bond portfolio; balanced portfolio (50% Lehman Agg, 50%
            US equities)*

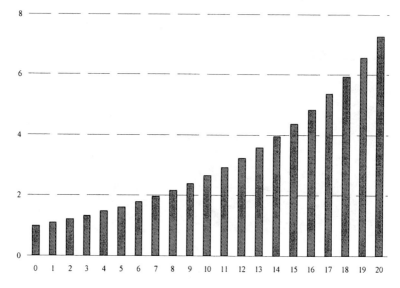

*Opportunity cost: government vs balanced
portfolio*

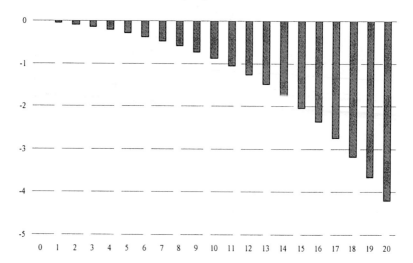

For national commodity funds, one again finds a tendency to invest in high-grade fixed income for 'capital preservation' reasons and lack of public understanding of the risk–return trade-off. Oil and other commodity funds are more akin to long term endowment funds, which seek both current income and capital preservation. In this case, a more appropriate strategic asset allocation would invest across asset classes including equities, bonds and so-called 'alternatives' (real estate, private equity, hedge funds). In this case the opportunity cost of investing in a sub-optimal strategy is even higher as can be seen in Figure 8.2 by comparing the cumulative wealth of a 1–3 year government-only US dollar portfolio versus a simple traditional portfolio of 50% broad fixed income and 50 per cent equities.

While there is broad understanding of the risk–return trade-off amongst central bank asset managers, there are significant obstacles to achieving more optimal investment strategies. As discussed in more detail below, there is a fundamental misalignment of incentives between wealth maximization and the central bank culture. Governments and central bank boards are, however, becoming more aware of the importance of generating higher returns and responding in both incremental and more fundamental ways

Governance

Central banks are unique in that their credibility lies in maintaining independence from their shareholders, their governments, to avoid a potential conflict of interest. While this conflict is most often cited in the context of monetary policy, it may also exist in the area of foreign currency reserves management whereby governments want to maximize short-term earnings for budgetary purposes at the expense of wealth accumulation. Governments also have a preference for stable income contributions to the budget. It is not unusual for governments to pressure central banks for greater investment returns but refuse to accept the occasional 'bad year'. This conflict is somewhat akin to the tension seen in the corporate world between investing to generate long-term earnings and pressure for short-term earnings and stable dividends. Corporations, however, typically have greater autonomy in financial policy decisions and managing variability in dividends, the private sector counterpart of government remittances. Specifically, a corporation can manage dividends and capital through a retained earnings capital account. When central banks set their own accounting policies, they were typically able to manipulate reported income so as to achieve their financial policy goals. As more central banks adopt market-to-market accounting standards, under IFRS, this is no longer the case. Problems are compounded when central banking laws dictate the policy for income remittances. Unless central banks actively adopt an independent financial policy akin to corporations, the result will be to retreat to low risk–return strategies to avoid year-to-year volatility in government remittances albeit at the cost of foregoing higher foreign currency investment earnings.

The central bank board is responsible for defining the preferred risk–return trade-off and agreed investment horizon. This decision forms the basis for both the strategic asset allocation and the appropriate benchmark structure. While this responsibility clearly resides with the Board, in practice, several issues can complicate such decisions. First, the central bank board's primary concern is monetary policy and it may not feel comfortable with developing a view on the appropriate investment horizon or risk tolerance of the institution. Second, the central bank may not have a quantitative team of financial specialists within the reserves management department able to present the expected risk–return trade-off of alternative investment strategies. These institutional gaps, however, are increasingly recognized and there is greater emphasis on establishing the capability and clear accountabilities for the strategic asset allocation decision.

Misalignment of incentives

Confidence in a central bank is its true asset as most central bank liabilities (issuance of bank notes) exceed international reserves. As such, central banks are extremely averse to any potential negative publicity, which constrains their risk tolerance and hence returns. This is most notable with respect to default risk as any loss from a default on an obligation is highly visible and can attract criticism, even if the loss is negligible relative to the portfolio's total return. A few central banks have overcome this constraint and espoused total return portfolio management, whereby results are measured based on the total return rather than on individual securities or asset classes. Such an approach, however, generally requires substantial education of the central bank board and the public at large.

The tyranny of the accounting cycle: 'no red ink'

The most significant obstacle to improving returns may be the accounting cycle, which requires a snapshot of financial results to be taken and published quarterly or at 12-month intervals. In principle, a central bank should determine the appropriate investment horizon based on reserves adequacy considerations and balance of payments stress-testing. The more stable the core reserves, the longer the investment horizon. In practice, however, central bank boards rarely accept an investment horizon longer than the 12-month accounting cycle. Table 8.2 offers one insight into the opportunity cost of this decision based only on the portfolio duration decision. This table presents the mean historical returns for government bond portfolios with increasing duration and, as expected, the mean return increases along with the risk, or volatility of returns. Most central banks interpret the capital preservation constraint as minimizing the probability of a negative total return over the 12-month accounting cycle or even within shorter periods. Table 8.2, which measures the frequency of negative total returns over different measurement periods, illustrates the relationship between the portfolio risk and the measurement period. Specifically, the shorter the measurement period, the riskier the portfolio as measured by frequency of negative total returns. If one constrains the investment horizon to a very short period, the portfolio will inevitably be forced into a low risk–return strategy. Note that for a country with very low reserves adequacy, this may be appropriate. For countries with ample reserves, however, such a stance would have a very high opportunity cost with respect to foregone returns.

Table 8.2 Frequency of negative total returns for US dollar government portfolios

Duration (years)	0.25	0.50	0.75	1.0	1.5	2.0	3.0	4.0
Average Return	5.3%	5.6%	5.8%	5.9%	6.2%	6.3%	6.5%	6.6%
Horizon	Frequency of negative total return							
3 months	0.0%	0.5%	0.6%	1.6%	3.7%	8.0%	16.0%	23.0%
1 year	0.0%	0.0%	0.0%	0.0%	0.0%	1.0%	3.7%	8%
3 years	0.0%	0.0%	0.0%	0.0%	0.0%	0.0%	0.0%	0.0%

Figure 8.4 shows the results of a fixed income portfolio optimization analysis, where eligible portfolios are expected to produce positive expected returns at a 95 per cent confidence level, over various horizons. Clearly, decreased tolerance for losses over shorter horizons will result in portfolios containing less risky assets, and correspondingly less expected return. Over time, such risk-avoiding decisions would result in significant opportunity costs.

Figure 8.3 extends the framework of this optimization analysis to include assets beyond the traditional high-grade fixed income universe prevalent in central bank reserves management. As in the previous analysis, shorter investment horizons will lead to portfolios that generate significantly less expected return than portfolios generated with longer horizons.

However, even in the case of the shortest horizons, expected returns are considerably higher than in the fixed-income-only analysis, and risky assets such as equities, hedge funds and commodities can be used (sparingly) to

Figure 8.3 Horizon-dependent fixed income portfolio optimization

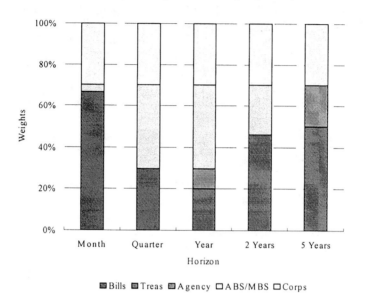

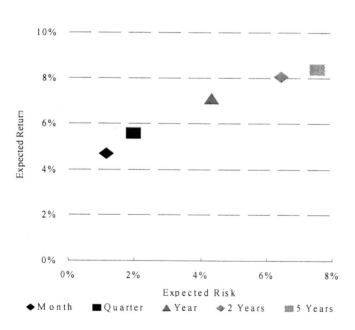

Figure 8.4 Horizon-dependent multi-asset class portfolio optimization

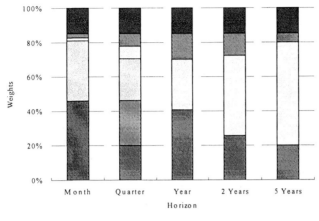

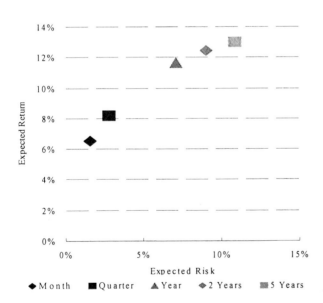

construct portfolios that exhibit favourable risk and return characteristics.

The ability to invest in 'risk assets' and accept the interim volatility is a resource that is ultimately rewarded in higher returns over the medium term. Failure to recognize and exploit this resource results in lower national wealth.

8.3   CENTRAL BANK RESPONSES: ADDING INCREMENTAL RETURN AND BREAKING OUT OF THE BOX

Capital preservation is typically enshrined as a portfolio constraint in the central bank's investment policy. Based on modern portfolio theory, capital preservation should be based on the market value of the portfolio as a whole over the appropriate investment horizon and not based on any single security or accounting period. Most central bank reserves managers understand the theory but have only partly put it into practice. Over the past decade or so, central banks in large part shifted out of cash equivalents into fixed income government securities with a portfolio duration of around 1–2 years and individual securities with maturities out to ten years. In doing this, they accepted that capital preservation could be measured on a portfolio basis – rather than on an individual security basis – with respect to interest rate risk, and they generally extended the measurement period to one year. Most still diverge from the industry, however, in two aspects. The first is a refusal to apply the same principle to credit risk as they have to interest rate risk. In other words, default risk on any individual security is unacceptable no matter the impact on the total market value of the portfolio from additional returns due to investment in credit sectors. Most central banks thus remain excruciatingly conservative in defining eligible issuers, again at a high opportunity cost, as was seen in Figure 8.1. Other central banks, albeit a minority, have fully accepted modern portfolio management theory and significantly expanded the universe of eligible assets. In addition, some have clearly defined a portion of central bank reserves as stable over a long-term investment horizon and adopted higher risk–return strategies for either a separate fund or tranche of the reserves.

Pushing out the yield curve

Historically, investors have always been compensated in higher returns over time by investing in longer duration portfolios. As central banks adopted modern portfolio theory, they tended to extend the target duration for the reserves portfolios to about 18 months. As can be seen in Figure 8.3, this allowed them to achieve higher mean returns and still minimize the probability of a negative total return over a 12- month period.

During 2003–4, however, historically low US dollar and euro interest rates caused many central banks to cut back their target duration to twelve months or less. Prevailing low yields did not provide sufficient cushion against price risk and the probability of a negative total return increased. This insight caused many central banks to adopt a 'constant risk' strategy rather than a 'constant duration' strategy.

*Figure 8.5 Mean historical return and variability of returns for USD
government portfolios of increasing duration*

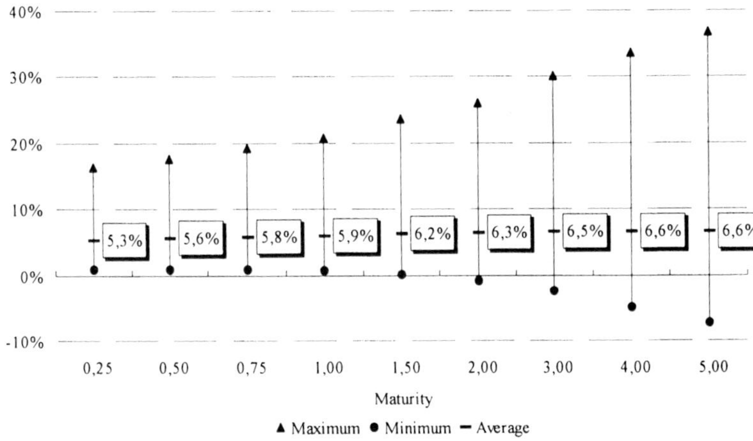

Rather than setting a targeted duration, the Board or Investment Committee would set an acceptable risk level based on minimizing the probability of a negative total return over the investment horizon. If yields changed significantly, the target duration of the benchmark portfolio would be changed to maintain the preferred risk profile. This new approach also implied the adoption of new risk measurement techniques. Forward-looking analysis using current market yields replaced was introduced to complement historical mean variance analysis in determining whether the benchmark risk was appropriate. The years of low yields had a second impact. As central banks cut back duration, attention turned to expanding eligible asset classes to enhance yield.

Widening the credit net

Central banks that wanted additional return without default risk focussed first on US dollar government mortgage-backed securities (MBS) and AAA corporate asset-backed securities (ABS), where structures were protected by over-collateralization. The addition of these securities to a government portfolio allowed for additional expected return at the same level of risk because of the impact of diversification. For example, as is shown in Figure 8.6, adding 30 per cent MBS to a US dollar Government 1–3 year portfolio has had a better risk–return profile than simply adding duration.

Figure 8.6 Historical mean return and risk of three portfolios

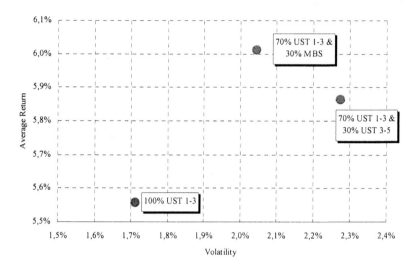

With only a few exceptions, however, official institutions avoided any class of issuer that could give rise to default risk, no matter how remote the chances of default actually were. Eligible asset classes were thus widened but only to allow issuers judged to have virtually zero default risk. A few exceptions existed with the Central Bank of New Zealand, Central Bank of Latvia and Banco de la Republica de Colombia and National Bank of Hungary, among others, allowing corporate bonds on a highly diversified basis as part of the international foreign currency reserves.

Engaging private sector partners

Central banks are increasingly engaging private sector partners for asset management, custodian services and, to a lesser extent, portfolio analytics such as risk measurement/performance and settlements/operations. Historically, central banks shied away from private sector engagements because of concerns regarding governance, confidentiality, reputation risk and their ability to oversee the risk and performance of external asset managers. Seeking greater return, however, they increasingly have turned to private sector financial service providers to gain exposure to new asset classes such as mortgage backed securities or corporate securities. Central banks also began to switch from official custodians to private sector custodians for broader and deeper services. In particular, many central banks want to earn extra income on securities lending and will frequently contract out this service to their custodian rather than setting up an internal desk.

Engagement of external managers, however, cannot add significant value unless the central bank has lessened the traditional constraints on eligible asset classes and adopted an appropriate strategic asset allocation for the totality of the reserves. A naïve view, which sometimes prevails amongst governments, is that one can simply outsource the management of the reserves to private sector asset mangers and that they can provide additional returns while underwriting the risk. If asset classes are constrained to government bonds, it is unlikely that external managers will generate any net return relative to central bank managers and the portfolio cannot benefit from diversification. In addition, the central bank will always 'own' the downside risk and so it is imperative that external mandates derive from the desired strategic asset allocation for the portfolio as a whole.

From active management to strategic asset allocation

Fortunately, another trend is greater emphasis on the appropriate strategic asset allocation rather than active trading. After central banks shifted from cash to portfolio management, the main focus was on 'beating the benchmark' or outright trading to try to make money on intra-day price changes. Relatively little focus was given to the strategic asset allocation and, particularly, the link between reserves adequacy and the appropriate risk–return profile. Most analytical and quantitative firepower focused on adding some 10 to 20 basis points over benchmark returns rather than achieving higher total returns through a more optimal strategic asset allocation. While this may seem irrational, it is understandable in the institutional context – both the general risk aversion of policy-makers discussed earlier and compartmentalization of functions within the central bank. Typically, reserves management is entrusted to a specialized 'markets' or investments department charged with investing the reserves and seeking to add value by beating the benchmark. While the markets department may propose benchmarks to policy-makers, such a proposal would not generally be grounded in an analysis of reserves adequacy and balance of payments trends – the purview of the research departments. The research department, on the other hand, would not be equipped to link reserves adequacy considerations to the appropriate strategic asset allocation for the reserves. The default option is thus to view risk and capital preservation over the accounting cycle rather than based on an analysis of sustainability of reserves. To date, the trend in central bank reserves management has been to add value by extending duration and adding new asset classes within the capital preservation constraint of no negative total returns over the accounting cycle and zero tolerance for default risk. The challenge for countries with stable reserves in excess of potential liquidity needs is to overcome these constraints.

Central bank reserves management departments are developing their analytical resources and setting up specialized quantitative teams, focused on developing appropriate strategic asset allocation decisions. In most cases, these teams are seeking to optimize the strategic asset allocation through choosing the duration and asset class composition with the highest expected return given the institution's risk constraints. This approach ensures that strategic decisions such as exposure to a given market segment, do not depend on the decision of an individual portfolio manager but rather are embedded in the institutional strategic asset allocation, which is approved by the Board. While portfolio managers may reposition the portfolio, within limits, versus the benchmark, they bear strict accountability for these decisions, as measured by their performance vis-à-vis the benchmark.

Breaking through institutional constraints: adding percentage points of return

Most central banks still operate within the institutional constraints discussed above, which are generally quite appropriate for foreign currency reserves liquidity portfolios. Some countries, however, have accumulated assets clearly in excess of any liquidity requirements and pressure to maximize returns has led to fundamental institutional changes. In many cases, these financial assets have arisen from the export of commodities and natural resources (oil, gas and precious metals) resulting in a transformation of commodities into financial assets. Traditionally, these resources accumulated as part of the central bank's foreign currency reserves and were invested according to the same criteria as the liquidity portfolio. As these reserves have increased, however, many governments have recognized the opportunity cost and fundamentally altered the investment management set-up. In most cases, this has been done by setting up a separate investment tranche (Central Bank of Botswana), a separate department within the central bank for management of the oil fund (Norges Bank) or a separate institution (Government Investment Corp of Singapore). Despite the different institutional arrangements, all of these national wealth managers have adopted multi-asset class investment strategies and have accepted interim volatility to maximize wealth over longer investment horizons.

8.4. CONCLUSION

What are some of the trends that are likely to persist? First, despite the trend towards a floating exchange rate system, the need for core liquidity reserves is bound to continue. While some have argued that in a world of freely floating exchange rates, there is no need for foreign currency reserves, most countries are not willing to accept sharp exchange rate moves and would normally intervene. Traditional liquidity tranches designed to support potential intervention requirements are likely to continue, although they would be relatively smaller than under a fixed exchange rate system. Second, foreign creditors will want to see sufficient foreign currency reserves to service short-term debt in the case of any crisis. The self-insurance function is thus bound to continue. Investment strategies, however, are likely to change along with the rationale for holding reserves.

The return criteria will become more important for reserves in excess of traditional liquidity needs. Diversification out of the US dollar – both into other major currencies and possibly commodities – is likely to continue for several reasons. From a portfolio perspective, diversification brings higher expected risk-adjusted returns and lower currency risk vis-à-vis the local currency (unless there is an external peg). For countries with 'super-size' reserves, however, any significant diversification is likely to be constrained by the relative size of capital markets versus the size of the reserves. As reserves are seen as a store of value, gold and other commodities may again gain favour versus debt obligations. China, for example, has invested a part of its reserves in commodities via the futures market to protect its global purchasing power for critical imports.

It is likely that the trend toward setting up separate funds or institutions to manage long-term financial asset portfolios is likely to continue given the misalignment of incentives between traditional central banking functions and asset management. Even within central banks, however, continued diversification into new asset classes is likely to continue as the concept of total return portfolio management is more broadly adopted. These trends may be checked by a 'hard landing' resolution of the current global imbalances if it were to result in an unwinding of reserves to support domestic spending or finance BOP deficits. Even in that case, however, there is still ample room for central banks to improve returns and enhance national wealth.

NOTES

1. Debt and Reserve-Related Indicators of External Vulnerability, IMF Board Paper, 23 March, 2003: www.imf.org/external/np/pder/debtres/index.htm.

9. Implications of Growing Reserves of Central Banks for Asset Allocation

Amy Yip

9.1 INTRODUCTION

Although the official reserves of Hong Kong have grown rapidly in the course of the 1990s their growth has stopped recently as a result of the budget deficit of the government. At approximately $130 billion the reserves of Hong Kong look smaller and smaller compared to the northern neighbour China, which in the course of 2006 became the largest reserve holder in the world. At the same time it has made the investment process of the Hong Kong Monetary Authority easier. China now faces the unenviable problem of not being able to invest fast enough as the assets roll in, while its performance is still measured against a benchmark, which is the way that most of central banks in Asia have gone.

In this article I will briefly describe the establishment and the workings of the Exchange Fund of Hong Kong which under the aegis of the Hong Kong Monetary Authority is the main investment vehicle for the official reserves of Hong Kong. I will then explain the development in asset management which has occurred over time as well as the various forms of asset allocation which have taken place over the past decade or so. Finally, I will deal with some of the practical issues which come up with asset management, including the management of the external managers.

9.2 THE EXCHANGE FUND OF HONG KONG

The Exchange Fund, which was established as early as 1935, is composed of the bulk of the government's reserves and is the result of the accumulation of the fiscal surpluses since the 1950s as well as of the income that has been generated on the investment of these fiscal surpluses. In Hong Kong all fiscal surpluses have been transferred to the Exchange Fund. All assets of the

Exchange Fund belong to the people of Hong Kong and they are managed by the Hong Kong Monetary Authority (HKMA) using powers delegated from the Finance Secretary to the HKMA under the Exchange Fund ordinance.

The investment objectives of the Fund are very clearly laid out. Under the Exchange Fund ordinance all assets have the following two primary purposes: to safeguard the exchange value of the Hong Kong dollar and to maintain the stability and integrity of the monetary and financial system of Hong Kong. Subject to these two primary objectives the Exchange Fund shall achieve an investment return that will preserve the long-term purchasing power of the Fund. The two major components of the assets of the Exchange Fund which can be invested are the accumulated surplus, e.g. the sum of the historical returns from the investments of the government reserves, and the fiscal surpluses of the Hong Kong government deposited with the Exchange Fund. At the end of 2005 total invested assets were slightly over HK$1 trillion or approximately $130 billion.

Initially the Exchange Fund was established in 1935 to maintain the stability of the financial system and the exchange rate vis-à-vis the pound sterling since Hong Kong formed part of the sterling zone. Consequently reserves were actually invested in sterling assets all the way through the 1960s and the early 1970s. Between the early 1970s and the mid 1990s there was a diversification away from sterling assets (actually most of the time this was in sterling deposits) into multi-currency global bonds and cash deposits. Up till 1993 almost all assets of the Exchange Fund were invested by external managers, in other words they were outsourced.

With the establishment of the HKMA in 1993 management responsibilities for the reserves were assumed and that is when the monetary authority started building up internal capabilities of asset management. In doing so most of the staff in the reserve management division has been hired from the market place, unlike our counterparts in the other central banks in Asia; the HKMA has very few career central bankers within the Reserve Department. It is very fortunate that in spite of our dismal pay we have been able to hold on to most of the staff. They are there for the intellectual challenge of managing public funds.

In 1997 and 1998 there was a great leap in the growth of the Exchange Fund, which was caused by the transfer of the funds of the Land Fund into the Exchange Fund. The Land Fund was a fund that was set up in 1986 by the British and Chinese governments. It constituted a store of value for the future of Hong Kong; half of the proceeds of land sale in Hong Kong, which at the time was the main source of fiscal income, went to the government and the other 50 per cent went into the Land Fund. In 1997, when the United Kingdom handed over Hong Kong to the Chinese government, the Land Fund assets were given over to the then Hong Kong government.

Figure 9.1 Growth in the size of the Exchange Fund (HK$ billion)

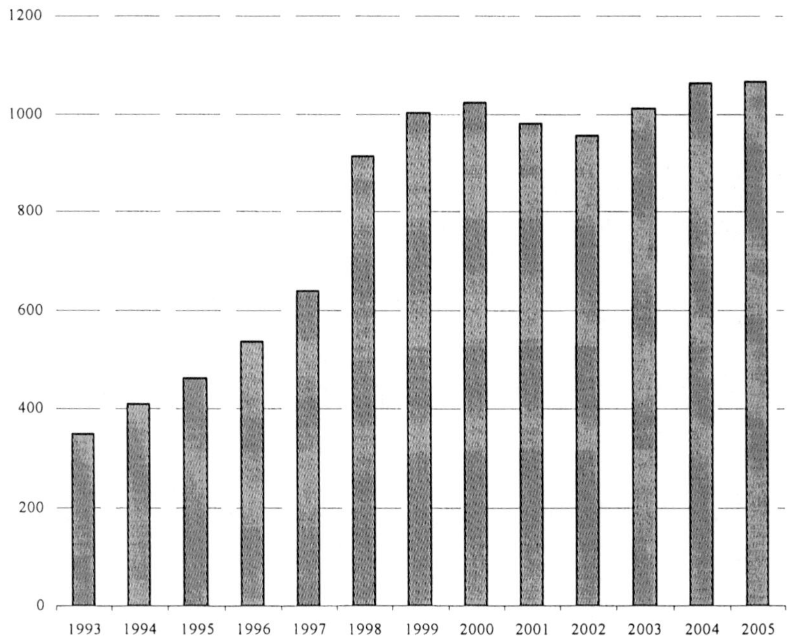

This explains the large jump in the size of the assets of the Exchange Fund in 1997 (see Figure 9.1).

9.3 RELATIONSHIP WITH THE TREASURY

The dynamic relationship between the Exchange Fund and the Hong Kong government Treasury deserves further explanation. The Treasury deposits all fiscal reserves into the Exchange Fund managed by the HKMA. The monetary authority then pays a dividend from the income of the managed reserves to the Treasury. Prior to 1998 dividend income was paid in the form of a deposit rate which was in line with the prevailing money market deposit rate. In other words, the Treasury parked its surplus with the HKMA and when the deposits had been there for six months the HKMA would quote a six-month interest rate. If deposits had been maintained for a year or longer a longer interest rate based on US treasuries was quoted.

In 1998 the government decided that this arrangement was enough. The government wanted a return above the deposit rate of return because at that time it was felt that the HKMA was generating a return in excess of deposit rates and the government felt cheated. The Treasury met with the HKMA

Governor Joseph Yam and a formula was agreed which spelled out that the cost of the liabilities in the form of the reserves placed with the HKMA in the Exchange Fund would be equivalent to the investment return generated for the entire portfolio. This agreement was the main driver for a number of major changes in reserve management over the following years.

Up till 1998 the portfolio was predominantly liquidity driven and over 90 per cent of the Exchange Fund assets were invested in deposits and (short term) debt securities. There was no pre-determined investment benchmark in operation. After the new income sharing arrangement with the government the discussion with respect to reserve management centered on the question whether the HKMA could have one overall investment benchmark to govern all invested assets and whether it was possible to remain predominantly short duration driven or whether equivalent liquid assets in other asset classes outside of cash and short duration bonds could be found. The conclusion at the time was that the financial markets had developed sufficiently so that we could lend our equities in the form of repurchase agreements in order to raise instant liquidity if called upon.

Another intense debate was held on the question how many reserves would be necessary to maintain the currency board. At the time all liabilities arising from the currency board were taken into account and were matched by assets in the form of very liquid high quality US dollar bonds, the HK dollar being pegged to the US dollar. This took care of the liquidity need. The balance was then to be invested in multi asset classes and in multi currencies in order to generate a long term return that would maintain the purchasing power of these assets. At the time we relied quite heavily on the advice of Goldman Sachs on the pros and cons of the asset allocation process. After intensive internal discussion HKMA decided to define one overall investment benchmark for the strategic long-term allocation of all assets and to carve out components into various different portfolios. In essence two portfolios were created, the 'backing' portfolio which held the assets backing the liabilities arising from the monetary base (needed for the operation of the currency board), and the 'investment' portfolio which would hold long-term investments in bonds and listed equities. With the help of Goldman Sachs various performance criteria were defined.

9.4   DEFINING THE INVESTMENT BENCHMARK

The construction process of the overall investment benchmark comprised five consecutive steps. First, the investment objectives for the Exchange Fund were defined; second, the investment objectives were converted into risk tolerance levels and return expectations; third the risk tolerance levels and return expectations were quantified into critical investment performance criteria; fourth the 'Litterman' model[1] was used to construct an efficient frontier of optimal portfolios; and, finally, from the optimal portfolios an appropriate portfolio on the efficient frontier was selected to be the investment benchmark for HKMA.

With respect to the definition of the investment objectives it was first of all considered absolutely critical that capital be preserved. Also it needed to be ensured that the monetary base is fully backed by highly liquid short-term US dollar denominated securities and that liquidity was preserved for maintaining monetary and financial stability. After having fulfilled the first three objectives HKMA was to achieve an investment return that would preserve the long-term purchasing power of the assets. In doing so HKMA became a return optimizer. This proved to be a good strategy all the way up to the year 2000. However, in 2000 the government ran into a fiscal deficit situation and HKMA came under increasing pressure from the Treasury as well as from the media and the legislative council and the people of Hong Kong to generate a return to help cope with the fiscal deficit. So, absolute transparency is not always a good idea!

HKMA announces its returns twice a year and this does affect its investment decisions. We would not be true to ourselves if we would say that we were true long-term investors. Because come end of the year, we cannot afford to show any capital losses. So far we have been very lucky, but one of these days the luck is going to run out. Usually by year-end the Reserve Department gets worried about year-end market prices because the portfolio is marked to market as all international accounting rules, including the latest changes under IFRS, are followed. All told, there is a minimal appetite for capital losses, even over short periods.

When the investment objectives were translated into the investment portfolio benchmark the question was asked what the expected long-term returns would be. As a minimum it would be expected that returns at least have to be in line with the domestic inflation rate. This is translated into the probability of outperforming the domestic inflation rate on a one-year basis, a two-year basis and a five-year basis. Furthermore the probability of a shortfall against the domestic inflation rate is determined. The most difficult issue in recent annual reviews is the need for capital preservation. Capital preservation is fine as long as one is looking at expected returns from the markets in high single digits, but now that we are looking at returns in the low to mid-single digits the probability of a positive expected return is not as easy, given the current volatilities. Consequently some of the capital preservation parameters had to be relaxed. Critical performance criteria are spelled out in Table 9.1. The first preferred neutral position (PNP) for the portfolio is actually the investment benchmark and it is a very simple one: 80 per cent is invested in bonds, 20 per cent in equities, and as far as currencies

Table 9.1 Critical performance criteria

	Return Parameters	
(1)	Expected annual return in line with the long-term domestic inflation rate	
(2)	Probability of outperforming domestic CPI-A (average past 5 years)	
	1 year	50%
	2 years	60%
	5 years	75%
(3)	Annualized average shortfall vs domestic CPI-A (average past 5 years)	1%
	Capital Preservation Parameters	
(1)	Probability of positive expected return	
	1 year	90%
	2 years	98%
	5 years	99.9%

---

are concerned: an overlay of 80 per cent in the US dollar-bloc and 20 per cent in the non-US dollar-bloc. The currency composition has to do with the heavy US dollar bias, because of the exchange rate being fixed to the US dollar under the currency board arrangement. The bonds and the equities are all issued in OECD developed markets, because of liquidity requirements.

9.5 IMPLEMENTATION ISSUES

As explained before, reserves are basically managed as two portfolios, the backing portfolio and the investment portfolio. The latter of course is the more interesting and the more challenging one. As to investment expertise, HKMA decided that there would be no way as a central bank to build up the in-house investment expertise that the outside world offers, so a model was adopted where very specialized portfolios were outsourced, including equities and anything outside plain US dollar investments, such as yen, sterling or European government portfolios. All in all approximately 40 per cent of the assets of the Exchange Fund are outsourced to external managers. The actual implementation and allocations differ from the benchmark. Benchmarks such as the MSCI developed markets index and the JP Morgan Government bond indices were used to approximate the permissible market in which to invest in the optimization process. However, in the actual investment process we diversify away from the benchmarks that are used in the construction of the investment benchmark.

The other deviation is that HKMA deploys active managers with large tracking errors, particularly on the equity side, in an attempt to achieve active return over market returns. 50 per cent of the equity allocations are passive and 50 per cent are active, high tracking error investments. Unfortunately, in the past three years most of the high tracking error has been negative for the active equity managers. There are a number of managers who have done well and who have outperformed the benchmark, but most of the active managers have not. We have looked into the reasons and done attribution analysis, and we have come to the conclusion that part of that has to do with our investment guidelines. Our guidelines are very heavily large cap-oriented because of the liquidity requirements. Until quite recently the rally in the equity market, particularly in the United States, has been predominantly mid to small cap driven. Therefore, our active equity managers in the US and to a certain extent in Europe and the UK have suffered because of our investment guidelines. The HKMA is now on the verge of deciding whether or not to review this large cap bias, with, as always, at the back of our minds the adage that 'we have to maintain absolute liquidity'. We will have to work out with the Board members of HKMA how much headline risk they can tolerate.

Another issue is the diversification into various asset classes. The HKMA itself has not gone down the credit curve for various reasons, one being that the Reserve Department is very small, with a headcount of 50 people. Some of these 50 people are deployed as the risk management team that prepares the benchmarking, the performance attribution, the risk analysis, etc. Then there is an external managers' team that searches, monitors and deals with all external managers. Since over 75 portfolios are managed externally, there needs to be a strong team of internal managers overseeing their activities. So there is a very serious constraint in terms of resources. If the HKMA reserve management activities were to go down into various types of asset classes there would be a need to build up internal understanding, if not the actual investment expertise, of the asset classes, what the risk is all about, what the returns are about, in order to communicate and monitor the external managers and ensure that they are doing what they are supposed to do.

At the HKMA we have maintained a very tight grip on credit. We have not gone into corporate credit, because it is a very complex area. It is felt that we are not able to develop the resources needed to understand the marketplace in order to work with our external managers. Since there is already a 20 per cent allocation to equities, credit risk is already on the books but then in the capacity of owner. The decision to become lenders (by investing in corporate bonds) in addition to being owners has been postponed for the moment. In order to generate additional returns we allow ourselves tactical deviations from the investment benchmarks. We can be overweighed, or underweighted, within certain defined parameters. These decisions are made principally by the investment professionals within the Reserve Department with approval from the deputy governors as well as the board members.

Actual performance is also helped by a very high element of luck. From 1998 to 2004 the HKMA was able to achieve positive active returns in addition to benchmark returns. The investment benchmark is regularly reviewed at the beginning of each year. The volatilities from the permissible markets from the prior year are incorporated, and in an optimization process we see if strategic asset allocation of the investment benchmark can comply with the figure of critical performance criteria shown earlier (see Table 9.1). When that does not work or seems to be deviating too much, we become more conservative – at least that is what we did in 2001, 2003 and now again in 2005.

The other asset class, the HKMA, has gone into is hedge funds. That is because we believe that this is an alternative source of alpha and that, properly managed, we should be able to see good quality returns. At the Reserve Department we have spent three to five years intensely researching this asset class, we have worked closely with many of the leading edge of hedge fund managers and we have taken the plunge. However, it will not be possible to get the sort of alpha that the whole hedge fund universe can offer because of the peculiarities of our needs. For example it would not do if the HKMA were found to be investing in hedge funds that were speculating against the Hong Kong dollar. The way it looks right now, the investment in hedge funds can be viewed more like an overlay to the long equity portfolio. The bulk of current investments in hedge funds will be in funds which are going equity long-short and some of it into some convertible arbitrage strategies.

9.6 CONCLUSION

The way reserves are managed in the Exchange Fund by HKMA has undergone tremendous change since return considerations have become more important, albeit subject to the primary objective of supporting the currency board arrangement and the maintenance of monetary and financial stability. Since 1998 the Fund has been managed as two main portfolios, i.e. the backing portfolio and the investment portfolio. The long-term asset allocation strategy is governed by the investment benchmark. About one-third of total assets and all equity portfolios are managed by external managers. Since there is already a 20 per cent allocation to equities HKMA has decided not to add corporate credit, e.g. corporate bonds, to its investment instruments. However, after careful study and research HKMA has gone into hedge funds which can be basically viewed as an overlay to the long equity portfolio.

NOTES

1. See also Chapter 15.

10. Setting the Strategic Benchmark Duration and Currency Allocation: A Developing Country Case Study

Vinod Kumar Sharma[1]

10.1 INTRODUCTION

In the present chapter, an attempt has been made to illustrate the application of the shortfall risk approach to identifying and recommending a policy and operating framework for setting the benchmark duration and currency composition of the foreign exchange reserves of a mid-sized central bank of a developing country. It is assumed that the central bank has reserves of $10 billion and has been traditionally managing its interest rate risk by benchmarking its fixed income portfolio to a 3-month Salomon Brothers Treasury Bill Index. In a typical developing country central bank's context, the purpose of foreign exchange reserves is primarily to support the pursuit of an appropriate exchange rate policy, with the management thereof becoming an adjunct to the main public policy purpose of pursuit and maintenance of an appropriate, competitive nominal exchange rate, whatever it may be determined to be. The raison d'être of foreign exchange reserve management, in other words, is its deployment in an optimal manner consistent with the need for intervention, i.e. as a last resort in financing the current account deficit of the balance of payments. Thus, it derives from the exchange rate policy objective i.e what to do with the foreign exchange reserves in the intermediate period pending their use.

10.2 INTERVENTION NEEDS AND INVESTMENT OBJECTIVES

In the context of a typical developing country, central bank interventions may take two explicit forms: a draft on the foreign exchange reserves for official external debt servicing and the sale of foreign currency to the domestic private foreign exchange market. In either form of intervention, the underlying policy objective is to pursue an appropriate exchange rate policy. But, nevertheless, there is a subtle but significant difference between the two forms of intervention: all else being equal the former always over-rides the latter. In other words, should the worse come to the worst, the available foreign exchange reserves would be pre-empted for official external debt servicing at the expense of the private foreign exchange market even if that meant jettisoning a particular exchange rate objective. In that extreme case, even though it might push up the cost of official debt servicing, the meeting of official debt servicing obligations becomes the overriding policy objective. Indeed, it is from the strait-jacket of the aforementioned intervention needs that the policy objectives of the investment of foreign exchange reserves derive. Therefore, given the very nature and purpose of foreign exchange reserves, these investment objectives are fairly universal across all central banks, viz. (1) preservation of the principal, (2) liquidity (being able to liquidate investments in a fairly large size without adversely affecting prices; also indicated by very narrow bid-offer spreads) and (3) return, in that order.

While these investment objectives are universal across all central banks, central banks, however, may and do differ considerably from each other in terms of the degree of relative emphasis placed on these individual investment objectives. In other words, different central banks have differing risk–return trade-offs. Typically, large central banks will have a higher risk-tolerance than the small ones, especially in large countries where Treasuries service their external debt obligations by going directly into the private market, or where the size of the foreign exchange reserves is structurally comfortable. Incidentally, the risk–return trade-off connotes the fact that a higher expected return requires the assumption of incurring a commensurately higher risk. If a central bank prefers higher return (the objective no. 3), then inevitably it must be prepared to bear so much higher incremental risk as signified by lower liquidity, and/or a higher potential loss in the value of the principal.

Having thus seen the risk–return trade-off in the correct perspective, the next real policy challenge is how to formalize, and quantify, the most desirable risk–return trade-off. It is in this that the latest, and state-of-the-art, analytical tool of 'shortfall probability' comes in extremely handy for the management of foreign exchange reserves of a central bank.

10.3 THE BENCHMARK DURATION DECISION

The first investment objective of preservation of the principal can be assured by investing the principal in nothing but the top-rated credit risk free fixed income instruments issued by G-5 industrial countries only, and a neutral currency mix. But then this step addresses only the credit risk, i.e. the default risk, but not the market risk. For example, if a central bank chooses to invest its reserves in a 10-year US Treasury note, while indeed there is no credit risk, it nevertheless carries considerable market risk; a rise in market yields will lead to erosion in the value of the principal amount of investment which may well swamp even the coupon income! When this happens, obviously the returns are negative.

A natural corollary of this proposition is that where the erosion in the value of the principal exactly balances the coupon earnings, the returns are zero and thus the principal's value remains intact. So the best way to quantify this investment policy objective is to specify the 'shortfall probability', i.e. the probability of the returns being negative over a given time horizon. It follows from this that the most extreme, conservative case would be where such probability is specified to be zero, where in practice, it would mean that no risk is being incurred and, therefore, expected return will be the risk free rate. A more realistic and practical policy stance, however, would be to admit of some probability of negative returns.

It is in the specification of this 'shortfall probability' that individual central banks differ regardless, of course, of whether they explicitly identify and specify such probability. Extremely conservative, and hence risk-averse, small central banks would perhaps accept no more than 1 per cent 'shortfall probability', i.e. a 1 per cent probability that returns would be negative. Stated differently, what this means is that only in 1 out of 100 times will there be erosion in the value of the principal amount of investment. Less conservative central banks will typically be comfortable with no more than 5 per cent shortfall probability.

Indeed, such 'shortfall probability', all else being equal, is a function of the maturity, or rather more accurately, the duration of the investment instrument. For instance, an analysis of US Treasury instruments over the period 1980–95 by Salomon Brothers showed that based on monthly returns, the shortfall probability of monthly returns being negative were 0 per cent for 3-month Treasury bills, 0.52 per cent for 6-month Treasury bills, 6.77 per cent for one year Treasury bills, and 19.8 per cent for two year US Treasury notes. An in-house analysis done by the central bank on a more recent limited three year-database (June 1996–May 1999) revealed that the corresponding 'shortfall probabilities' were 0 per cent, 0.001 per cent, 1.7 per cent and 16 per cent, respectively. Thus, it is readily seen that the two year US Treasury note will be ruled out as a benchmark maturity for most central banks across the risk-spectrum. The one-year US Treasury bill could be acceptable to some central banks, based on recent data. As regards, however, the six month duration, the 'shortfall probability' of the monthly returns being negative, based on both analyses, was much less than 1 per cent. In other words, even for the most risk-averse, conservative central banks, six months is an ideal benchmark duration.

If this benchmark duration for the foreign exchange reserves portfolio is accepted by the central bank, it would mean that the bank is reasonably comfortable with the policy stance that there will be no more than a 1 per cent probability that monthly returns will be negative, i.e. there will be no more than 1 per cent probability of the value of the principal amount of investment being not preserved. This then is the state-of-the-art way to quantify the 'strategic' risk-preference/tolerance of a central bank.

10.4 THE CASE STUDY

In the present chapter, we consider a case study of a typical central bank in a mid-sized developing country, where the foreign exchange reserves are being managed in-house, including a fraction by an external fund manager against the implicit benchmark of the three month Salomon Brothers Treasury Bill Index. This implies a benchmark duration for its fixed income portfolio of three months. The central bank has on its asset side foreign exchange reserves of a total of $10 billion, mostly held in US dollars. The country has a substantial external debt, denominated in foreign currency, which is partly owed to official international organisations. For the case study, market data up till 1999 have been used.

As for the strategic benchmark duration decision, a risk-return trade-off analysis of the Salomon Brothers three month US Treasury bill index and the six month US Treasury bill for the three year period from June 1996–May 1999, throws up some compelling conclusions. Over that period the average annual yield of three month US Treasury bills was 5 per cent per annum as against 5.1561 per cent for six month US Treasury bills, i.e. there would be an annual pick-up of 16 basis points (0.16 per cent) per annum by choosing the six month bill as a benchmark, rather than the three month bill, and indeed at the expense of an incommensurately small increase in the 'shortfall probability' from 0 per cent to 0.001 per cent. By choosing the six month US Treasury bill as the benchmark, a yield pick up of 16 basis points would amount to an additional annualised return of US$ 16 million on a total size of reserves of US$ 10 billion. This could be achieved at no more than practically insignificant incremental risk, both risks being much below the conservatively maximum acceptable risk of 1 per cent shortfall probability.

Having made the strategic benchmark duration decision, the next most critical policy decision would be to specify the constraints for the tactical management of the reserve portfolio around the strategic benchmark for the in-house managers or the external portfolio managers. The idea is to challenge the internal and external portfolio managers to outperform the benchmark in a risk-adjusted sense. But the idea is certainly not to give the managers unfettered freedom to deviate from the benchmark. In accomplishing this, again, a maximum acceptable 'shortfall probability' of 'excess' returns being negative is to be determined, and specified, for meticulous observance by the 'tactical' portfolio managers. Typically, for the monthly evaluation period, a reasonably conservative 'shortfall probability threshold' of the excess returns being negative would be 2.5 per cent. The chief merit of such a 'shortfall probability' specification, instead of prescribing the maximum duration, is that it provides flexibility in duration management, depending upon the actual yield curve and perceived yield volatility. A higher yield environment can, for a given shortfall probability, accommodate relatively longer duration and vice versa. The above reasoning leads to the first recommendation.

Recommendation 1
Adopt the Salomon Brothers six-month Treasury bill as a benchmark with 2.5per cent being the maximum acceptable shortfall probability of the excess returns (actual portfolio returns less benchmark returns) being negative (<0).

For the purpose of structuring the actual reserve portfolio, which would conform to the benchmark duration, the prescription of mandatory guidelines as to the permissible investments would also be necessary for the guidance of the operational staff.

10.5 THE BENCHMARK CURRENCY ALLOCATION DECISION

A typical central bank benchmark portfolio inevitably needs to address three types of risks: credit, interest rate and currency risks. The first two risks have already been captured in the first part of this chapter. Equally intellectually and professionally challenging is the determination of the strategic currency allocation of the benchmark portfolio.

The best way to approach this critical decision is to align the currency allocation of the foreign exchange reserves portfolio exactly with that of the stock of foreign currency liabilities, i.e. the outstanding external debt stock of the country. Here it is assumed that the individual market players have not hedged their currency exposure. Conceptually, and operationally, this approach is by far the most robust in efficiently and effectively addressing the currency risk concerns of a developing country. This approach avoids the serious pitfalls associated with continuous tracking of the currency composition of the periodically projected debt service outflows; the latter exercise in fact does not avoid the currency risk but, on the contrary, actually incurs it. The reason is that the actual underlying currency risk exposure does not arise from the currency of initial disbursement or notified currency of repayment, but the currency of denomination of the debt amounts outstanding. In other words, interestingly, even though the exposure to Japanese yen may not sometimes be visible, for certain countries there will be some considerable actual exposure to Japanese yen, not because of loans from Japan but on account of the Japanese yen having a 17 per cent share in the SDR, the SDR being the currency basket in which loans of international institutions such as the IMF and the World Bank are denominated. Indeed, international official creditors routinely raise supplementary bills if the exchange rate moves between the day of billing and actual payment.

Based on the above, the outstanding official external debt stock of the country under reference is disaggregated and regrouped according to the underlying currency exposures. In our case study, we assume that, after having decomposed the SDR exposure in underlying currencies, the total debt stock is composed of US dollar debt at 75 per cent, euro 12.5 per cent, sterling 8 per cent and Japanese yen 4.5 per cent. It must, however, be noted that these weights are subject to change over time as the relative currency values change and, therefore, there would be a need for periodical monitoring and review so that necessary changes can be made if there is a substantial change in relative currency values.

The currency allocation of the strategic benchmark portfolio should, therefore, correspond to this currency distribution. It is insightful and revealing to consider the currency structure of the existing reserve portfolio which is almost entirely denominated in US dollars. In order to bring out the extent of the currency risk implied by the existing almost 100 per cent US dollar based reserve portfolio structure, a historical simulation spanning the daily exchange rates over the six-month period from January–June 1999 was done. Using this time series, standard deviations and correlations of the three currency pairs were computed and plugged in the overall portfolio risk formula to arrive at the portfolio currency risk as measured by its annualized standard deviation of 1.92 per cent. At this stage, it is interesting to look at what actually happened in this six-month period. Indeed, there was a windfall gain by virtue of having the reserve portfolio almost entirely in US dollars. But it could have given an equally big loss with almost the same probability. Indeed, the historical time series-based portfolio risk covering exactly the same period throws up 4.4 per cent as the probability that the potential gain could be $229 million, or more. In other words, what had just a small probability of 4.4 per cent in fact eventuated!

Significantly, the same log-normal distribution also gives 4.75 per cent as the probability that the potential loss could be $229 million, or more. This clearly shows that a loss of $229 million on a portfolio size of $10 billion was, and will be, almost equally likely. Although currency risk is far more serious than other types of market risks like interest rate risk, the existing currency and maturity structure of the central bank in our case study implies a disproportionately greater tolerance of currency risk relative to interest rate risk (as captured by the actual duration profile).

To see this vividly and graphically, suffice it to compare the standard deviations of currency and interest rate returns. As we have seen, the portfolio currency risk is 1.92 per cent annualised. As against this, since the standard deviation of three month T-bill yield was 11.6 per cent annualized and as the average three month T-bill yield was 5 per cent during June 1996–May 1999, one standard deviation of absolute yield change corresponded to 0.6144 per cent per annum. Given the duration of 0.25 years of the three month T-bill, this gives one standard deviation of price returns as 0.1536 per cent per annum (0.6144 x 0.25%). The ratio of 1.92/0.1536 $\cong$ 12.5 shows that the currency risk embedded in the current/existing structure of the foreign exchange reserves portfolio is about 12 to 13 times the interest rate risk[2]! As empirical research also shows that, unlike other asset classes, the bearing of currency risk is not rewarded in the long term, there is a very strong case for the elimination of the very substantial currency risk present in the existing currency composition of the foreign exchange reserves.

At first sight, it would appear that this can be accomplished only by realigning the currency composition of the official reserves so as to have 75 per cent US dollar, 12.5 per cent euro, 8 per cent sterling and 4.5 per cent Japanese yen. This will impose additional transaction and logistical costs related to having to open new foreign currency accounts, e.g. for Japanese yen. But thanks to leading edge quantitative techniques, this is not necessarily so, and it is entirely possible to construct an optimum currency basket without Japanese yen which almost tracks the target currency composition. Indeed, given the currency correlations, it turns out that a currency basket, with 75 per cent US dollar, 17 per cent euro and 8 per cent sterling, almost completely tracks the risk of the target currency structure; the portfolio currency risk of the target currency basket, as we have seen, is 1.92 per cent per annum as against the portfolio currency risk of 1.94 per cent for the tracking currency basket. But a warning should be in order: the tracking currency basket would need very careful monitoring to detect incipient divergence due to shifts in the correlation structures, and consequential review. This problem is, however, completely avoided if the actual currency composition is exactly matched with the target. Thus, the trade-off involves balancing the savings in logistical and transactions costs against the risk of escalation in tracking error. This, however, applies to a do-nothing scenario; a dynamic monitoring review and adjustment will avoid this danger. From this analysis a second recommendation follows:

Recommendation 2
Adopt a strategic benchmark currency allocation comprising 75 per cent US dollar, 17 per cent euro and 8 per cent sterling for the central bank in the case study. Such a currency allocation would entail almost zero currency risk in a strategic sense.

Interestingly, this has a very significant policy implication that such a currency basket, and not any single currency, will be the numeraire in terms of which to stabilize, preserve and maintain the purchasing power of foreign exchange reserves!

After deciding on the strategic benchmark currency allocation, as in the case of the strategic duration decision, the next most critical policy challenge would be to quantify, and prescribe, constraints for *tactical* currency play, whether in-house or externally managed, with a view to adding incremental value to the portfolio, for a maximum acceptable risk. The best way to quantify the maximum currency risk-tolerance would be to limit it to no more than that acceptable in the case of the benchmark duration in a strategic sense. This we have identified as a six month duration. The six month US T-bill benchmark corresponds to a maximum principal loss of approximately 0.2 per cent over a monthly horizon, with only 1 per cent probability that such loss will exceed 0.2 per cent. This is obtained by the formula: modified duration × absolute yield change corresponding to a 2.33 standard deviation of six month yields. The standard deviation of six-month yields, as we have seen, is 3.35 per cent per month, and since the average six month T-Bill yield is 5.1561 per cent, we get for 2.33 standard deviations of absolute yield change 0.41865 per cent ($5.1561 \times (e^{0.0335 \times 2.33} - 1)$). This, when multiplied with modified duration (duration/1.051561 = 0.4755) gives 0.4755 × 0.4186% = 0.199% ≅ 0.20%. This, it must be noted, exclude the coupon/interest income component.

Trial and error calculations show that US and the non-US currency allocations of ± 2.5 per cent, i.e. currency portfolios with a US dollar share of 77.5 per cent and a non-US dollar share of 22.5 per cent, or a US dollar share of 72.5 per cent and non-US dollar share of 27.5 per cent, more or less give the same order of maximum principal loss as does the 6-month Treasury Bill with 1 per cent probability of such loss being exceeded. In particular, the US dollar 77.5 per cent portfolio carries an absolute risk of 1.73 per cent (annualized standard deviation) versus 2.24 per cent for the US dollar 72.5 per cent portfolio. Therefore, relative to the benchmark allocation, the two portfolios carry a risk of 1.94 − 1.73 = 0.21% and 1.94 − 2.24 = 0.30%, respectively. The first portfolio has a 1 per cent probability of loss exceeding 0.14 per cent and the second one, of loss exceeding 0.20 per cent. This leads to the third and last recommendation.

Recommendation 3

The maximum permissible deviations in the currency allocations relative to the currency benchmark should not exceed ± 2.5 per cent.

In the case study, the actual currency allocations, therefore, can vary between US dollar –72.5 and 77.5 per cent, euro –15.30 and 18.70 per cent and pound sterling –7.20 and 8.80 per cent. The idea is that the portfolio managers are challenged, subject to the maximum acceptable downside risk, to endeavour to earn a gain of 0.14 – 0.20 per cent, based on an active view-taking on the international currency markets. For instance, over the short to medium term, if the view is that the euro would weaken against the US dollar, then depending upon the degree of confidence in such view, portfolio managers in the central bank would increase the US dollar share to no more than 77.5 per cent. If their view came right, they could add incremental value, otherwise, the potential loss would be limited to no more than 0.20 per cent with 99 per cent probability, which was considered acceptable anyway.

10.6 SUMMARY AND CONCLUSION

In this case study we have examined the typical case of a developing country central bank, where official reserves have been held predominantly in US dollars at very short duration. We have seen that it is useful to define clearly a desirable risk-return trade-off. The concept of 'shortfall probability', i.e. the probability of returns being negative over a given time horizon, is a useful device in helping central bank management to formulate such risk tolerance. It was shown that an interesting yield pick can be achieved by extending the duration of the portfolio at insignificant incremental risk, which would still remain below a conservatively defined maximum acceptable risk of 1 per cent shortfall probability. As for the tactical management internal and external portfolio managers should be challenged to outperform the benchmark in a risk-adjusted sense. Here again, a maximum acceptable 'shortfall probability' of 'excess' returns being negative should be determined. This would provide for flexibility in duration management, depending upon the actual yield curve and the perceived yield volatility.

Although currency risk is far more serious than other types of market risks, the existing currency and maturity structure of many central banks implies a disproportionately greater tolerance of currency risk. As the bearing of currency risk is not rewarded in the long term, there is a very strong case for the elimination of substantial currency risks by aligning the currency composition of foreign exchange reserves to the outstanding external debt of the country. Since a major part of developing countries' debt is denominated in SDRs it is preferable to decompose the currency risk of external debt into the underlying currencies. In the case study it is shown that a major reduction in currency risk can be achieved by switching from a mainly US dollar denominated portfolio to a portfolio which would be comprised for 75 per cent of US dollars and for the remainder of euro and sterling (assuming that the Japanese yen would be strongly correlated to the euro). For the tactical currency management of the reserve portfolio around the strategic benchmark again a maximum acceptable shortfall probability should be determined.

In conclusion, the case study vividly illustrates, in the context of central banks' foreign exchange reserves management, the nuts-and-bolts application of the current frontier and state-of-the-art analytical tool of 'shortfall probability' in formalizing, and quantifying, the most preferred risk–return trade-offs as regards interest rate and currency risks. In particular, without at all being pedantic, or pontifical, the 'shortfall probability' approach presented in the paper lets the top management in central banks choose, in their absolute discretion and judgement, the most appropriate strategic and tactical 'risk–return trade-offs' that best correspond to the degree of their risk aversion/risk preference/risk appetite!

NOTES

1. The views expressed in this chapter are those of the author and not of the Reserve Bank of India.
2. The interest income component of the returns has been excluded, i.e. only the price risk has been considered.

11. Observations on the Return versus Liquidity Debate: The Canadian Perspective

Donna Howard

11.1 INTRODUCTION

Central banks face a number of trade-offs or opposing objectives that arise in reserve management. These include modern versus traditional approaches of reserve management, liquidity considerations versus storage of national wealth considerations and micro versus macro risks, among others. Furthermore, central banks have to weigh the trade-off between credibility and the possibilities of reputation loss if they venture further on the risk scale in managing reserves. The weight of these trade-offs is partly determined by the institutional setting in which the central bank operates, where a corporate model can be distinguished from an agent model. In the corporate model the central bank has a clear and precise mandate that requires it to assume certain risks in the autonomous conduct of operations through its own balance sheet. In this model, a central bank acts as a separate legal entity with its own capital that serves as a buffer to absorb potential future losses. At the other extreme of the spectrum, the agent model, a central bank acts as an agent for the government and the main risks associated with its activities are borne by the government. The following overview of the Bank of Canada's role in reserve management clarifies the bank's position in the corporate/agent model structure and highlights the unique perspectives that Canada brings to its decision-making process.

11.2 RESERVE MANAGEMENT AT THE BANK OF CANADA

As with most central banks, price stability is the Bank of Canada's objective: the best way that a central bank can contribute to the domestic economy is by preserving the value of its money. In order to achieve that objective, the Bank has only one instrument, the overnight rate of interest. By not having a target for the exchange rate, i.e, by having a floating exchange rate since 1970, the Bank does not have a need for foreign reserves for its own balance sheet. (Its domestic liabilities (banknotes) drive the size of the Bank's balance sheet and they are offset primarily by holdings of Government of Canada bonds and treasury bills.)

The Bank of Canada does not own Canada's foreign reserves – it manages them on behalf of the Minister of Finance within a well-defined governance framework (see below). Given this perspective, it is relatively easy to see that the management of reserves is ultimately done for the government on behalf of the taxpayers. It is therefore more difficult to make the distinction between a corporate model and an agent model, since under both, a public service is being provided. The arrangements with the government differ however. Perhaps the principal-agent arrangement that Canada has brings the advantage that the government understands the issues that are being dealt with and needs less 'education'.

Canada holds foreign reserves in case they are required for intervention in the currency market or to provide foreign currency liquidity for the government. This contrasts with the situation in countries that use their foreign reserves as a national store of wealth. Thus in principle, the entire portfolio is there to be mobilized if the need arises. That being said, the use of reserves is expected only under exceptional circumstances. In fact, the Bank of Canada has not intervened to support the Canadian dollar since 1998, and even before then, significant events were rare during nearly three decades of a floating exchange rate.

Almost by definition, it is hard to say what an exceptional or tail-event period would look like. Nonetheless, the need to prepare for an exceptional event implies that part of the portfolio of assets would need to be very liquid under any circumstances. Most of the remainder should be in assets that could be mobilized quickly, but not necessarily immediately, under possibly adverse circumstances.

What would this look like? A diversified portfolio of highly-rated assets from well-known issuers, where the issue size is large and secondary markets are active. The diversification would be across issuers as well as major currencies. And it also suggests holding a tranche of that portfolio in short-term assets.

Highly-rated assets are indicated because the liquidity of low-rated assets is likely to dry up during periods of financial stress, hence the term 'flight-to-quality' seen in periods of corporate defaults or downgrades. Highly-rated assets also minimize the risk of capital loss for the government due to default or downgrade of the counterparty. The credit composition of the assets in

Canada's Exchange Fund Account (EFA), which forms the largest proportion of the foreign reserves, is illustrated in Figure 11.1.

Figure 11.1 Investments in Canada's Exchange Fund Account, by credit rating (December 31, 2004, percentage of market value)

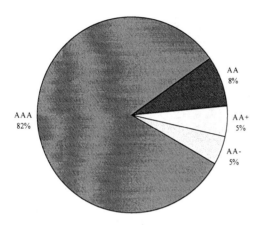

Currency diversification is indicated in case the exceptional circumstance that triggers the need to use the reserves involves difficulties in particular geographic markets. In Figure 11.2 the currency composition of the EFA is illustrated. Diversification across issuers guards against the situation where a normally easily-traded asset becomes illiquid if leveraged investors are forced to rapidly liquidate large positions in that asset (e.g. the Long-Term Capital Management episode). Finally, a tranche of short-term assets helps satisfy immediate liquidity needs while other assets are being mobilized.

One could say that this portfolio is so constrained by liquidity considerations that returns could be foregone in achieving that liquidity. However, the management of Canada's reserves involves more than asset management. In fact, Canada's foreign reserves are fully funded by its foreign-currency liabilities. The framework of well-defined asset and liability matching minimizes both interest rate and currency risk.

*Figure 11.2 Currency composition of Canada's Exchange Fund Account
         (31 December , 2004, percentage of market value)*

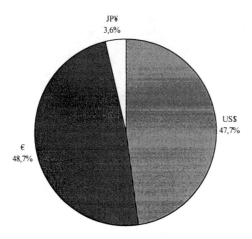

So while the total return on Canada's foreign reserve portfolio may be low on a relative basis through time, the total cost of the liabilities that finance that portfolio has been even lower given our AAA rating, a rating that is supported by a foundation of sound monetary and fiscal policies[1]. As a result, we have been earning a positive net total return on the combined portfolio, even during the recent period of low yields.

While unique, Canada's reserves management shares a number of features with other countries that hold modest amounts of reserves exclusively for intervention and foreign currency liquidity needs. By contrast, countries that hold large reserves as a result of exchange rate policies or as a store of wealth, and those that do not benefit from a strong credit rating, are likely to have a different view of the trade-off between liquidity and return.

11.3 GOVERNANCE ASPECTS AND ACCOUNTING ISSUES

Governance and accounting standards influence the management of reserves. Recall that there is a standard model for governance set out in the IMF's Guidelines for Foreign Exchange Reserves Management (2004). It comprises the strategic level (establishing the parameters and risk control), an Investment Committee (establishing the operational framework, investment strategy, and the portfolio benchmarks/performances ratios) and the front office (which operates on a day-to-day basis within the pre-established guidelines and is monitored by an independent risk office).

The Bank of Canada and the Department of Finance recently completed a governance review which clarified roles and responsibilities and resulted in the creation of an independent Financial Risk Office and Risk Committee (Department of Finance Canada, 2003). While the Minister of Finance is ultimately accountable for the foreign reserves, the Bank of Canada is a full participant in the decision-making process.

One of the challenges facing some central banks is the shift in objectives, i.e. from countries required to hold reserves for potential foreign currency intervention to those holding reserves as a store of wealth (generally independent of the government's liabilities). To frame the decision-making process it is important to first clarify the county's objectives in holding foreign reserves and then determine the appropriate investment policy, relying on an appropriate governance structure in making those decisions.

Finally, one brief word on accounting standards and transparency: the issue of changes in standards is one being faced by the public and private sectors in all countries, particularly as international standards are converging. Perhaps it is timely to step back and recognize that accounting is the globally accepted means for recording and reporting the financial position and activity of entities, providing a tool and a language that supports understanding, accountability and effective management. Adherence to standards and principles allows a consistent and comparable presentation of financial information over time. That is why there is a strong push to international standards in an increasingly globalized environment.

Central banks are leaders in the public eye and have made great strides with respect to transparency of their monetary policy decisions. It is hard to make a compelling case that central banks should not be held accountable for the management of their financial assets. The leadership role that they carry points to moving towards meeting the new standards whenever possible. This avoids the potential criticism that central banks are saying 'do what I say and not what I do', especially as they enter into new areas that were traditionally associated with the private sector, such as active asset management! Some comfort can be taken from the words of a private sector banker who noted that market analysts and others who care about financial reporting are aware of the implications of the changes in accounting standards and are intelligent enough to interpret the facts correctly. However, this does not take away the communication hurdles with other stakeholders. Investing in the education of stakeholders throughout the change process can minimize reputation risks, although some risk will always remain.

11.4 CONCLUSION

Central bank reserve management raises a number of very interesting perspectives, which can be grouped into the following broad themes. First, as not all central banks are homogeneous, it is very important to understand the underlying objectives of the reserve portfolio before deciding on an investment policy. Second, central banks are ultimately accountable to the taxpayer (whom the government represents), irrespective of whether a corporate or an agent model is applied. Under both models central bank reserve management is a public service involving public funds. Third, central banks can play a large role by leading by example, in particular in meeting international accounting standards whenever possible.

NOTES

1. An asset/liability matching framework effectively excludes investment in MBS where the prepayment risk precludes matching with offsetting liabilities. However, even if these were eligible assets, an assessment would need to be made as to whether the liquidity of these assets in the current environment would be sustained in a period of financial stress.

12. A European View on Return versus Liquidity[1]

Pentti Hakkaraïnen and Mika Pösö

12.1 INTRODUCTION

Global central bank reserves, especially reserves held in foreign assets, have grown rapidly in recent years. This growth has taken place mostly in Asia which today accounts for more than two-thirds of the global foreign exchange reserves. In addition to Asia, where foreign exchange reserves have accumulated for foreign exchange policy reasons, reserves have risen significantly in oil-producing countries too, where increased export revenue has been funnelled into the balance sheets of the respective monetary authorities. The increase in central bank reserves has not gone unnoticed by market participants. Indeed, the volume and flows of the central bank reserves are today so significant that a proper understanding of financial market developments requires understanding of the composition of the major central bank reserves and the way in which they are managed. When assessing the reasons for holding reserves and the way they are managed, central banks are often seen as a relatively homogeneous group. It is fair to say that many central banks share the same motives and objectives for holding and managing reserves. At the same time, however, one should note that not only the level of reserves, but also their composition in terms of currencies and the types of assets differ significantly from one country to another. Similarly, the way in which the reserves are managed differ, sometimes to a significant degree.

12.2 RESERVE MANAGEMENT FRAMEWORK IN THE BANK OF FINLAND

The reserve management framework in the Bank of Finland has remained largely unchanged since Finland joined the euro. After the introduction of the euro, the Bank of Finland invested in corporate bonds, increased duration of investments and begun 'active investment management'. In accordance with its strategic policies, the Bank of Finland takes a long-term perspective on managing its foreign reserves and handles them in a professional and active manner on the basis of strict risk management principles.

The Bank of Finland holds foreign reserves in order to meet any additional transfer requirements of foreign reserves to the European Central Bank (ECB) and to meet the financing requirements of the International Monetary Fund (IMF), as well as to prepare for contingencies, such as serious disruptions in the financial markets. When measured in euro terms, the size of the Bank's foreign reserves has remained fairly stable. The key objectives of the Bank's investment policy – security, liquidity and return – have remained unchanged. The security objective refers to the requirement that the market value of foreign reserves must not fluctuate excessively as a result of the various risks involved. In addition, part of the reserves must be sufficiently liquid, in that they can be converted into cash sufficiently quickly and at low cost, whenever needed. Within these constraints, the aim remains to obtain the best possible return.

The portfolio that is assessed as being best suited to the Bank of Finland's long-term investment objectives is expressed in terms of currency distribution and currency-specific benchmark portfolios. The currency distribution and the structure of benchmark portfolios largely determine the return on invested reserves. The aim of active investment is to obtain a return on invested reserves that is higher than the return on the benchmark portfolios. The cornerstone of the investment policy is effective portfolio diversification. The benchmark currency distribution is reviewed at two- to three-year intervals.

Interest rate risk is measured and managed in terms of duration and the value-at-risk (VaR) method. The target duration of two-and-a-half years is applied to all the currencies included in the foreign reserves. The VaR method has been used comprehensively in the risk management framework since the end of 2004. In addition, interest rate risk is restricted by spreading investments among debt instruments with different maturities in all reserve currencies.

Most of the reserves are invested in government (sovereign) papers, but approximately a quarter of the foreign reserves are invested in debt instruments issued by entities with a high credit rating, such as non-financial corporations (see Figure 12.1).

In the long run, these investments generate higher returns than corresponding government debt instruments because of the credit risk attached to them and the fact that they are less liquid than government debt instruments. The credit risk inherent in the credit portfolio is also measured using the VaR method. Effective portfolio diversification is crucial in the management of credit risk. Diversification is achieved by setting maximum limits and minimum credit rating criteria for issuers and counterparty banks and maximum limits for the VaR figures derived for the credit risk on the credit portfolio (see Figure 12.2).

Figure 12.1   Distribution of the Bank of Finland's foreign reserves
excluding gold, as of 31 December, 2005

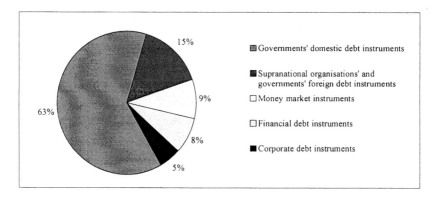

Figure 12.2:   Distribution of the Bank of Finland's credit portfolio by credit
rating, as of 31 December 2005

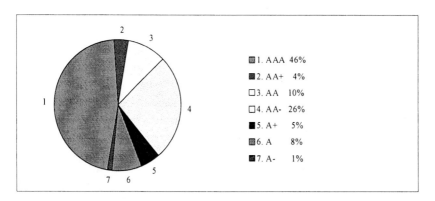

12.3 DETERMINANTS AND POLICY REQUIREMENTS FOR CENTRAL BANK RESERVE MANAGEMENT FRAMEWORKS

In a simplified framework, the objectives for holding central bank reserves can be seen as stemming from two types of risk; macroeconomic and microeconomic. Macro risks will always remain the primary risks for a country – or a central bank – against which reserves are held, as they concern not only risks to monetary, foreign exchange and financial stability, but also risks to the safe functioning of the national economy or currency area. The fact that it is normally the central bank that is the holder of the country's reserves against macroeconomic risks originally results from an innate division of labour in society. Due to the nature of its objectives and functions, the central bank can be seen as the natural institution for the task of holding reserves on behalf of the society it serves.

Although micro risks are also very important, they can be only secondary to macro risks, as micro risks 'merely' concern the financial result of the central bank. In this respect, micro risks have implications not only for the financial result of the central bank itself but also its stakeholders, such as the government, to whom at least a proportion of the financial result of the central bank is transferred.

In order to realize fully the relative importance of macro and micro risks, it is worth emphasizing the causality between them. Macro risks are the reason for holding reserves, whereas micro risks are a consequence of holding reserves. One should also note an implicit trade-off between macro and micro risks in this context. When eliminating micro risks, the central bank may increase the country's exposure to macro risks. Similarly, by trying to minimize the country's exposure to macro risks, the central bank may end up facing more micro risks

Changing weights of macro and micro risks in Europe

Managing macro and micro risks, and the above mentioned trade-off between them, is complex since these risks are not perceived as being fixed over time. The weights given to these risks by society and decision makers vary over time. As macro risks normally materialize during financial turbulence or hard times, the weight given to them tends to decrease when good times prevail.

When considering the framework for defining the level, liquidity and composition of central bank reserves, it is crucial to identify the relevant macro and micro risks and the weights placed on them. Although there are many sophisticated tools, techniques and frameworks that can be used to approach this problem, one cannot hide from the fact that these weights are often only defined implicitly and characterize how the world is perceived. Assessment of the risks is, to a significant degree, a highly subjective matter. The reason that this task is often entrusted to central bankers probably results from the expectation that central bankers have a more distant horizon than other decision makers and, therefore, have a comparative advantage in avoiding myopia when times are good.

Looking at global and European experiences in this respect, three general observations can be made. First, when total reserves increase – deliberately or otherwise – the central bank becomes stronger in facing macro risks, but at the same time, potentially more exposed to the micro risks that could affect the financial result of a central bank.

Second, it appears that in many euro area countries macro risks are now deemed smaller than they were before the monetary union. The specific reasons for this view may differ from one country to another, but the creation of the ECB and the Eurosystem is widely seen as a factor that has decreased some macro risks and correspondingly, the need for reserves against macro risks.

We do not believe that macro risks as such have significantly decreased since the introduction of the euro. However, we do see that within the monetary union the euro area central banks are provided with more tools with which to manage macro risks. The best example of this is the ECB which, with the foreign reserves that have been transferred to it, now takes primary responsibility for possible foreign exchange interventions. On top of which, for many euro area central banks, the euro is a more usable currency to hold against macro risks than their previous, legacy currencies.

The third observation concerns the increased freedom that the euro area central banks have in arranging their financial assets. Indisputably, the euro area central banks have an independent position from which to carry out their tasks, in comparison to other European or governmental bodies. Independence has not only offered freedom, but also an obligation to maintain a more efficient, skilful and careful approach to managing micro risks. Euro area central banks are more accountable than ever for demonstrating, through their actions, that they fully deserve their independent status.

12.4 LIQUIDITY AND RETURN CHARACTERISTICS OF CENTRAL BANK RESERVE MANAGEMENT

Although the specific words and their order may differ from one central bank to another, safety, liquidity and return are the objectives of reserve management which are most often set by central banks. The Bank of Finland is no exception to this rule.

In order to simplify the task of characterizing investment policy for total reserves on the basis of these three objectives, there is a tendency to divide total central bank reserves into two parts, at least metaphorically[2]. In the following, these two parts are referred to as liquidity reserves, which are held primarily against macro risks, and investment reserves, which can be managed by concentrating more on maximizing return at the chosen level of financial (i.e. micro) risks.

Liquidity reserves should be managed in a way that keeps the probability of losses very low over the short term. Therefore, liquidity and safety take priority over the search for return, when the investment policy for liquidity reserves is formulated. The reason for emphasizing liquidity and capital preservation is that were macro risks to materialize, it would be excessively costly for a country not to have access to reserves – and especially foreign assets – at that time. The inability to liquidate foreign assets in stress situations and turbulent market conditions can have drastic effects on the real economy and lead to a significant reduction in national income and wealth.

Having determined the level and the currency distribution of liquidity reserves, the very nature of the reserves obliges the implementation of a conservative investment policy that puts a relatively large emphasis on minimizing micro risks. Liquidity reserves are thus invested in a manner that guarantees, as far as possible, that the assets are usable virtually immediately once the central bank or the country needs them. For this reason, liquidity reserves are normally allocated to a small number of major international currencies and invested in the most liquid and creditworthy assets in those currencies. For instance, the Bank of Finland concretizes the liquidity requirement by ensuring that 25 per cent of invested reserves are highly liquid. In this context, only government securities, repurchase agreements with up to one month's maturity and up to one-month deposits in the reserve currencies are defined as highly liquid.

Investment reserves and how to manage them

As regards investment reserves, the investment horizon and holding period are longer than for liquidity reserves and restrictions regarding safety and liquidity are therefore looser. When managing investment reserves, more emphasis can be put on maximizing return.

When setting an investment policy for investment reserves, central bankers should probably listen more carefully to what asset management professionals, investment bankers and even other long-term investors have to say. Although the optimization of a central bank's investment portfolio still comprises restrictions that are not common to the private sector's long-term investors, the objective of aiming for an efficient frontier is in fact not that different. So, what advice do asset management professionals give us central bankers today? The following three recommendations, at least, have often been mentioned[3].

First, investment bankers recommend differentiating the currency allocation from the country allocation. Placements can be made separate to managing the foreign exchange exposure thereby making use of the best characteristics of both markets. As the currency and bond returns, at least historically, have had a relatively low correlation, this would provide a significant opportunity to reduce risk without having a negative effect on the return of the total portfolio. What makes this advice especially interesting is the fact that following it would not necessarily increase the cost of liquidating the portfolio, even in distressed conditions.

Second, investment bankers recommend relaxing the individual duration constraints within each country sector and focussing more on total portfolio risk. Being more efficient in taking advantage of the various shapes of yield curves and different covariance amongst the maturity sectors creates opportunities to both increase return and reduce risk. In essence, this also means higher durations.

Third, investment bankers advise relaxing the credit constraints on the portfolios and widening the array of instruments. Allowing the portfolio to extend into investment-grade credits or even beyond and into instruments such as asset and mortgage-backed securities, would again allow improvement in the efficiency of the total portfolio, as measured by the Sharpe Ratio criterion. Moving away from government risk to credit risk may actually allow a reduction in the total risk of the portfolio while increasing returns. This is supported by the Bank of Finland's experience with its credit portfolio.

The advice given by investment bankers is, of course, correct when judged on the basis of the models and assumptions used. However, advice may often be derived from too narrow a framework, especially if the advice is asset management-oriented rather than being backed by a more comprehensive asset and liability management framework.

Intuition tells us that central banks that are separate legal entities, and increasingly like private companies, with their own balance sheets and income statements, cannot overlook their liabilities when formulating asset management and investment policies. Even though central banks have unique tasks and objectives that differ from those of the private sector, it should not mean that central banks become complacent about their implicit funding structures, their obligations or about what is done in the world of investment management in general. It appears fair to say that more attention should be paid to comprehensive asset and liability management in central banks too. The liability side of the balance sheet always contains crucial information on the dependencies between different balance sheet items, and understanding them fully is a prerequisite for setting an investment policy that maintains a strong central bank balance sheet. The characteristics of liabilities naturally have an impact on the entire interest rate risk of the balance sheet and certainly on defining the duration of the invested assets.

In this respect, a number of open questions arise. How should the central banks generally see their balance sheet liabilities, such as banknotes and equity? What are their costs and interest rate characteristics? Should the way in which central bank assets are financed affect the way in which they are invested? For instance, should we see banknotes as having a redemption obligation and if so, should this have an effect on duration guidelines when setting investment policies? Should part of the assets be earmarked as being financed through equity?

An opponent to this approach could argue that what suits pension funds, for example, is not applicable to central banks. Central banks are entities which actually set the cost structure of their balance sheets by, for example, deciding on policy interest rates. Central banks also create funds through issuing banknotes. In addition, on-balance sheet liabilities do not fully characterize the total liabilities of the central bank, for instance, at a time of serious financial stress.

However, there are a number of similarities between central banks and private sector long term investors, such as pension funds. Both have long-term liabilities and objectives. Confidence is the core element in both businesses and both have to reliably demonstrate that future obligations will be met. Since obligations materialize in the distant future, both institutions require decent returns on assets to maintain or increase the real value of the assets. Both also face increased demand for transparency.

Perhaps one weakness in the usual recommendations offered to central bankers is the fact that these suggestions are often derived from simple mean-variance optimization frameworks. The models use historical data to estimate parameters, such as correlation coefficients, which are often treated as stable. This can be a serious weakness, since central banks' investment policies have traditionally been chiefly defined for those periods of financial market stress when these parameters tend to break down. Central banks are not prepared to accept major losses from micro risks in circumstances where macro risks materialize.

It is important to remember that central bank-specific restrictions significantly limit setting investment policies for investment reserves. Again, these restrictions probably vary among central banks in their nature and number. Also the size of the central bank and its role in the global scene has an effect on how restricted it feels, as recent developments in Europe seem to confirm.

In general, it can be said that European national central banks have probably fewer restrictions and have more room for manoeuvre than 10 years ago. However, Even though the trend in reserve management has provided more freedom, there is one abstract and important restriction; so-called reputation risk. For instance, reputation can be damaged when a central bank incurs losses due to the default of a debt security, even though the effect on the total portfolio return may be marginal.

Some practical hindrances to the implementation of a modern investment policy for investment reserves may exist, such as limitations in IT systems, experience and skills. In some cases, it may not be possible to include a new financial instrument in the investment universe, due to limitations in an IT system or the lack of a skills base, even though it would be optimal from the portfolio optimization point of view. Of course, these kinds of restrictions could sometimes be circumvented through outsourcing, for example, such as in the use of external asset management.

A central bank's justification in managing liquidity reserves is clear and often even written into national legislation. The justification for managing investment reserves, i.e. assets not held against macro risks, is not as clear. In fact, if the central bank does not manage its reserves efficiently and following the highest professional standards, one should not be surprised to hear occasional comments questioning the birthright of the central bank to manage them. One can also expect more regular comparisons with the performance of similar investors managing wealth, such as pension funds. As a result of increased transparency and accountability requirements, central banks cannot and should not avoid this kind of exposure.

12.5 CONCLUSION

It appears clear that liquidity requirements, in their strictest form, are applicable to a smaller proportion of central bank reserves in the euro area today than before the introduction of the common currency. The euro and its track record support the notion that the macro risk burden, which previously was carried wholly by national central banks, is now partly carried by the European institutional framework. Therefore, the need for holding very liquid foreign reserves against macro risks has probably been reduced somewhat and as a result, the euro may have substituted foreign assets in some balance sheets of the euro area central banks. Of course, this does not mean that the euro would not have characteristics as favourable in crisis situations as any other major currency.

At the same time, one can observe that the balance sheets of the euro area national central banks are not becoming smaller. On the contrary, the continuous growth of the Eurosystem liabilities, mainly due to the strong demand for euro banknotes, has meant that the asset side of the Eurosystem balance sheet has also continued to grow.

Following these two developments, both of which interestingly result from the success of the common currency, many euro area central banks are facing a situation where their investment reserves are on a progressive path. This has meant, and probably will continue to mean, that the portfolio-theoretic thinking and the return objective will play a larger role in the future when setting investment policies in the euro area central banks. In this environment concentrating on asset management techniques alone is probably too narrow an approach and more attention should be paid to the liability side of the central bank balance sheet. In any case, euro area central banks have become increasingly accountable for managing national wealth through the exercise of prudent stewardship.

NOTES

1. The opinions expressed in this article are those of the authors and do not necessarily reflect the views of the Bank of Finland or the Eurosystem.
2. See e.g. Putnam, (2004), pp 29–46.
3. See also Fisher and Lie (2004), pp 75–96.

13. The Composition of Central Bank Reserves: The Market Perspective

Joachim Fels

13.1 INTRODUCTION

The rapid growth of official currency reserves in recent years, especially in Asia, the Middle East and Russia, raises important issues for both central banks and financial markets. For reserve managers, the main issue is how to efficiently manage their swollen reserves, given the peculiar policy constraints they face. Put simply, the key trade-offs for reserve managers are between liquidity, safety and return. To what extent should central banks diversify their reserves across currencies, maturities and asset classes?

On the other side of the fence, financial markets worry about the impact of such reserve diversification on exchange rates and asset prices, especially since official reserves (excluding gold) have soared to more than $4,000 billion by the end of 2004. For example, US dollar bears point to potentially large-scale future diversification by central banks out of the Greenback to justify their dire predictions for the US currency; currency traders often cite alleged central bank flows as causes for exchange rate moves; and analysts have offered Asian central banks' purchases of US Treasuries as one explanation for Alan Greenspan's 'yield conundrum'. In short, the actual and prospective composition of central bank reserves has become a hot topic for central bankers and markets alike.

This chapter discusses the composition of central bank reserves along three dimensions: (1) currency, (2) duration and (3) asset classes. Is it reasonable to expect massive diversification out of the dollar into the euro or other currencies in the coming years? Should central banks extend the duration of their portfolios, which in most cases are still heavily concentrated in short- and medium-term bonds? Does it make sense for central banks to move into riskier assets such as private-sector bonds, emerging markets, equities, commodities and hedge funds? And is there a role for inflation-linked bonds and derivatives in central bank portfolios? One possible approach to these questions is to use quantitative models to construct optimal asset allocations for central banks based on their specific constraints and degrees of risk tolerance. By contrast, this chapter will offer some general thoughts on reserve composition based on the observations and biases of a financial market economist.

13.2 SOME STYLIZED FACTS

While many central banks have made big strides towards more transparency in monetary policy over the past decade or so, the composition of official currency reserves is still shrouded in secrecy. Not even the IMF and the BIS, the two most frequently used sources for data on official reserves, know for sure. For example, the IMF in its Annual Report 2005 released revised estimates of the currency composition of official reserves for 2003 and 2004 (see Table 13.1). But the authors admitted that they lacked compositional data on no less than $1,300 billion, or almost 33 per cent of total reserves, by the end of 2004 (the so-called 'unallocated reserves' in the IMF tables), mainly because many key central banks in emerging Asia do not report the composition of their reserves to the IMF (nor to anybody else).

Dollar still reigns supreme (probably...)

Looking at the currency shares for the member states that do report the currency composition of their reserves, the US dollar accounted for 65.9 per cent of official reserves, the euro for 24.9 per cent, the yen for 3.9 per cent and the pound sterling for 3.3 per cent at the end of 2004. Note that the dollar's share in total reserves, while down from a peak of 71 per cent in 1999, actually rose marginally during 2004 (from 65.8 per cent in late 2003) despite the dollar's depreciation against most currencies. Needless to say, this contrasts sharply with the market chatter about large-scale central bank diversification out of the dollar that was so popular recently. However, keep in mind that these estimates have to be treated with a great deal of caution as, again, the currency composition of about one-third of the world's total currency reserves is undisclosed.

Mostly short- and medium-term government bonds, but this may be changing

While we have at least a rough idea about the currency composition of reserves, we know next to nothing concrete about the duration of central banks' bond portfolios and the distribution across asset classes. Traditionally, central banks have held most of their reserves, apart from gold in government

Table 13.1 Share of national currencies in total identified official holdings of foreign exchange, end of year

	2003	2004
All countries		
U.S. dollar	65.8	65.9
Japanese yen	4.1	3.9
Pound sterling	2.6	3.3
Swiss franc	0.2	0.2
Euro	25.3	24.9
Industrial countries		
U.S. dollar	70.5	71.5
Japanese yen	3.8	3.6
Pound sterling	1.5	1.9
Swiss franc	0.2	0.1
Euro	22.1	20.9
Developing countries		
U.S. dollar	60.7	59.9
Japanese yen	4.4	4.3
Pound sterling	3.9	4.8
Swiss franc	0.2	0.2
Euro	28.9	29.2
Unallocated reserves		
All countries	29.8	32.6
Industrial countries	0.2	0.3
Developing countries	47.2	50.2

government bonds and, within that, mostly in short maturities. But more and more central banks are broadening the set of asset classes in which they are prepared to invest. The quest for return in a low-yield environment certainly plays an important role here, as does the fact that in many cases the level of reserves by far exceeds the amount deemed necessary for intervention purposes, which is usually held in highly liquid assets. For example, a recent survey among central banks conducted by Central Banking Publications

(Pringle and Carver, 2006) shows a general move towards riskier bonds and spread products. Three-quarters of the central banks surveyed said they had introduced new asset classes to their investment management processes in the last one to two years including, in a few cases, equities and hedge funds.

Table 13.2 Central bank survey: which of the following 'new' asset classes is your central bank currently invested in?

	Central banks	% of respondents
Government Bonds (AA)	36	75
Government Bonds (A)	18	38
Government Bonds (BBB)	6	13
Government Bonds (below BBB)	4	8
Corporate Bonds (above BBB)	10	21
Corporate Bonds (below BBB)	2	4
Agency paper	32	67
Asset-backed bonds	12	25
Mortgage-backed bonds	12	25
Index linked bonds	12	25
Equities	4	8
Hedge fudns	0	0
Property	0	0
Alternative investment	4	8

Source: Pringle and Carver (2006)

13.3 THE END OF THE DOLLAR'S DOMINANCE?

Is it reasonable to expect large-scale diversification out of the US dollar into the euro and other currencies over the next several years? Could even the dollar's status as a reserve currency be challenged in the foreseeable future? The arguments of the dollar sceptics are well known: they mostly revolve around America's record current account deficit of more than 6 per cent of GDP, which is widely viewed as unsustainable. Hence, the argument goes, central banks and private investors would start to shed dollar assets at some stage in the search for another reserve currency. Given the size of the euro area's economy and financial markets, the euro is widely seen as the leading contender for the next reserve currency. However, as I see it, rumours of the imminent death of the dollar as the leading reserve currency are grossly exaggerated, for several reasons.

Reserve currencies don't lose their status that easily

Convenience and 'network externalities' tend to favor the incumbent lead reserve currency. It took several decades of severe monetary and economic mismanagement in Britain plus two costly wars in Europe before the British pound lost its reserve currency status to the dollar. By contrast, the US economy has weathered several severe external shocks in the past five years remarkably well and has remained the engine of growth for the world economy. The Greenback is issued by a highly credible central bank, and the US remains the only military superpower in the world. All of these considerations – economic, monetary and political – are important in determining the status of a currency as a reserve medium. This is not to say that the US current account deficit is irrelevant or that future monetary and economic mismanagement by the US authorities is impossible. But the burden of proof is on the dollar sceptics, as the dollar rally in 2005, despite a widening US current account deficit, has shown.

Large-scale currency diversification is difficult for dollar-peggers

Much of the debate about potential reserve diversification out of dollar denominated assets has been sparked by the sharp rise of Asian central banks' dollar reserves in recent years. The increase in reserves has been largely due to the Asian authorities' policy of pegging to the dollar (e.g. China until July 2005) or their desire to lean against an undesirable excessive appreciation of their currency (e.g. Japan). As long as a dollar peg or quasi-peg is the overriding domestic policy goal, the level of reserves is endogenous and adjusts passively to the net flows in the balance of payments. Thus, a separate target for the level of dollar reserves would conflict with the exchange rate target. Large-scale diversification out of the dollar by countries that wish to maintain a peg or a quasi-peg to the dollar would put upward pressure on these countries' currencies against the dollar, which in turn would be incompatible with the overriding policy goal. Thus, fears that Asian central banks would all of a sudden move large amounts of their reserves out of the dollar, thus sparking a dollar-crisis, have always been and are likely to remain overblown.

The euro is not a glaring alternative

Moreover, large-scale diversification out of the dollar presupposes that there is a good alternative reserve currency. Clearly, given its economic size and the size and depth of its capital markets, the euro is the leading contender to the dollar. However, there are two reasons why the euro is likely to remain a distant second to the dollar in reserve portfolios (recall that it currently takes 25 per cent of official reserves, versus 66 per cent for the dollar). The first reason may be of a transitory nature, but is clearly an argument against large-scale diversification in the near-term: the low level of interest rates in the euro zone compared to those in the dollar zone. Short-term interest rates are way below US short rates, and 10-year bond yields in the euro area currently trade 125 basis points below US Treasury yields. Yield considerations matter for central banks, as can be seen in the low share of yen assets in central bank portfolios. Thus what looked like an attractive investment proposition up until the middle of 2004, when euro area short rates were twice as high as US short rates and longer-term bond yields were at roughly equal levels, has turned into a disadvantage for the euro. More important and of a less transitory nature, in my view, is the euro's second disadvantage: the euro remains a currency without a state as a closer political union in Europe is very unlikely to emerge in the foreseeable future. Europe's widening political fractures and economic divergences raise the specter of an EMU break-up over the next five to ten years. I don't believe (and I certainly don't hope) that this is the likely outcome, but the break-up risk is larger than generally perceived. In my view, the lingering risk of an unravelling of the euro project implies that the euro will not be able to rival the dollar as a reserve currency, despite the dollar's own problems.

Diversification into risky assets may benefit the dollar

A further argument for a continued dominance of the dollar in official reserves has to do with central banks' desire to diversify into riskier assets than government bonds. Dollar-denominated asset markets are still much broader and deeper than those in the euro area when it comes to mortgage- and asset-backed securities, investment-grade and high-yield bonds, and equities. Thus, diversification into riskier assets could actually increase the weight of dollar assets in official reserves, simply because the dollar zone offers superior liquidity and breadth in risky assets.

Taken together, central banks should and are likely to think twice before shifting large parts of their portfolios out of the dollar. Fears of a dollar-crash due to currency diversification are overblown. There are several good reasons why central banks are, on aggregate, heavily invested in dollars and are likely to remain so in the foreseeable future.

13.4 LENGTHENING THE DURATION OF BOND PORTFOLIOS

Central banks' portfolios have traditionally been concentrated heavily in short- and medium-term government bonds. This largely reflects the low tolerance for capital losses that would result if bond yields rise. However, to the extent that central bank reserves are not only a pool of liquid assets potentially needed for currency intervention or other emergencies, but a store of national wealth that is to be preserved for future generations, extending the duration of bond portfolios would be a natural step. Once one accepts the idea that reserves are a means of intergenerational wealth accumulation, it makes sense to consider matching the long-term liability central banks have to future generations with long-dated assets. This suggests that central banks should incorporate asset-liability-matching considering in their investment process, similar to what pension funds and life-insurance companies are doing, even though both the nature and the duration of central banks liabilities to future generations are, of course, much less clearly defined.

There are two caveats, however, that have to be considered in extending into long-dated bonds. The first is that currently yield curves are extremely flat, especially in the US bond market. Thus, the yield pick-up to be obtained from extending into long-dated bonds is extremely low at present. The second caveat is the risk of unanticipated inflation in the future, which would reduce the purchasing power in the investment currency for future generations. Hence, if central banks decide to extend duration, they may wish to consider investing in inflation-linked government bonds to address this particular risk. This point will be further covered below.

13.5 DIVERSIFICATION ACROSS ASSET CLASSES

The arguments for spreading official reserves over a broader range of asset classes are well-known. Many central banks have seen their reserves swelling well beyond the levels that are deemed necessary for intervention purposes.

Thus, the liquidity constraints are more easily met and a growing number of central banks is separating their reserves into a liquidity tranche and an investment tranche. In the latter, the focus is on return and portfolio efficiency, which automatically leads to the consideration of a broader range of asset classes. As noted above, surveys among central banks show that this move out of government bonds is underway. Central banks are increasingly diversifying into Agency bonds, mortgage-backed securities and corporate bonds. Agencies and MBS not only offer a yield-pick-up but, in contrast to corporate bonds, are highly liquid, which even makes them attractive also for central banks that mainly focus on the liquidity constraint. Apart from fixed income securities, some central banks have ventured into equities, and a few say they are considering hedge funds.

Figure 13.1 Spread between corporate BBB and government bonds

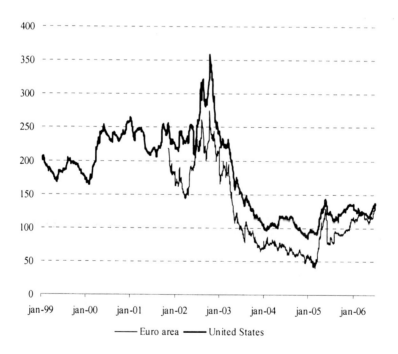

It is difficult to argue against a broader diversification of official reserves across asset classes, especially for those parts of the portfolio that are intended as a store of wealth for future generations (see Figure 13.1).

However, it is questionable whether it makes sense to extend into riskier assets at this particular point in time. The reason is that risk spreads are extremely compressed by the combination of a goldilocks global economy – strong economic growth and relatively low inflation – and an unprecedented amount of excess liquidity. The latter has been created by easy monetary policies around the globe in the last several years and, to some extent and somewhat ironically, also by the rapid pace of official reserve accumulation (to the extent that the increase in reserves has not been sterilized by open-market operation in domestic assets). Low short-term interest rates have induced investors to move out on the yield curve, thus leading to flatter curves, and to move out on the risk curve, thus compressing risk spreads. After several years of massive out-performance, the potential for an under-performance of risky assets in the period ahead is large. Reserve managers should keep this in mind when looking at the excess returns earned by some of their peers who have ventured into risky assets already in the last few years.

13.6 THREE SUGGESTIONS

This chapter concludes with three thoughts on investment instruments that central banks might want to consider, which are slightly away from the trodden path of diversification out of the dollar, along the yield curve, and into MBS, corporate bonds and equities.

Currency hedging

If central banks are concerned about currency risk because they have a large dollar exposure, but are reluctant to diversify out of dollar assets for various reasons, they may wish to consider hedging some of that risk via forwards or currency options. While some central banks already use derivatives to hedge currency risk (for example, the Netherlands central bank has hedged away all of its currency risks), many reserve managers are currently not authorized to do so. Assuming that appropriate risk management procedures are in place (or being put in place), these constraints should be relaxed. Naturally, activities in foreign exchange derivatives could have repercussions on spot foreign exchange markets and hence, central banks need to tread cautiously. But the same is true in the case of outright diversification out of the dollar. More generally, just as many private asset managers use a separate currency overlay management in their asset allocation, it would make sense for central banks to unlink their currency allocation from the bond allocation.

Gold

Recommending gold as an investment vehicle to central banks may sound like carrying owls to Athens. As a matter of fact, many central banks have over the past several years reduced their gold holdings and put the proceeds into higher-yielding assets. By the end of 2004, gold accounted for some 9 per cent of officially held reserves, down from around 50 per cent in the early 1980s. One important reason is that gold has not been a good hedge against inflation in the past 20 years or so as the real gold price has trended down. However, gold is a good neutralizer for currency variability, especially versus the pound sterling and the Japanese yen, but also against the dollar and the euro. With the big four Asian central banks (Japan, China, Korea and Taiwan) holding only a little more than 1 per cent of their assets in gold, raising their allocations to gold would seem to make sense.

Inflation-linked bonds

Apart from currency risk, the biggest long-term risk for central bank reserve portfolios is an unanticipated increase in inflation in the investment currency, which would erode the purchasing power of the nominal assets that central banks hold. Traditionally, gold was thought to be a good hedge against that risk, but that has not been true for the last 20 years or so. A more appealing instrument to hedge against inflation are inflation-linked bonds, which have become an important new asset class for many private investors in the last several years. In a way, government inflation-linked bonds are the ultimate 'risk-free' asset (unless, of course a government defaults) and should thus have natural appeal for central banks that take a very long view in their investment decisions. True, inflation linkers are less liquid than nominal bonds, but the size of the linker market is growing rapidly, especially in Europe. This recommendation is usually met with much scepticism by central bankers. While acknowledging that inflation-linked bonds are a good diversifier in portfolios, central banks believe that it would send a strange signal if they invested in such products as it could send a signal to markets that they do not trust their own peers to keep inflation in check.

13.7 CONCLUSIONS

Large-scale reserve diversification out of the US dollar is facing important hurdles, and diversification along the yield curve and along the risk curve, while reasonable in principle, is not very attractive at a time of flat curves and tight risk spreads. On aggregate, central banks' current asset allocation would thus seem to come close to the one often recommended to institutional clients under current market conditions: short duration, cautious on risky assets, cautious on the euro. Again, a broader diversification of official reserves makes sense in principle, but this is not the right time. Elsewhere, reserve managers may want to consider a more prominent role for the following three investment instruments: currency options to hedge away some of their currency risk; gold as a good diversifier in portfolios; and inflation-linked bonds as a hedge against what central banks generally consider to be their enemy number one: inflation.

14. Central Bank Risk Management: The Case of the Czech National Bank

Luděk Niedermayer

14.1 INTRODUCTION

There has been a remarkable convergence of the monetary policy goals and targets in the central banking community in the last decades. Even the instruments and the monetary policy know-how as well as the communication strategies of central banks are getting very similar. Transparency has become a generally accepted practice that is required by market participants.

Less of such convergence is seen in the area of foreign exchange reserve management. There is less exchange of information, there is not a very clear and well-established 'best practice' and transparency is not always very high[1].

We can expect that there will be more discussions on this subject in the future. Such discussions could address not just very technical questions related to asset allocation or risk appetite of a central bank, but they can also address some very general questions. First, how to measure 'success or failure' in the area of asset management? Second, how do losses or poor returns on reserve management affect the credibility and the reputation of a central bank? Third, are there special challenges for reserve management in emerging countries and is there a link with their monetary policy? And last but not least: even if we, as central bankers, want to be efficient, adopt best market practices, etc., there is the issue of feasibility. Can the central bank in practice compete with a 'state of the art' asset manager in the commercial sector and achieve similar results?

While there are no clear answers to these questions, there are still some implicit answers through the comparison of some aspects of reserve management in different countries.

14.2 A COMPARATIVE ANALYSIS OF RESERVE MANAGEMENT

Size of the reserves

There are a lot of articles and statistics dealing with the optimal size of reserves and with comparisons of different indicators. But the size of reserves is not always set by a decision of the central bank. This is not only true of the countries with different kinds of fixed exchange rate regimes and implicit intervention responsibilities. There are also many countries without a fixed exchange rate regime for which fluctuations in the size of reserves is not a matter of choice, but the outcome of monetary or even economic policy. In most of these cases central banks are not able to sell[2] 'undesired' reserves[3]. There could be two reasons. In some cases the inflow of foreign exchange is very big in comparison with the size of the foreign exchange market in local domestic currency. This would not only imply that the effort to sell foreign exchange would cause some appreciation of the currency, but it could also have as a result that the market would 'seize to function' when the size of foreign exchange offered for sale by the central bank or by market participants is high. In countries with a more developed market, central banks often prefer some increase of their reserves to an appreciation of the currency as they believe that appreciation would harm the economy much more than the possible cost of reserve accumulation in their balance sheet.

The case of emerging market countries with a successful macro policy is a very interesting one. These countries are often facing a fast decline of the risk premium. The implication is that domestic assets, even when yields are low and on the decline, can be very attractive for global investors. The currency can appreciate very fast and often central banks prefer interventions to a rapid rise of the currency. Any appreciation of the domestic currency willcause a loss for central banks with an open foreign exchange position[4]. And it is not likely that interventions would completely stop this economically justified process. However, the more reserves the central bank accumulates when intervening, the higher the eventual loss is when there is in the end some appreciation of the currency.

Benchmarks

Different central banks have different structures in their balance sheet and a different system of profit sharing with their stakeholders/governments. Even the reasons for the holding of reserves are different. So there is no 'natural common' benchmark for reserve management. In most cases there are no corresponding liabilities in the balance sheet, and even the holding period of the reserves remains an unknown. So it is not surprising that the central bank boards are in many cases the bodies that are deciding on the main parameters of the asset allocation[5]. Such a discretion should be counterbalanced by clarity and transparency of the decision making process, at least inside the central bank.

Taking into account the relative liberty in the setting of the benchmark parameters, and on the other hand the relative restrictiveness of the rules for active trading imposed by most central banks, it is clear that the majority of the profit from central bank reserve management is coming from the asset allocation itself (beta) rather than from active asset management (alpha).

Asset allocation

Any discussion of the subject of asset allocation starts with a paradox accompanying the decision to employ active management tactics in reserve management by central banks. While in the implementation of monetary policy central banks often assume that the market is efficient, in the case of reserve management the same decision-makers believe that there is an added value in the active management of reserves as markets are deemed to be not efficient. Some central banks were able to avoid this paradox and the Bundesbank, the German central bank, is a good case of consistency in its belief that markets are efficient.

For the majority of the central banks that are trying to find an appropriate asset allocation, we can observe the following development.

From short duration to long duration
The lengthening of duration is a natural move as nowadays in most cases the holding period of reserves is very long. Nevertheless, even in the case of unexpected sales of reserves, the central bank's balance sheet need not be hurt, as the sale would likely take place at the time of a depreciation of the currency. During such a period the central bank with an open foreign exchange position is experiencing high profits, so it can 'afford' some realized losses from the sale of long-term assets[6] (not mentioning the option that the central bank does not sell securities and would use the repo market).

From government bonds to 'lower' credits
The move down the credit ladder is a logical outcome of 'the search for yield'. There are credits (supra nationals, agencies) that are offering some yield pick-up while still meeting the high security concerns of the central banks.

From agencies and commercial credit risk to equities
While central banks often end up accepting non-bank corporate credit risks,

until recently there were just a few cases of central banks investing actively in equities. Recently we can see a reversal of the trend, and more and more central banks are considering this option. In some cases, there is an effort to avoid the holding of specific shares and central banks are looking at derivatives or synthetic products.

From external asset managers to hedge funds

Many central banks are using external managers for different reasons. As hedge funds are overcoming the period of their 'bad reputation' and have now become standard market players (sometimes not very different from money managers), it is no surprise that central banks can consider[7] the employment of hedge funds and eventually accept the increase of the leverage on their funds. In many central banks some of these processes are now under way. This could be a source of some concern. Firstly, a massive move of central bank assets from government bonds to agencies (for example) can change the pricing of these assets and change the risk/reward assumptions of the central banks. Secondly, as the central banks are rather conservative institutions that are not very fast in changing policies, there is the risk of some cyclicality of their moves.

14.3 A CASE STUDY OF THE CZECH REPUBLIC

Institutional setting of the central bank

The central bank (Czech National Bank – CNB) is set by the constitution and its rules of operation are set out in the Central Bank Act. As a member of the ESCB the CNB has a very clearly defined mandate which among other things excludes the financing of the government by the central bank. Financially, the Czech National Bank is independent. The profit of the central bank is primarily used by the bank for a transfer to its internal funds (including the offset of previous losses or the financing of reserves and provisions); the rest is transferred to the government. In contrast, the case of losses being borne by the central bank is not solved by the law and in practice it is up to the central bank to cover possible losses with future profits. Currently, the balance sheet of CNB shows an accumulated loss of €3,6 billion (end of 2005). In addition, in only one out of last five years did the bank not suffer a loss[8] (see Figure 14. 1).

Size of the reserves

The foreign exchange reserves of the Czech National Bank have been growing very fast.

Figure 14.1 Profits and losses of the Czech National Bank (end of 2005, CZK billions)

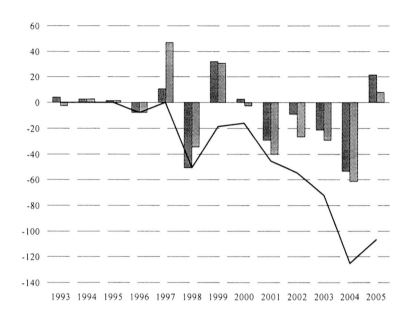

P/L in current year   FX P/L ——— P/L cumulated

There were several different causes of this reserve accumulation. Until 1997, CNB was operating various kinds of fixed exchange rate regimes (with a widening fluctuation band and decreasing intervention activity). During this regime, the growth of foreign exchange reserves was a reflection mainly of capital inflows[9]. Since that time, the Czech crown (CZK) has been a floating currency. CNB was occasionally buying reserves in an effort to slow down the appreciation of the Czech crown in three periods during 1998–2002. Afterwards, there were no direct interventions in the foreign exchange markets but CNB was buying large foreign exchange revenues of the government caused by the privatization of Czech public enterprises. These transactions are covered by an agreement between CNB and the Ministry of Finance. In addition to that, CNB has done some foreign exchange transactions on behalf of its clients and recently has been selling part of the interest earned on reserves.

Figure 14.2 Size of reserves of CNB

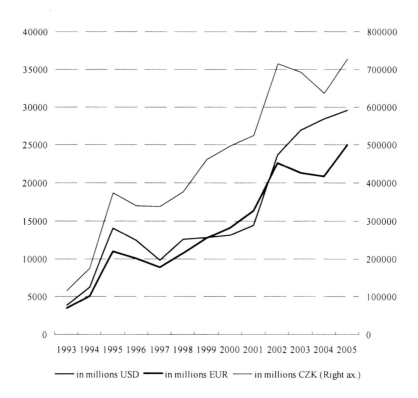

Balance sheet and sustainability

A simplified structure of the balance sheet of the Czech National Bank is presented in Figure 14.3.

Foreign exchange reserves are 90 per cent of the assets of the central bank, whereas at the other side of the balance sheet the most costly component, i.e. sterilisation repos, are just around 45 per cent, while the proportion of interest-free liabilities in the form of notes and coins is 32 per cent. It is clear that given the higher size of the interest-bearing assets compared to interest-bearing liabilities, the balance sheet generates profit in case of no appreciation of the currency and a similar level of domestic and international interest rates.

It should also be noted that an appreciating currency is not just a source of loss for the central bank's profit and loss account but at the same time does imply a lower level of domestic nominal interest rates.

Figure 14.3 Balance sheet of the CNB (end of 2005, CZK billions)

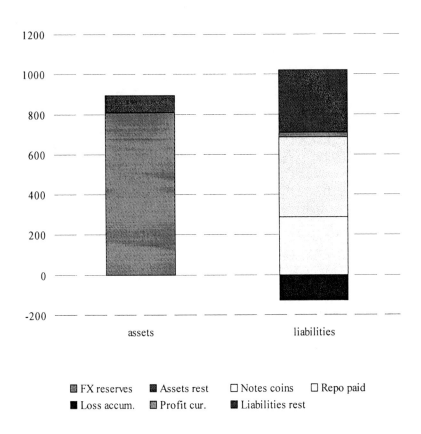

FX reserves   Assets rest   □ Notes coins   □ Repo paid
Loss accum.   Profit cur.   Liabilities rest

Overall, as the chart shows, the P/L of the CNB, net of foreign exchange P/L (in most cases losses), has been positive since 1999.

Because of this underlying profitability of the central bank[10] the sustainability and credibility of CNB has not, so far, been undermined by the losses it has incurred. So far the CNB has not seen any negative side-effect of these losses for the implementation of monetary policy.

Reserve management strategy

The accounting rules applicable for reserve management are based on marked to market reporting and there is a high transparency of disclosure. The investment process is 'top down', where the main rules of the asset allocation are set by the Bank Board. The actual structure of the benchmark is defined

Figure 14.4 Exchange rate and P/L of CNB

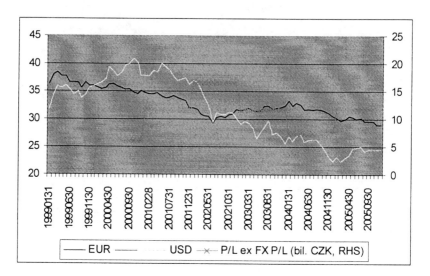

by the head of the Risk Management department.

The CNB believes in added benefits of active trading (positive alpha), and there is room for dealers to deviate from the benchmarks. The existence of relatively tight limits is a reflection of the asymmetric perception of profits and losses, which can be interpreted as giving relatively high weight to the preservation of reputation, and to some extent is a reflection of the limited resources for reserve management. In practice, dealers tend to use even a smaller part of their limits in trading. A likely explanation is the asymmetry of the gain/loss balance of each trader in an institution that does not pay bonuses for higher profits.

The main risks accepted by the CNB

Credit risk
The reserves have been diversified out of government bonds. The counterparty limits reflect the size of the reserves (small limits are not included). While in theory the goal is to minimize and manage the credit risk, in practice the bank is trying to avoid credit risk losses (default risk).

Liquidity
The CNB, like many central banks, has been overestimating the significance of liquidity risk. After the currency crises in 1997[11], it was clear that the 'investment portfolio' (of long but liquid government bonds) was more liquid

than the 'liquid portfolio' (of short-term bank deposits). Since that time, the requirements for the liquidity of investments have been included in the general benchmark setting and in the allowed deviations from the benchmark.

Active trading
Traders of the CNB are delivering almost systematic outperformance, even within their small limits (on average 20 basis points). In practice, it is not easy to decompose the additional return to active trading or to position taking and to imperfections in the benchmark. Nevertheless, the CNB values the market intelligence brought by the traders to the know-how of the central bank and considers this as part of the benefits from active trading.

14.4 CONCLUSION – CENTRAL BANKS IN SEARCH OF YIELD

Although convergence in the field of reserve management is not as fast as convergence in the area of monetary policy, there is a clear trend of `chase for yield` in many central banks.

In this search for yield the central banks are facing many obstacles, starting with the absence of clearly defined goals and objectives or a natural benchmark. There is also the specific problem of the motivation of the central bank reserve management staff, when the central bank board wants to preserve 'fair and transparent' salary rules across the organization.

A similar problem of motivation is relevant for the top management level of central banks. The central bank board is faced with the issue whether it should strive for an increase in the return (and the risk), when often all profits of the central bank are turned over to the government. Central bank boards are acutely aware of the fact that in case of bad outcomes of more risky strategies, a loss of credibility for the central bank and even possible reputation harm for the board members are likely. So a 'weak but stable return' is a very tempting reserve management choice. Nevertheless, over time we will likely see a further shift down the road towards more aggressive central bank reserve management and towards more transparency in this area.

NOTES

1. Not a big surprise in a policy area, where even the name of 'foreign currency reserves' is not very correct. These 'reserves' are not a reserve at all since they are assets in the central bank balance sheet; in most cases they are not held in the form of cash or currency deposits and in some cases they are not only foreign currency denominated but also held in the form of domestic assets.

2. It should be clear that where we are talking about the sale of reserves, we mean true sale or hedging, as the second method has the same impact on the market and on the currency.
3. There is some symmetry also for purchases, the only difference being that some central banks are in the position not just to buy, but also borrow reserves from the market.
4. In the case of unhedged reserves or if the size of foreign exchange liabilities is smaller than foreign exchange assets.
5. As a result, it is not surprising to find examples of central banks in the same region with very similar institutional settings and operating in similar economic conditions, that have a different asset allocation.
6. Obviously, profits can also be realized on long-term investments.
7. The only likely and logical restriction is that a central bank would try to avoid the situation where a hedge fund is using central bank money to challenge the monetary or exchange rate policy of its client. I should be also noted that under 'normal reserve management practice' the investing central bank is often taking positions (speculating) against decisions of another central bank.
8. In the mid 1990s, some of the losses were related to the bail-out of commercial banks, as well as, lately, to the high cost of sterilization. In recent years, the appreciation of the domestic currency is the main source of loss. The appreciation of the currency took place despite some massive interventions by the central bank that caused a large build-up of reserves. So the CNB does not believe that it is a realistic option to sell a substantial part of its reserves. Recently, there is an effort to sell at least the profits on reserve holdings, but so far, the amount of actual sales has not reached this goal.
9. The size of the reserves was volatile in 1997, as the CNB was intervening in the first half of the year to prevent currency wakening during currency crises and then bought back part of the reserves.
10. Another way to look at the balance sheet is to consider how big a depreciation must take place to offset the loss caused by the earlier appreciation of the Czech crown (end of 2005 data):

Current loss of the CNB	CZK 105 billion
Size of reserves	EUR 27.8 billion
Current FX rate of CZK	29.0 CZK / EUR
FX rate, offsetting the loss	32.8 CZK / EUR

11. CNB intervened with billions of US dollars in just a few days during that episode.

15. Returns from Alpha and Beta: An Equilibrium Approach to Investing

Robert Litterman

15.1 INTRODUCTION

One of the issues central banks face in reserve management is whether they should passively manage their portfolio once the asset allocation has been decided upon or whether they should strive to generate additional revenues by actively managing their portfolio. In the finance literature the passive management is referred to as beta, which is the return received on market risk, whereas alpha is realized by actively managing the portfolio and thus outperforming the markets. Central banks can learn from modern portfolio insights, especially in cases where the size of reserves has grown well beyond what is required on the basis of traditional indicators.

15.2 MODELING INVESTMENT DECISIONS

The equilibrium approach that Goldman Sachs takes toward asset management has relevance for central banks. It is based on the capital asset pricing model and in particular on the global version that Fisher Black developed and which he called universal hedging. The basic idea of the approach is to separate market risk from active risk. The beta, which is the return one gets from market risk, is the dominant return that investors globally can expect and it is largely determined by the risk embedded in global equities and the asset and maturity mix.

It is the business of an active manager, such as at Goldman Sachs Asset Management, to focus on creating alpha from active risk. However, with central banks managing over $4 trillion of reserves one has to be mindful that alpha is a zero sum game. Therefore, it would be hard to promise that all of these assets managed by central banks could generate alpha. Still, there is a phenomenon that could be called the active risk puzzle. Most institutional investors around the globe do take active risk, but they take only a very little amount of active risk. It is a puzzle not that they take so little, but if one has confidence in being successful then one should take more. If one recognizes that alpha is a zero sum game and that there are inefficiencies and transaction costs to carry, so that the average investor will under perform, then why not be passive? Perhaps there should be more bifurcation and certainly in large institutional portfolios a passive approach may be the best approach.

A number of issues are associated with generating alpha, which can be grouped under the heading of the five Cs – correlation, consistency, capacity, capital and cost. In generating alpha it is important to have as little constraints on the forms of investment as possible. From this point of view there is nothing wrong in central banks moving into hedge funds. They are not more risky than traditional forms of active management. Actually hedge funds are more of a pure form of active management, effectively trying to separate alpha from beta. Hedge funds apply a typical performance fee structure, but asking an investor to pay 20 per cent of the upside for beta risk is very expensive and inappropriate. A good hedge fund would be concentrating only on active risk, creating alpha and only then is the performance fee appropriate.

Modern portfolio theory and in particular the global version of the capital asset pricing model is a good framework for thinking about investments, both for central banks and for other institutions. Starting from the risk return paradigm where risk is on the horizontal axis and expected excess return on the vertical axis, we usually think of the highest expected return for a given level of risk as being the efficient frontier. We think of indifference curves if utility moves towards the northwest in this diagram, so one is looking for the portfolio on the efficient frontier that maximizes the expected utility (see Figure 15.1). The efficient frontier has a curved shape but, of course, if there is a risk free rate then one can move anywhere along the linear frontier that touches the portfolio with the highest ratio of expected return to risk. The optimal portfolio is now somewhere along the linear frontier rather than necessarily on the curved frontier.

A couple of issues come up in this context. First, we use a one-period model, but nowhere is the actual period specified. Supposedly, in theory we think of that period as being a very short period, but in practice we always

The optimal portfolio is a single point where the frontier is tangent to the curve. Any deviations from equilibrium will tend to be arbitraged away. These would be the source of alpha where investors will try to take advantage of anomalies in the market place which in turn will push prices toward equilibrium. So it is very useful to think what happens in equilibrium and how one can best benefit from that.

*Figure 15.1 The optimal portfolio is a point where the frontier
is tangent to a utility curve*

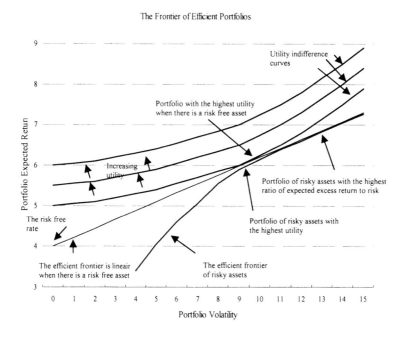

In equilibrium, the portfolio of risky assets with the highest expected return is the market portfolio. The set of returns will have to equilibrate to that point. All investors should hold the portfolio somewhere along the line that connects the risk-free rate with the market portfolio. Central banks historically have tended to locate very close to the risk-free rate, that is holding very low-risk liquid assets because they do prefer liquidity and low risk, although some central banks have divided their reserves into a liquidity component and a separate endowment component which really represents the wealth of the country. A number of other central banks are still holding tremendous amounts in reserves in US treasuries and this is a very risky asset from the point of view of long-term wealth creation.

15.3 GOVERNANCE ISSUES

A major governance issue is what really constitutes the purpose of these reserves and whether it is possible to define a benchmark that represents real wealth creation in the long run. Inflation linked bonds are probably the most appropriate benchmarks. If inflation linked bonds are used as the benchmark then one can think about risks relative to that and about the rewards for the risk that one is taking. In this context nominal bonds look very risky and have a very low expected return.

Thinking about the benchmark is a first step towards having appropriate policies.

In this context there are three basic sources of return (see Figure 15.2). There is the risk-free rate, which would be an inflation linked bond. Then there is the additional return, which is generated by the market exposure which would come in equilibrium from exposure to the global capital markets. And there would be alpha if the market is not in equilibrium and if one has the ability to perform above average.

The key to generating optimal portfolios is to define the benchmark appropriately. Typically a starting point is formed by the three basic sources of risk: the interest rate risk from liabilities, the market risk from exposure to the capital markets and the active risk. If a component of central bank reserves is being viewed as an endowment or a long term store of wealth, then it probably makes sense to think about those as long-dated real obligations and therefore, again, inflation linked bonds are probably the appropriate benchmark.

Figure 15.2 Three basic sources of return

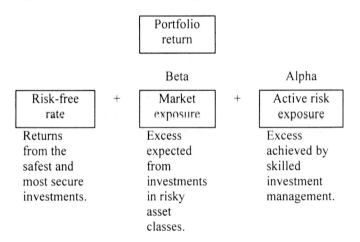

That kind of return is realistic in equilibrium? We have created one form of the market portfolio in terms of various different asset classes. What is shown here is the weight and the equilibrium excess returns along with volatility and Sharpe ratios (see Table 15.1). Basically, in equilibrium the expected excess return is proportional to an assets covariance with the market portfolio. Given our assumptions that the equity risk premium is around 3.5 per cent per year, the expected excess returns reflect the betas of various asset classes. For central banks it is appropriate to focus on the line labeled 'Fixed Income', which has virtually zero equilibrium expected excess return. In fact it is somewhat sensitive to the time horizon for which the covariance is measured, because basically fixed income instruments are uncorrelated, or may even be negatively correlated, in the last five to ten years with global equities.

The bottom line is that investors cannot expect to earn a positive return from holding treasuries. One is unlikely to keep up with inflation. Therefore, one is taking a fair amount of risk by holding treasuries. It is uncompensated risk and it is not a good idea for the store of wealth of a country. On the other hand, taking the total portfolio one gets 1.8 per cent excess return in a portfolio that is roughly equally split between equities and fixed income, a volatility of 8.4 per cent and a Sharpe ratio of 0.2 and 0.25 as a reasonable assumption about the return per unit of risk.

Table 15.1 Equilibrium: market-capitalization-weighted portfolio

Asset class	Gross excess			
	Weight (%)	Return (%)	Volatility (%)	Sharpe ratio
U.S. equity	28.20	3.30	16.20	0.21
U.K. equity	5.70	2.90	16.20	0.18
Europe equity, ex-U.K.	9.80	3.60	19.00	0.19
Asia Pacific equity	6.80	2.30	16.40	0.14
Canada equity	1.50	2.90	16.80	0.17
Emerging markets equity	2.70	3.80	23.60	0.16
Fixed iicome	42.30	0,050	3.20	0.01
High yield	2.80	1.00	7.70	0.12
Total portfolio	100.00	1.80	8.40	0.22
Equilibrium stock / Bond split		55% / 45%		

Moving along the efficient frontier more or less determines how much risk one is taking, but it does not affect the Sharpe ratio.

15.4 CONCLUSION

Given the sheer size of central bank reserves around the globe central banks cannot rely on active management of the portfolio, i.e. generating alpha, to drive returns. However, central banks can increase substantially return by creating a market portfolio with different asset classes, moving away from the more traditional portfolios of treasuries. Although US Treasuries are rightly viewed by central banks as 'safe and liquid' investments the nation's wealth could be put to better use and earn a higher return by diversifying in global capital markets.

16. The Conservative Approach to Central Bank Reserve Management

Hans-Helmut Kotz and Isabel Strauss-Kahn

16.1 FOREIGN RESERVE MANAGEMENT: A NEW BACKGROUND

Foreign exchange reserves have been accumulated on a substantial scale and even with an accelerating pace over the last half decade. In particular emerging market economies have felt obliged to buttress these cushions against external shocks. For those countries, the academic literature emphasizes two main motives: taking out an insurance against volatile international capital markets; more precisely, against sudden stops of capital inflows and the pursuant financial crises with all their devastating consequences. At the same time, the rapid rise in foreign assets is deemed to be related to some degree to containing the domestic currency's appreciation in order to safeguard export-oriented development strategies (Rodrik, 2006).

Industrial countries' reserve holdings, on the other hand, have shown a much more moderate evolution[1]. In their case, the old rules of thumb for the appropriate level of reserves, developed under the fixed-rate skies of Bretton Woods, still appear to apply empirically. Indeed, the dawn of Bretton Woods, that is, the early 1970s, was the last time that the optimal level of reserves was discussed in academic literature. In a nice survey article the German–French economist Emil-Maria Claassen (1975) posed the question, whether 'central banks (do) behave rationally with respect to their holdings of international reserves? (Or, whether they are characterized by) an insatiable appetite for foreign reserves, somewhat reminiscent of "Mrs. Machlup's Wardrobe Theory of Monetary Reserves"?' The appropriateness of reserves was judged against a number of scaling variables: level of imports, net international liabilities etc. Robert Triffin (1960), relying on his awe-inspiring experience, held that 'major countries would aim at maintaining a reserve level of not less than 40 per cent (of import) in most years. A 20 per cent level of gross reserves would be regarded as an absolute minimum'.

Hence, quite evidently, this was a debate about the ultimate purpose of holding reserves – why do we need them? – as well as what level is needed in order to achieve the purported objectives in a cost-effective manner. Thus, the argument was mainly about the opportunity costs of foreign exchange reserves. Consequently, the appropriate amount of reserves was derived from a cost–benefit analysis. Following Robert Heller (1966), benefits arose from the fact that faced with a deficit on the current account, the need for adjustment could be delayed, if temporarily only. (And here the old issue of the appropriateness of buying time – finance and/or adjust – arose.) Costs, on the other hand, were measured in terms of benefits foregone, that is, the possible and foregone return on alternative uses of funds locked into reserves that were. This debate re-emerged nevertheless in the Eurosystem with the advent of the euro. As an upshot, in most countries, as well as for the Eurosystem as a whole, the optimal level of foreign exchange reserves was intensely discussed – without coming to a conclusive answer.

As usual, optimality exists where marginal costs equal marginal benefits. Viewed from this (economists') angle, obviously there can be too many reserves. Acknowledging this, central bankers showed nonetheless a substantial risk aversion, i.e. they opted for a significant margin of safety – we do believe, with an eye on the multitude of crises having happened ever since, most probably for good reasons. But this question of politics – the appropriate level – is beyond the remit of this chapter. Thus, we take the amount of reserves as a given, determined on a political level. What we will deal with in these remarks, however, is an issue of policy or, put differently, technique, namely, given their primary purpose(s), the appropriate structure of reserves.

There's yet an additional limitation. Rather evidently, the management of foreign exchange reserves is secondary to monetary policy considerations, at least in the case of industrial countries (Hildebrand 2005). Hence, following a sequential logic, monetary policy purposes, defining the ultimate objectives of central bank policy, make for binding constraints. Consequently, f/x-reserves should be invested in assets with (very) low risk and (very) high liquidity. Following modern portfolio theory this implies, as an almost logical corollary, a commensurately modest level of returns. Nonetheless, given the opportunity costs implied, the drive towards a more active f/x-management in order to generate higher returns is undeniable. Moreover, conducting one's business in an 'investment banking way', which, inter alia, means investing in new instruments or asset classes, seems to be an inexorable part of this development towards professionalization.

In the following, however, we beg to disagree – conservatively, or, put differently, to argue from a cautious and, one might add, modest, perspective. In order to build our case for the cautious management of foreign exchange reserves, in the next section we will briefly reiterate the arguments for a basically passive approach. Then, since foreign exchange management is mainly about generating abnormal returns (in view of risks implied), we sketch the essential prerequisites to outperform consistently the average or representative investor. As a case in point, we put an emphasis on the fixed-income universe. Finally, in our concluding section, we ponder what purpose new instruments (or, in the current lingo: new asset classes) could serve and we draw some policy or technical conclusions.

16.2 PORTFOLIO ALLOCATION – A CONSERVATIVE CENTRAL BANK's VIEW

Rather generically, in weakly efficient markets opportunities to exploit mis-pricing should be very much in short supply, existing very transitorily only. In such a world, *cum grano salis*, generating consistently above average returns – whilst controlling, appropriately, for risk – appears to be very difficult to achieve indeed. Essentially, disciplined active management is about translating one's model's forecasts into the structure of one's portfolio; and then about predicting – or, in more operational terms, timing – the market's move correctly. Therefore, consistently producing returns above those the equilibrium model would deliver requires predictability of the trajectory of asset prices from which returns derive. This is, using standard results, over short periods of time, i.e. up to an annual or bi-annual basis, only at best very marginally the case. Waging bets on those results (for stock returns), however, would, after accounting for transaction costs, barely be profitable. In the long run, however, mean reversion implies predictability. Alas, again, after all costs are acknowledged, this is deemed not to be relevant in terms of an active investment policy since such predictions come with high risks attached.

Therefore, looking at the long haul of data makes one circumspect – or modest. As concerns equities, data on which have been scrutinized most thoroughly, stock indices in real terms have a mean and a variance that are time-dependent. In other words, they are non-stationary – integrated of order $1 : I(1)$ –, that is, they rise over time. Returns, on the other hand, appear to have, over long horizons, constant means and variances, that is: they are $I(0)$. In addition, looking at return data, one immediately detects periods of calmness or turbulence, that is, pools or clusters of volatility. And those periods appear to be self-reinforcing. Hence, volatility seems to be (conditionally) auto-regressive (see for a concise overview with regard to stocks Cuthbertson and Nitzsche (2004), pp. 73–114).

From this important observation, quite obviously, volatility forecasting takes its cue (in particular with the ARCH model in its numerous guises).

Moreover, histograms of real stock returns for most markets do sport fat tails: there is, relative to a standard normal (or bell) curve, more probability mass at the margins. In addition, again with reference to a norm, return distributions usually have more large negative returns, that is, they have a negative skew. As an upshot, in accounting for these characteristics of the data, one is entitled to be sceptical about our average capacities to forecast consistently correctly. This holds true, to repeat, most strongly for shorter time spans, below the annual or bi-annual frequency, i.e. those time horizons under which central banks render their accounts.

Equivalently, the same sceptical attitude arises out of research on the capacity for market timing. Indeed, there is precious little evidence to show in its favour. Graham and Harvey (1997), for example, have established that 'fewer than 25 per cent of investment letters achieve returns greater than a volatility-matched buy-and-hold equity/cash portfolio. In addition, the newsletters' ability to time the market is unimpressive'. All of this is, of course, not surprising in almost (nearly) efficient markets after all.

Scepticism, in our case, implies modesty. Building on the conclusions of modern portfolio theory, ample research – as well as practical knowledge – convincingly tells us that on average, the median of portfolio managers is not better than the market, in fact, average managers regularly under-perform markets[2]. Being extraordinary, as a rule, is simply impossible! Essentially, this is the logical consequence of the zero-sum character of this game of active managers betting against active managers.

This structural underperformance has been shown, for example, for institutional investors in the pension fund industry by Lakonishok et al, 1992[3]. Those funds, 'actively pick(ing) stocks, an activity not predicted by standard finance models yet enthusiastically pursued by virtually all financial market participants' (Lakonishok et al 1992, p. 341) fell significantly short of the S&P 500 Index. In another careful analysis, dealing with mutual funds, Burton Malkiel (1995) held that his 'study of mutual funds does not provide any reason to abandon a belief that securities markets are remarkably efficient' (p. 571). Bearing witness to this evaluation is the fact that 'in the aggregate, funds have underperformed benchmark portfolios both after management expenses and even gross of expenses' (p. 549). Finally, Greenwald et al (2001, p. 7) write that 'approximately 70 percent of active professional investors have done worse than they would have by adhering to a passive and low-cost strategy of simply buying a share of the market as a whole...'

To be brief: the quite unanimous result of substantial research into the issue is that active management, as a rule and on average, subtracted value! Incidentally, one does not have to buy concurrently into the belief of the permanent efficiency of markets to come out in favour of passive management. Even if and when existing, inefficiencies or mis-pricing might simply not bear the costs and risks of exploiting them – this is the limits-of-arbitrage point as developed convincingly by Shleifer and Vishny (1997).

16.3 BOND PORTFOLIO MANAGEMENT – A CASE IN POINT

Because (conventional, i.e. without new asset classes) foreign exchange management is mainly about fixed-income portfolios it appears to be appropriate to illustrate our point within a fixed-income environment. This is of some relevance since one constantly reads claims to the fact that active bond-portfolio management can time and again generate value on a relative basis. In order to check for such a capacity, performance attribution is a useful device. It highlights the channels through which this contribution could come. Active fixed-income management implies bets on the evolution of (see for the following Leibowitz 1986):

- interest rates (levels) – thus is about evaluating the stochastic behaviour of interest rates, more precisely about taking directional positions;
- yield curves (shape) – hence suggests to capture mis-pricing in implied forward rates;
- spreads – therefore claims to profit from mis-pricing opportunities;
- credit risk – is about betting on reversion to model-consistent default premiums.

Given benchmark and duration constraints, additional returns therefore would, in a more operational vein, result from the active management of (de la Grandville, 2001):

- duration – that is: taking (or controlling through immunization) market risk;
- convexity – again for return enhancement or risk containment purposes;
- illiquidity – meaning investments in assets with a premium due to their reduced fungibility;
- plus a residual – which captures the effect of a change in the shape of yield curves.

All of this could – on an individual investor's level – pan out if theory would provide us with a blueprint for disciplined activism, allowing investors to profit from duration as well as convexity positioning. But, unfortunately, theory does not give us this especially attractive Rosetta's stone. Alas, even if academia were so cooperative, such knowledge would only be precious if not common. If it were public, however, then it would, quite naturally, be of no avail and opportunities would be competed away quickly.

Unfortunately but not surprisingly, with regard to active management's capacity to outfox the market, sobering results have been produced for the case of bond funds as well. Here, again, the average mutual fund has been unable to consistently generate positive abnormal returns (Blake et al, 1993). Moreover, as Blake et al found out '(f)or most of the models and fund subgroups, this underperformance was approximately equal to the average management fees, indicating that, pre-expenses, the surviving funds performed about on par with the indexes' (p. 402). As a matter of fact, more than two-thirds of mutual bond funds had negative abnormal returns. From these analyses we take the view that, in principle, it amounts to a very substantial challenge to not opt for a passive strategy.

But then, to confuse our case, there are investors who seemingly possess those superior skills. If appearances were not deceiving, this would fly in the face of an argument which Bob Litterman makes in Chapter 15: alpha is in short supply. (We would add: acknowledging commissions and fees, it is most probably in negative supply.) But this point is statistically straightforward to prove. Asset returns are noisy. Therefore, with alpha being rather small while its standard error is rather high, we would need many data points to establish with conventional confidence such superiority. That is, to tell the difference between skill, on which one could bank, and luck, on which one would not like to bet, is very difficult indeed. In the meantime, before accepting purportedly proven superior capacities, one would check the sample size as well as being aware of a possible survivorship bias. Some investors – but not the representative – are always making money out of pure luck.

Then, particularly relevant for those venturing into stocks or corporate credit, and reiterating an aspect already alluded to, the data-generating process is non-normal. Since the end of World War II investors witnessed 17 days when the Dow fell by more than 4.4 per cent, i.e. more than five standard deviations (see Figure 16.1). These events happened 4,000 times more often than they should according to normally distributed price assumptions.

The same holds true for the return of basically all other assets in which one might consider investing: assuming normally distributed returns, we should see one daily downturn beyond five sigma in a financial market every 14,000 years. Thus, there should have been no – or precise: only 0.002 – such outliers over the past 34 years. Instead, we have seen 12 of those in the DAX since 1971, 10 in the yen/US dollar-market and so on (see Table 16.1).

This implies the need to safeguard against low-frequency/high-severity events. In particular central banks are loath to accept such eventualities.

Figure 16.1 Daily Dow Jones Industrial changes

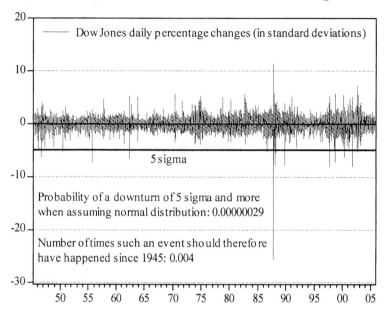

Daily Dow Jones Industrial Changes

This comes from the fact that in their objective function the actual level of their resources plays a dominating role. Ultimately, they attempt to prevent the level of reserves falling below a certain margin of safety.

In other words, central banks' objective functions are not defined over returns but an appropriate level of assets in a multi-period context. Therefore, the danger central banks want to avert is a shortfall risk, i.e. a portfolio value that is below the value a central bank would like to hold at a minimum as a cushion to accommodate possible shocks. Here it is important to reckon that while the variance of returns decreases over time, this does not hold true for the level of wealth. Therefore, it is not implausible that over a certain interval, faced with a negative run, the level of reserves of an actively managed fund is vulnerable to a possibly substantial shortfall problem.

16.4 POLICY CONCLUSIONS

For foreign exchange reserves management, moreover, an additional challenge arises: Given the functionally unavoidable currency exposure, we

Table 16.1 Return distribution of various financial assets

	Skewness	Kurtosis	5 sigma downturns
S&P 500	– 0.9792	25.3656	9
Dow Jones	– 1.2089	32.8748	8
Dax	– 0.2608	6.7234	12
GBP/USD	– 0.0505	4.5006	6
JPY/USD	– 0.6987	11.4374	10
DM/USD	0.0322	4.4315	3
NLG/USD	0.0574	4.9351	7

Note: Daily percentage changes for the period between January 1971 and May 2005. As a reminder: the normal function has a Skew of 0 and a Kurtosis of 3.

would like to minimize other dimensions of risk as far as possible. That is, we start from very conservative preferences/a very significant risk-aversion (a position close to the origin in a static return-risk optimization plane). However, this entails in no way a reluctance to deploy current, state-of-the art instruments. In fact, in order to control risk cost-effectively, the use of modern analytical techniques and procedures is a *conditio sine qua non*. Otherwise, the immunization of the portfolio against adverse shocks would be difficult to achieve. And here, derivatives or structured products, seen in a portfolio-context, are especially helpful.

This bears on the debate about new asset classes or instruments for reserve management. Most of those instruments are, of course, well-known and very much seasoned. Hence, they are new only relative to the traditional asset allocation of central banks. Nonetheless, there are indeed innovations which serve traditional purposes of f/x-reserve management more cost-effectively. Those instruments concern in particular the hedging of portfolios. Whilst looking at f/x-reserve management's mission from a purely functional perspective – how do we achieve our purposes most efficiently? – there is no reason why conservative, that is, value-protecting central banks should not apply those instruments. In fact, cautious management even requires using these devices in a disciplined fashion.

Coming back to our main point, we favour a conservative approach because theory and empirics are unfortunately sobering with regard to activism. In fact, the debate would be grossly misrepresented if framed in terms of modern versus. traditional approaches. Consistently beating the market – what average opinion perceives average opinion to be – is beyond most of us mortals. Thus, prudence implies a cautious - or, in the academic lingo a (mainly) passive management. Moreover, the characteristics of data – not being generated from a time-invariant distribution, hence being non-stationary – suggest being cautious as well.

From here the general orientation of conservative central banks (like the Banque de France or the Bundesbank) immediately follows:

- on a practical or institutional level foreign exchange reserves should provide for further calls of the ECB – hence, implicitly, underwrite the ECB's potential intervention power;
- in light with the conceptual approach, foreign exchange management chooses a risk–return profile consistent with the hierarchy of objectives of a central bank;
- and a historical and more marginal aspect: foreign exchange reserves should underwrite international liquidity (particularly for payment obligations of the government).

All of this translates straightforwardly into a structured or principled (conservative) investment process.

- safety is first – this dovetails with a low tolerance for credit risk as well as a high aversion to reputation risk[4],
- in this line of reasoning, liquidity reigns supreme; the tranching approach chosen by some central banks does make a difference between a liquid segment of the overall portfolio (foreign exchange reserves, in fact) and an investment portfolio that does not have the characteristics of foreign exchange reserves pure and proper;
- and, finally, as a logical upshot, return is a third-level priority, which, it is true, has gained in importance.

To wrap up: while the juxtaposition of active versus passive management and new versus standard instruments seems to rapidly translate into state-of-the art versus old-fashioned approach, this would be simply misleading. In fact, activism should, on average, be less conducive to a central bank's primary functions or obligations than a passive but nonetheless (or, more precisely therefore) analytically disciplined approach. Cautious management acknowledges the limits to our collective capacity to foretell market developments. At the same time, it rests on sophisticated new techniques to control and contain risk in an ever-evolving financial environment.

NOTES

1. In fact, after the introduction of the euro, numerous central banks within the ESCB, the European System of Central Banks, have reduced their level of reserve holdings, thereby taking account of the bigger inside currency area after the implementation of the euro. This holds true, for the Banque de France as it does for the Bundesbank, which has cut down its foreign exchange reserves by about 20 per cent.

2. Keynes used to portray this zero-sum set-up with an instructive quip: 'Why are New York bankers so successful?' Answer: 'Because they compete with New York bankers.'

3. We have replicated their approach, applying it on an extended period, that is, including data covering the period between 1995 and 2003. And we can basically confirm their results. Results are available on request.

4. Central Banks, as a rule, do not maintain the internal capacities of analysing credit risk products. This would require the deployment of substantial resources (technical expertise, infrastructure). But outsourcing credit-risk analysis is not a panacea.

PART THREE

Implications for Central Bank Balance Sheets

17. Central Bank Balance Sheets: Comparisons, Trends and some Thoughts

Francesco Papadia and Flemming Würtz[1]

17.1 INTRODUCTION

The balance sheet of a central bank is important for many reasons, not least because it provides important information on the central bank's institutional framework and its operating procedures. However, the most obvious reason why the central bank balance sheet is important is its size, which shows that the central bank has large amounts of financial resources at its disposal. Most prominent on the liabilities side of the balance sheet is the issuance of banknotes. However, one should also consider 'equity' (the sum of capital, revaluations and provisions) and reserve holdings of the banking system, in the form of current accounts. In the case of the Eurosystem, these three core financial resources totalled around €900 billion in 2005, which approximately corresponds to 12 per cent of annual euro area GDP, 4 per cent of the aggregated liabilities of monetary financial institutions and 17 per cent of total government debt. Moreover, it is interesting to note that the single largest 'funding source' of the Eurosystem, namely banknotes, has grown, on average over the last three years, by as much as 16 per cent per annum, which corresponds to nearly 1 per cent of euro area GDP year after year.

The mere size of the central bank balance sheet immediately raises the possibility that its composition, and the ensuing possible mismatches between assets and liabilities, could have a non-negligible effect on the overall allocation of resources in the economy. Against this background, it is somewhat surprising that public opinion and economists pay more attention to the way in which central banks employ human resources, in particular to check whether they are efficiently used, than to the way they use financial resources.

The fact that the issue of central bank balance sheets is under-researched means that the economic profession is very far from having identified in a precise way what a central bank balance sheet should look like. This means, in turn, that it would be premature to aim at defining the characteristics of an 'optimal' central bank balance sheet. More modestly, in this chapter an attempt is made to identify the main characteristics of an 'appropriate' balance sheet, thus moving in the domain of what is satisfactory, rather than in the domain of what is optimal. Still, an appropriate balance sheet should ideally result from some well defined objectives. A first and natural attempt in this regard is to focus on the objective of price stability, which, in the case of the Eurosystem, has a lexical priority that is stipulated by law. It is however very interesting to note that central banks – at least those, such as the Eurosystem, which do not pursue a foreign exchange target – can equally well pursue this task with very different balance sheets, both in terms of size and composition. Hence, even though the objective of price stability and the related needs for credibility and clarity constrain the central bank balance sheet, they still leave significant degrees of freedom, hence the need to take into account other criteria to determine an appropriate balance sheet.

The observation that a monetary policy implementation targeted at achieving price stability imposes only few constraints on the balance sheet follows from the fact that monetary policy implementation is nowadays synonymous with steering a short-term money market interest rate – normally the overnight rate – and this depends solely on the way in which the central bank calibrates its total assets and liabilities at the margin (see e.g. Woodford, 2001)[2]. Even if this conceptual scheme may become more complex once all practical details are taken into account, still it illustrates clearly that there is not a one-to-one correspondence between the size and composition of the balance sheet and the steering of short term rates. A corollary of this is that the amount of financial resources flowing to the central bank, because of the exogenous demand for banknotes as well as current accounts held by banks, is not necessarily justified by the need to implement monetary policy, nor is the composition of the assets side determined one-to-one by monetary policy considerations. Indeed, a central bank enjoys a significant degree of freedom when deciding on its assets side. There are limits, however, to this freedom: in practice, not only monetary policy considerations but also historical developments bind central banks when setting up their balance sheets.

Once one takes into account both the importance of the topic of the central bank's balance sheet and that the needs deriving from monetary policy implementation only partially determine its size and, particularly, its structure, the amount of economic research dedicated to the topic looks surprisingly small. This is probably for two reasons. First, it is only rather recently that most central banks have committed so strongly to the overnight rate as an operational target (see e.g. Bindseil, 2004) and hence have realized the degree of freedom that they enjoy – from a monetary policy implementation perspective – in designing their balance sheets. Second, once the implementation of monetary policy appeared insufficient as an overarching and comprehensive principle to design an appropriate balance sheet, economists have not been able to substitute it with another encompassing criterion.

The purpose of this chapter is to contribute to closing the gap between the importance of the subject of central bank balance sheets and what economic analysis can say about them. To do this, the chapter first reviews, in Section 17.2, the (limited) literature relating to central bank balance sheets. In Section 17.3, it presents a simplified balance sheet classification to support the subsequent analysis. Using this classification, Section 17.4 compares the balance sheets of the G3 central banks, i.e. of the US Federal Reserve, the Eurosystem (and, before Economic and Monetary Union, the Deutsche Bundesbank) and the Bank of Japan. In particular, the differences between the first two central banks provide proof that central banks have significant degrees of freedom in setting up their balance sheets, even if they pursue the same overriding objective of price stability through the steering of short-term rates. Section 17.4 also sheds some light on the variety of approaches and concepts that can be used to understand the observed differences across the G3 central banks. As a way of exemplifying how the analysis leading to an appropriate balance sheet would look. Section 17.5 attempts to identify which conceptual constraints the overriding objective of price stability actually imposes on the balance sheet. Moreover, it puts forward some first ideas about the criteria that could complement these constraints in identifying an appropriate balance sheet. The ideas presented in this section are, however, very tentative and purely qualitative. Indeed, it would be premature, at this stage, to try and move to a quantitative treatment that would necessarily have to be more precise. Finally, Section 17.6 concludes.

17.2 LITERATURE RELATED TO CENTRAL BANK BALANCE SHEETS

The statement in the introduction that the issue of central bank balance sheets is under-researched may appear, at first sight, surprising. In fact, there is very abundant economic research on specific items of the balance sheet. A first example is the extensive literature on the optimal volume, or optimal rate of growth, of base money or its various components. This literature was written under the assumption that either base money or commercial bank reserves are the operational target of the central bank (see e.g. Lindsley et al, 1984) and has lost much of its relevance since this assumption, as mentioned in the introduction, has been abandoned in favour of an interest rate-based implementation of monetary policy. Of course, this literature may still have some relevance for the (so far) exceptional case in which short term interest rates reach the zero lower bound, as it has been the case in Japan between 2001 and the spring of 2006. In this case, there is a closer relationship between monetary policy implementation and the balance sheet, which may linger on some time after short-term rates will have returned to positive levels. This case, however interesting, is not further considered in this chapter, which will limit its analysis to the 'normal' times when short-term interest rates are above zero.

A second item of central bank balance sheets which has been the subject of much analysis is the level of foreign exchange reserves, in particular as regards emerging markets. This literature, however, has struggled to come to definitive conclusions, even though it has presented some interesting results and some useful rules of thumb (see e.g. Ben-Bassat and Gottlieb, 1992).

The common characteristic of the analyses dealing with base money and international reserves is that they look at one particular item in the balance sheet without considering the balance sheet as a whole or the fact that balance sheets must balance, i.e. that a change in one item must be reflected in a change in another item.

This limitation is partially obviated in the, not numerous, analyses that have been carried out of another balance sheet item: the 'equity' of central banks. Although these analyses still concentrate on a specific item, they comes closer to the focus of this paper because 'equity' is in many ways a balance sheet item that is intrinsically intertwined with all the others. In particular, several papers, including Bindseil et al (2004) and Ize (2005), have assessed the level of equity needed by the central bank, taking also into account the relationship with other items in the balance sheet. Bindseil et al (2004) argue that central banks, in principle, do not need equity in order to carry out their tasks, because they can settle their liabilities by issuing legal tender and hence never need to care about their solvency. On the other hand, the authors recognize that this conclusion relies on an extreme, and unrealistic, version of the concept of central bank independence and that it is inconsistent with the empirical relationship observed between the financial strength of some central banks and their inflation performance (Stella, 1997). In fact, they argue that central banks have incentives to care about their financial position if their independence falls short of the theoretical extreme which they assume as limiting case. In this more realistic setting, central banks' equity holdings reinforce the credibility of their inflation control, reducing the likelihood that they will reach a point of financial distress at which they would need to deviate from their target in order to boost monetary income. The higher the central bank's financial risks (on and off the balance sheet), the larger, logically, the amount of equity needed to ensure credibility.

Without much argumentation, Ize (2005) makes the rather extreme assumption that the critical point of financial distress, which the central bank should avoid, is when its 'net worth' reaches zero. Note, however, that the concept of net worth does not correspond to the concept of on-balance-sheet equity used in this chapter. While the latter only reflects the difference between the market value of assets and that of non-equity liabilities in the balance sheet, 'net worth' is defined as the market value of the total 'central bank business'. In addition to on-balance-sheet equity, this also comprises the market value of all off-balance-sheet items, including the permanent right to issue legal tender, which increases net worth, and the obligation to ensure price stability in all circumstances, which has the opposite effect of normally reducing net worth[3].

Obviously, it is very difficult to calculate the net worth of a central bank in practice. For instance, following the logic of Bindseil et al (2004), this calculation would need to take into account not only the risks associated with the assets and liabilities recorded in the balance sheet but also the risks resulting from the fact that central banks are in practice never totally independent. Still, the concept of net worth can explain how some central banks can temporarily sustain negative equity in their balance sheet: a positive net worth, deriving from the fact that their 'core income' is sufficiently large to reverse the position some time in the future, supports their financial strength.

As a clearer exception to the item-by-item approach, Bindseil and Würtz (2005) briefly discuss whether the assets side of the balance sheet of a central bank should consist of short-term refinancing operations or outright holdings. They argue that the former have the advantage of market neutrality because the repurchase contracts underlying open market operations, as documented in Bindseil and Papadia (2006), have a minimal, if any, effect on the price of the assets given as collateral to the central bank. However, the central bank may decide to 'sacrifice' the neutrality of temporary operations and hold outright assets to achieve what it perceives to be the optimal duration, or interest rate risk, of its assets side. From an investment perspective, this depends on the risk preferences of the central bank. If the central bank has the same risk preferences as the aggregate of market participants, the duration of its assets should be the same as that of the fixed income market portfolio, which is around five years in the case of the United States and the European Union. However, the issue of central banks' risk preferences is not discussed in this paper; neither is the equally crucial and broader issue of the macroeconomic effects of the composition of the assets side of the central bank balance sheet.

Broaddus and Goodfriend (2001) discuss extensively the composition of the assets side of the central bank balance sheet, albeit from a completely different perspective, which centres on the issue of central bank independence. Focusing on the case of the US Federal Reserve, they put forward two principles that should guide the central bank's choice of assets. First, the asset acquisition should respect the integrity of the fiscal policy-making process by minimizing the central bank's involvement in credit allocation. Second, assets should be chosen to enhance the central bank's independence. They argue that the best way of complying with these two principles is to hold only Treasury bonds. Thereby, all financial resources are effectively channelled to the Treasury and the central bank does not have to take any fiscal decisions, defined as the allocation of credit in the private market. At the same time, this approach prevents outside pressure – stemming either from the Treasury or from private entities – on the central bank to make certain credit allocations, which would always be disputable. Following this logic, the transfer of the central bank's financial resources to the Treasury is not seen as a fiscal decision, which may appear somewhat counter-intuitive.

Gros and Schobert (1999), in a study that probably marks the clearest exception to the 'item-by-item' approach, concur with the viewpoint of Broaddus and Goodfriend, although they are somewhat less specific on the need to hold government paper only on the assets side. Focusing on the situation of the Eurosystem at the beginning of monetary union, they argue that a central bank should not act as an 'investment manager' and propose the so-called 'lean balance sheet' as a guiding concept. According to this concept, which we put into a broader context in Section 5, the central bank balance sheet should not, for instance, hold more foreign exchange reserves and equity than is needed for policy purposes. Moreover, the size of the 'lean balance sheet' should be determined by the size of the liabilities side, which in turn should almost exclusively consist in the monetary base.

As we shall see in the next section, this viewpoint corresponds closely to the actual composition of the Federal Reserve's balance sheet, while the Eurosystem has chosen a different approach.

Another strand of literature, which also comes close to the topic discussed in this chapter, is the one arguing that the central bank's asset composition is likely to affect the overall pricing of financial assets and consequently to have some broader macro-economic effect. For instance, while emphasizing that the new operational framework of the Bank of England indeed aims to control short-term money market rates, Tucker (2004) hints at the existence of such an effect, which could operate via risk premiums and the quantity of money. Furthermore, the current Chairman of the Federal Reserve, Ben Bernanke, pointed out an influence of asset composition on risk premia as a possible tool for providing monetary stimulus. Indeed, Bernanke (2002) has explicitly suggested that the Federal Reserve could, if interest rates were to hit the zero lower bound, provide monetary stimulus by reducing risk premiums on long-term interest rates via outright purchases of long-term debt. To ascertain the empirical foundations of this statement, Andres et al. (2004) found empirical evidence, using US data, that the central bank can indeed affect risk premiums by changing the stocks of financial assets it holds. This aspect should be kept in mind by a central bank designing or making large reforms to its balance sheet. In addition, it should be noted that this effect implies that short-term temporary operations are not completely market neutral because their size affects the maturity structure of the financial assets held by the general public and thereby potentially risk premiums.

17.3 A STYLIZED CENTRAL BANK BALANCE SHEET

For convenience, we present a central bank balance sheet in a greatly simplified, though still illustrative, form (see Table 17.1).

Table 17.1 A stylized central bank balance sheet

Assets	Liabilities
Outright holdings	Exogenous factors
- *Foreign exchange portfolio incl gold*	- *Banknotes*
- *Domestic assets portfolio*	- *Government deposits*
- *Net residual*	- *Equity*
Temporary operations	Current accounts

The various items in the stylized balance sheet and some of their main properties are discussed below.

Consider first the liabilities side, which comprises the sources of finance for the assets held by the central bank. Two main items are distinguished. Under the first main item, four exogenous or autonomous factors are listed, so called because the central bank can, if at all, influence them only to a limited extent and/or with significant time-lags. First, there are banknotes, which are purely demand driven and are the most obvious, and normally by far the largest, liability item; second, government deposits, which denote the working balances of the governments held with the central bank. The arrangement for government deposits, which differ substantially across central banks, is normally an integral part of a central bank's institutional setting; and, third, equity (comprising capital, provisions and revaluations), which is determined by the cumulated level of profits of the central bank and by its 'dividend' policy (as mentioned in the previous section, equity corresponds, in a full marking-to-market approach, to the difference between the value of the assets and the value of the liabilities).

The other main item on the liabilities side is the current account holdings of the banking system. The level of these holdings is normally dominated by reserve requirements, the role of which mostly consists in absorbing temporary liquidity shocks through their so-called averaging provision.

Now consider the assets side. Also on this side of the balance sheet, we distinguish between two main items. The first main item is denominated outright holdings, which may consist of either foreign exchange (including gold) or domestic currency-denominated portfolios. For the sake of simplicity, we also treat the net residual as part of the outright holdings. This residual contains the net sum of all the other miscellaneous items that are not explicitly contained in the simplified format. These items, which may appear on both the assets and the liabilities side, but which are here netted on the asset side, can for instance stem from payment system-related activities. Within the outright holdings, one can somewhat arbitrarily distinguish two types of portfolios, depending on the extent to which they are coordinated with temporary operations on the basis of monetary policy considerations. If the outright portfolio is not subject to a strict coordination, which one could also call 'monetary policy influence', it can be labelled as an investment portfolio'. Conversely, a so-called 'monetary policy portfolio' is indeed subject to such strict coordination, comprising, as a minimum, those assets that are held explicitly for policy purposes, such as foreign exchange interventions.

The second main item on the assets side is denominated temporary operations. This is defined as net collateralized refinancing (reverse) operations, which, for practical reasons, normally have a short maturity and are used to steer liquidity at the margin, so that the resulting overnight rate is in line with the target level. This item also includes the net use of the marginal lending facility, which in the case of the Eurosystem, as well as in the other two G3 central banks, play a role in the formation of short-term interest rates. Note that temporary operations (including standing facilities) may also appear on the liability side, but are here for simplicity netted on the assets side.

17.4 THE G3 CENTRAL BANK BALANCE SHEETS

Figure 17.1 provides a graphical overview of the G3 central bank balance sheets, using the data shown in Table 17.2. For each central bank, the chart shows the share of the main items of the simplified balance sheet in total assets and liabilities. Hence, it gives information on the relative composition of the balance sheet. To also give an indication of the size of the balance sheet, the ratio of total assets to banknotes is reported (in the circles), which indicates by how much the size of the balance sheet exceeds its absolute minimum. Moreover, since banknotes are also related to economic activity in the respective countries, this ratio can also be seen as a rough proxy for the size of the central bank relative to the total economy. In this regard, it is however an important consideration for both the Federal Reserve and the Eurosystem that a large stock of banknotes is circulating outside their domestic economies.

Figure 17.1 Graphical overview of the G3 central bank balance sheets

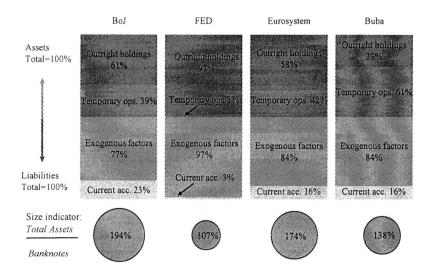

Specific features of the US Federal Reserve's balance sheet

The balance sheet of the Federal Reserve immediately stands out as a 'corner solution' for central bank balance sheets. First, the size of the balance sheet is

Implications for Central Bank Balance Sheets

Table 17.2 Balance sheet data for the G3 central banks

	Absolute numbers				Share out of total assets and liabilites			
	BoJ JP¥ trillion	FED US$ billion	Eurosystem € billion	Buba DM billion	BoJ percent	FED percent	Eurosystem percent	Buba percent
Assets								
Outright holdings	88	752	524	136	61	97	58	39
- *Foreign exchange portfolio, incl. gold*	5	31	297	116	3	4	33	33
- *Domestic assets portfolio*	85	727	219	0	59	93	24	0
- *Net residual*	-2	-6	8	20	-1	-1	1	6
Temporary operations	56	26	377	216	39	3	42	61
Total assets	144	778	901	352	100	100	100	100
Liabilities								
Exogenous factors	111	758	754	294	77	97	84	84
- *Banknotes*	74	727	519	255	52	93	58	73
- *Government deposits*	32	5	58	0	22	1	6	0
- *Equity*	5	26	177	22	4	3	20	6
Current accounts	33	20	147	58	23	3	16	16
Total liabilities	144	778	901	352	100	100	100	100

at a minimum, with banknotes accounting for 93 per cent of liabilities (i.e. almost all the exogenous factors stem from banknotes). This also reflects that, as shown in Table 17.2, the Federal Reserve only has a small amount of equity and that it only imposes a small reserve requirement on banks. The latter observation is related to the fact that (most) reserve balances are unremunerated, because the Federal Reserve is, by law, prohibited from paying any direct remuneration on deposits. Second, turning to the assets side, almost all liquidity is injected through outright holdings, the size of which mirrors, almost one to one, the size of banknotes (see Figure 17.2). Therefore, in the case of the Federal Reserve, the balancing item (which over the medium term adjusts endogenously to all other items) is clearly the outright portfolio. The volume of temporary operations is kept to the minimum sufficient to steer liquidity at the margin. Third, and closely related to the latter point, the outright portfolio is clearly a monetary policy portfolio: a close coordination between the management of the outright portfolio and the temporary operations must take place so as to ensure that there will normally be a small net need for liquidity to be satisfied by the latter operations (see also FRBNY, 2004). Moreover, the Federal Reserve is very transparent about the composition of its domestic outright portfolio (see for instance, FRBNY 2003), which consists in government papers and makes up the bulk (93 per cent) of the outright holdings. Detailed information on this so-called SOMA (System Open Market Account) portfolio is published regularly on the internet and sales and purchases are organized via auction procedures. Finally, only the remaining 7 per cent of the outright portfolio is made up of foreign exchange reserves[4].

The balance sheets of the three other central banks appear to have a rather similar structure among themselves, with current accounts making up around 20 per cent of the liabilities, and outright holdings making up around 50 per cent of the assets. However, the size of the balance sheet, as well as the extent to which the outright holdings consist of monetary policy or investment portfolios, show some important differences among the three other central banks considered.

Figure 17.2 Selected items of the US Federal Reserve's balance sheet

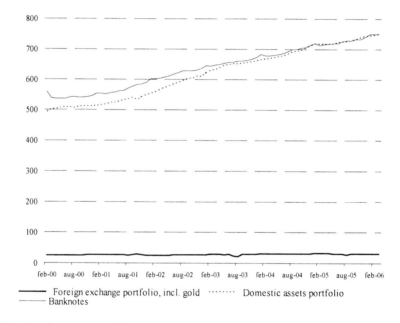

Note: the chart shows monthly averages

Specific features of the Bank of Japan's balance sheet

First, it can be seen from Figure 17.1 that the Bank of Japan, according to the size indicator, has the largest balance sheet relative to the outstanding amount of banknotes, in spite of the fact that the country's foreign exchange reserves are held by the government[5]. The large balance sheet is the result of two factors: 1) large government deposits and 2) large current account holdings, which of course result from the policy of quantitative easing followed between 2001 and 2006 (see also Figure 17.3, below). After the discontinuation of this policy in March 2006 (not covered by Figure 17.3), there has, however, been a reduction in the current accounts holdings.

During the quantitative easing period, the Bank of Japan did, as part of an initiative to secure financial stability, acquire several other types of domestic assets (which are not distinguished in our stylised format), such as shares and asset-backed securities, which the other central banks normally do not hold (see for instance BoJ, 2004). The holdings of such assets, however, have remained relatively modest at around ¥20 trillion, or 1.5 per cent of total assets.

It is interesting to note that the increased 'excess reserves' of commercial banks – reflected in higher current accounts – had a counterpart more in outright purchases of domestic assets than in refinancing operations (see Figure 17.3). While the increase in domestic assets was, until 2004, due to an expansion of the portfolio of long-term domestic government bonds, the latter has been slightly declining over the last couple of years, when instead there has been a rather strong increase in the holdings of short-term government bonds, which are more flexible and which entail less interest rate risk. Hence, for the Bank of Japan the domestic outright portfolio is also an important monetary policy instrument. The size of the portfolio of long-term domestic government bonds is close to, but does not exceed banknotes in circulation and is therefore, in relative terms, comparable to the portfolio of the Federal Reserve. Moreover, as the Federal Reserve, the Bank of Japan is also quite transparent about the composition of its outright portfolio.

Specific features of the Bundesbank's balance sheet

The Bundesbank's balance sheet is an alternative corner solution to that of the Federal Reserve. While its liabilities side was, with the exception of larger reserve requirements, comparable to that of the Federal Reserve, the assets side was fundamentally different: there was huge emphasis on temporary operations, which accounted for no less than 61 per cent of all assets (in comparison to 3 per cent for the Federal Reserve), and there was no domestic asset portfolio in place (compared with a 93 per cent domestic asset portfolio for the Federal Reserve). On the other hand, the Bundesbank had a relatively large foreign exchange portfolio, accounting for 33 per cent of all assets. Hence, in the case of the Bundesbank, outright portfolios did not play an active role in the steering of domestic liquidity conditions. Temporary operations were the only tool available for absorbing both structural and short-term movements on the liabilities side, and hence were the balancing item.

Figure 17.3   Selected items of the Bank of Japan's balance sheet

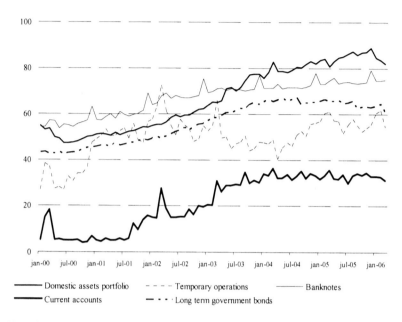

Note: the chart shows outstanding amounts at the end of each month

Specific features of the Eurosystem's balance sheet

It is not surprising that the Eurosystem's balance sheet is similar to that of the Bundesbank, with sizeable volumes of both temporary operations and outright portfolios on the assets side, and significant amounts of equity and reserve requirements (current accounts) on the liabilities side, in addition to the autonomous factors. Still, the balance sheet, and notably the composition and the management of the outright portfolios (i.e. investment versus monetary policy portfolios), are obviously heavily influenced by the fact that the Eurosystem is composed of 12 national central banks.

First, the balance sheet is somewhat bigger in relation to banknotes, than that of the Bundesbank, mainly owing to government deposits. Second, outright holdings are managed on a decentralized basis by individual Eurosystem national central banks and are not held for monetary policy purposes. Hence, as exemplified in ECB (2006), they are to be mostly regarded as investment portfolios[6], and significant heterogeneity in the (relative) size of the investment portfolios of individual Eurosystem national central banks can be observed. This heterogeneity (see also Gros and Schobert, 1999) reflects the fact that the national central banks only share monetary policy while they do not have a common responsibility on financial matters. Moreover, the national central banks have inherited very different balance sheet structures from the pre-EMU times when they were, in some cases, subject to rather strong government influence. As a result, the volume of the temporary operations is the balancing item, which not only adjusts to the autonomous factors on the liabilities side – as was the case for the Bundesbank – but also to the size of the investment outright portfolio, which is basically determined by the action of individual Eurosystem national central banks. Still, some coordination between the temporary operations and the size of the outright portfolios takes place in the context of an agreement which limits the expansion of the latter so as to ensure a certain minimum liquidity deficit. That is, a minimum volume is ensured in the regular temporary operations, which are only liquidity providing and hence only appear on the assets side of the Eurosystem. Third, in contrast to the case of the Bundesbank, the Eurosystem also holds a large domestic asset portfolio. Finally, it should also be noted that the Eurosystem has a much larger amount of equity (around 20 per cent of total liabilities) than the other central banks considered.

Trends in the Eurosystem's balance sheet

As shown in Figure 17.4, the balance sheet of the Eurosystem has recently strongly grown as a result of the strong upward trend in banknotes. The steady growth in current accounts (i.e. reserve requirements) has also contributed, albeit in a more limited way, to this growth, while the sharp decline in equity, which is mainly due to a decrease in the euro valuation of the foreign exchange portfolio, because of the appreciation of the euro, has worked in the opposite direction.

Turning to the assets side, the size of the outright portfolio has remained almost unchanged (at around €385 billion). This results from two offsetting phenomena: while the above-mentioned revaluation effect and a real reduction of foreign reserves by central banks brought about a reduction of net foreign assets by around €80 billion since 2003, domestic assets increased by the same amount. As a consequence, the strong increase on the liabilities side was matched by a comparable increase in the temporary operations, which have grown by 75 per cent since 2003.

A possible interpretation

The above description has highlighted several differences across central banks, which can be summarized as follows:

Differences on the assets side

The Federal Reserve matches its liabilities almost one to one with outright holdings of domestic government bonds, which are used actively in the Federal Reserve's monetary policy implementation. While not matching its entire (and much larger) liabilities side with outright holdings of domestic government bonds, the Bank of Japan also holds a sizeable portfolio of such bonds, which, as in the case of the Federal Reserve, corresponds to the outstanding amount of banknotes. Likewise, the Bank of Japan has also used purchases of government bonds as a tool of its monetary policy implementation. In contrast, the Eurosystem's portfolio of domestic government bonds is much smaller and is not used for the purpose of monetary policy implementation. In its case, structural changes in the liabilities side are matched by temporary operations.

Figure 17.4 Recent trends in the Eurosystem's balance sheet

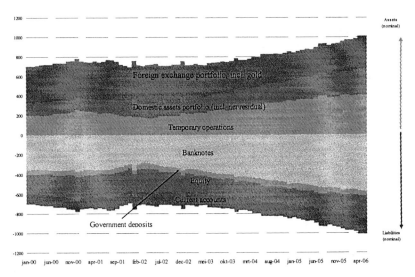

Note: the chart shows monthly averages and excludes other assets and liabilities, which were strongly inflated by TARGET gross balances in the first year of EMU

The Eurosystem holds much larger amounts of foreign exchange reserves and therefore also faces larger exchange rate risk than both the Federal Reserve and the Bank of Japan.

Differences on the liabilities side

The Eurosystem has significant amounts of equity resulting from retained profits, while the Federal Reserve transfers on a continuous basis most of its profits to the government, thereby only retaining a minimum amount of equity. The Bank of Japan also holds only a relatively small amount of equity. This difference in the amount of equity closely mirrors the difference in exchange rate risk mentioned above. However, it is important to also emphasize that the three central banks use different accounting standards, which, for instance, imply that movements in the market value of assets are recorded differently in the equity item. Therefore, it is in fact rather difficult to compare this item across the three central banks.

The Eurosystem has established much larger reserve requirements than the Federal Reserve and therefore has much larger current accounts on the liabilities side. The reason for this difference is twofold. First, it owes, in part, to the fact that reserve holdings are fully remunerated by the Eurosystem while they are unremunerated in the case of the Federal Reserve. Second, as further explained below, it owes in part to the differences in operating procedures. The huge current accounts on the liabilities side of the Bank of Japan's balance sheet are due to the policy of quantitative easing and not to particularly large reserve requirements.

The Eurosystem and in particular the Bank of Japan have larger 'other items' on the liabilities side, mostly resulting from government deposits, than the Federal Reserve.

As a first remark, it should be noted that the substantial differences between the balance sheet of the Federal Reserve and that of the Eurosystem prove the statement made in the introduction that monetary policy implementation is possible with different balance sheet structures. In spite of the differences, the two central banks are equally successful in steering their operating target, short-term interest rates (see e.g. Blenck et al, 2001) and in achieving their monetary policy objective. The case of the Bank of Japan is different in this respect since, over the sample period considered, it has targeted the quantity of bank reserves (current accounts) in its quantitative easing policy.

Note, however, that the existence of differences between the balance sheet of the Federal Reserve and that of the Eurosystem does not mean that the balance sheet composition is irrelevant for monetary policy implementation and vice versa. The operational framework, the liquidity policy and the balance sheet dynamics must be seen as parts of a whole and must be consistent with each other. Yet, central banks enjoy several degrees of freedom in choosing one approach or another for the implementation of monetary policy, consisting of different combinations of the operational framework, balance sheet structure and liquidity policy. For instance, the Eurosystem's choice to only carry out (regular) liquidity-providing temporary operations on a weekly basis (see ECB, 2002) requires higher volumes of reserve requirements and temporary operations. These higher volumes also depend, however, on the dynamics of the autonomous factors in the balance sheet: the more unstable the autonomous factors, the larger the necessary volumes in weekly operations and/or reserve requirements to offset temporary liquidity shocks without generating volatility in the overnight rate. This illustrates that the Eurosystem could not simply adopt – at least not completely – the balance sheet structure of the Federal Reserve, with minimal volumes in both reserve requirements and temporary operations, without also changing its operating procedures. In particular, if it wanted to adopt a balance sheet with the same structure as that of the Federal Reserve, the Eurosystem would need to carry out more frequent temporary operations, moving closer to the almost daily frequency of the operations of that central bank (see FRBNY, 2004).

Yet, exemplifying the degrees of freedom mentioned above, the Eurosystem could move somewhat closer to the balance sheet structure of the Federal Reserve without sacrificing any precision in the steering of the overnight rate, while the converse would also be true.

Behind the observed differences in the balance sheets, there also seem to be different interpretations of the concept of central bank financial independence. As explained in Section 2, the Federal Reserve perceives this to be best achieved by transferring continuously practically its entire financial surplus to the Treasury and holding no other assets than Treasury securities. The Bank of Japan seems to follow a somewhat similar approach, even though, in contrast to the Federal Reserve, it is not allowed to buy government papers in the primary market. Hence, both these central banks hold small amounts of equity and huge portfolios of Treasury paper, which are approximately equivalent to the amount of banknotes in circulation. Following the logic of this approach, it makes sense, when analysing the central bank balance sheet, to simply aggregate it with that of the government into a public sector balance sheet, given the close relationships between the balance sheet of the central bank and that of the Treasury.

Instead, in the case of the Eurosystem, safeguards against the governments' access to the financial resources of central banks are seen as an essential component of financial independence and are clearly reflected in the Treaty. As a consequence, the Eurosystem retains large amounts of equity on the liabilities side, indicating overall lower 'dividends' paid out to the governments, while on the assets side it mostly holds foreign exchange reserves and temporary operations instead of domestic government bonds. Obviously, according to this approach, an aggregation of the balance sheets of the central bank and the government is much less natural, since their financial resources are clearly separated. However, even though there are safeguards against monetary financing in the Treaty establishing the European Community and these safeguards could be invoked to explain the preferences for holding other assets than domestic government debt, the Treaty contains no explicit limits on the amounts of government debt which the Eurosystem can purchase and hold[7]. Indeed, as mentioned above, the outright portfolio of the Eurosystem is largely investment based and there has lately been a shift from foreign assets to domestic assets, including government bonds. Hence, the present structure of the Eurosystem's assets is not strictly determined by institutional reasons limiting the purchases and holdings of government bonds. Still, the Eurosystem emphasizes the importance of not being constrained by government interests, as well as the importance of its capability to hold sufficient financial buffers in the form of equity, thus making clear its attitude towards financial independence[8].

The different underlying perception of how to best achieve financial independence, which in the case of the Eurosystem is reflected in the Treaty, and the correspondingly different attitude towards an integration between the balance sheet of the central bank and that of the government, are probably partially explained by the different historical relationships between the government and the central bank. In the case of the United States, this relationship has been rather close and parsimonious, including during war time, and the easy access of the Treasury to the financial resources of the Federal Reserve has not led to rampant inflation, as was the case in Germany in the 1920s and in Italy in the 1970s and 1980s. These precedents may have argued in favour of a clearer financial separation between the central bank and the government in Europe than was considered necessary in the United States. Of course, this was reinforced by the overall design of Monetary Union in Europe, since a fully federal function, such as monetary policy, takes place in an institutional framework which is by no means completely federal. The latter observation is probably also another important reason why the Eurosystem, in clear contrast to the two other central banks, has so far not used outright operations in domestic bonds as an active tool for monetary implementation. Not only could this be seen as being somewhat against its approach to financial independence, but it could also force the Eurosystem, one way or the other, to make a difficult distinction between government bonds issued by the different Member States.

17.5 SOME NORMATIVE THOUGHTS ON THE CENTRAL BANK BALANCE SHEET

So far in this paper, we have compared the balance sheets of the G3 central banks, ascertained the trends in the balance sheet of the Eurosystem, examined the relationship between monetary policy implementation and the structure of the balance sheet, and offered the thought that the specific interpretation of the concept of financial independence also influences the structure of the central bank balance sheet.

The exercise has, however, proven that considerations relating to two fundamental concepts of monetary policy, namely monetary policy implementation and financial independence are alone insufficient to establish the basis for an exhaustive normative treatment of the central bank balance sheet. First, this follows from the fact that central banks with large differences in their balance sheets are equally successful in their monetary policy implementation. Second, even though specific interpretations of financial independence are reflected in some balance sheet structures, again there are a number of different balance sheet compositions that are consistent with a given interpretation of financial independence. This seems to be particularly the case for the Eurosystem. In fact, in the case of the Federal Reserve, the link between the chosen interpretation of independence and the composition of the balance sheet is, as explained above, more precise: the assets side should be mainly composed of outright holdings of government bonds. In contrast, the Eurosystem approach, in principle, only implies that government assets should not have a preferential status over private assets and this gives only limited guidance in determining the assets side of the balance sheet.

As an example of a possible normative analysis, this section focuses on the Eurosystem balance sheet. In doing so it takes as given its objective of maintaining price stability, which, according to the Treaty, has an overriding importance and can not be traded off with any other objective. At the level of generality chosen for this chapter, this objective, consistently with the findings and interpretations put forward in the previous section, only gives rise to two broad constraints: first, the Eurosystem's approach to financial independence must be preserved, with the resulting requirement that the balance sheet must be strong enough and clearly separated from that of the government sector; second, its specific approach to monetary policy implementation must be maintained, which, in turn, implies the preservation of its operational framework, which allows steering short-term interest rates sufficiently precisely to achieve its primary objective.

To complement these two overriding constraints three criteria are suggested that are plausible possibilities for addressing the issue of the appropriate composition of the central bank balance sheet. The exercise consists, first, in deriving from the two constraints and from the three criteria preliminary normative considerations about the balance sheet structure and, second, seeing what can be said about the size of the different items of the simplified balance sheet presented in Table 17.1.

When considering the three criteria listed below, it is important to keep in mind that they may yield different conclusions and therefore may need to be traded off one against the other. This will apply in particular to the discussion about the appropriate level of current account holdings.

Criterion 1: Operational efficiency

According to this criterion, the central bank should compose its balance sheet with a view to achieving the highest possible degree of operational efficiency. This criterion derives naturally from the central bank's institutional role. By way of example, it comprises the minimization of transaction costs for both the central bank and the market when rolling over the different items in the central bank's balance sheet, notably (short-term) temporary operations. A relevant element in this regard is the link between the central bank's balance sheet and the operational efficiency of commercial banks' balance sheets, specifically their liquidity management and, related to that, the functioning of the short-term money market. Crucial for these issues, for example, are the size of reserve requirements and of short-term temporary operations.

Criterion 2: Efficient allocation of financial resources

The central bank, given the size of the resources at its disposal and its responsibility towards society with regard to their use, must carefully ensure that it contributes to an efficient overall allocation of resources. In the case of the ECB/Eurosystem, this is explicitly foreseen in the Treaty, which establishes that: 'the ESCB shall act in accordance with the principle of an open market economy with free competition, favouring an efficient allocation of resources ...'. While one possible and intuitive interpretation of this criterion is that the central bank should aim at 'market neutrality', i.e. aiming to avoid distorting the relative prices of assets, it is not obvious whether in fact this is the most efficient approach. This depends, among other things, on the central bank's risk-taking capabilities. A more operational corollary to this principle is that the central bank should, in general, aim to minimize the financial resources that it uses to accomplish its mandate. This corollary, which can be reformulated as the principle of a lean balance sheet, makes the reasonable assumption that agents other than the central bank can, from a strictly financial point of view, normally get a higher return than the central bank itself. This is due to the fact that the investment universe of the central bank is, for good reasons, more limited than that of private institutions, thus yielding inferior returns.

Criterion 3: Enhancement of shareholder value

It is a fundamental principle that the purpose of a central bank is not to maximize financial return for the benefit of its shareholders. In the case of the Eurosystem, this principle is clearly specified in the Treaty, and it is taken into account in this analysis by taking for granted the Eurosystem's approach to financial independence, as specified in the first constraint mentioned above. Nevertheless, whenever the two constraints and the two more relevant criteria mentioned above would not be sufficient to determine one or the other item of the balance sheet, the central bank may take into account shareholders' preferences.

In the light of the two constraints and the three criteria mentioned above, what can be said about the size of the different items of the simplified balance sheet presented in Table 17.1 and about their reciprocal consistency?

Let us start with the liabilities side. There is not much to be said about banknotes, the value of which is strictly exogenous and determined by the demand of the public. It can just be recalled that the value of the banknotes also defines the minimum size of the central bank balance sheet (see Section 4). In Section 3, government deposits, equity and other liabilities were also defined as exogenous, as they clearly cannot be changed by the central bank over the time horizon that is normally relevant for monetary policy. Even if, over a longer time horizon, the central bank can have some influence on their level, it is probably accurate enough to consider government deposits and other liabilities as exogenous, since their level is basically determined by laws and regulations, which are difficult to change and which are not determined solely by the central bank.

Equity deserves a somewhat longer mention. The first observation is that equity should comply with the first constraint, i.e. should not be lower than what is necessary to safeguard central bank independence and credibility. The second criterion mentioned above, and notably the principle of a lean balance sheet, further adds that the level of equity should neither be higher than the minimum required to preserve independence. Unfortunately, it is not straightforward to identify in practice the minimum level of equity consistent with central bank independence and credibility. In fact, while the minimum threshold for equity is easily defined for commercial banks on the basis of regulatory requirements, it follows from the literature review in Section 2 that this is much more difficult to define for a central bank. A further complication in this regard, is that some central banks, including some national central banks of the Eurosystem, may also carry out non-monetary tasks, for instance within the fields of supervision and oversight of payment systems, which may require additional amounts of equity. Nevertheless, if we assume, notwithstanding the aforementioned uncertainty about this point, that the central bank should protect itself against the risk of negative equity, it is in principle straightforward to calculate the minimum amount of equity it needs. This is the amount which is needed to ensure, with a given degree of confidence and over a given time horizon, that equity will not become negative. In principle, given a certain confidence level and time horizon, one can calculate the Value at Risk of the entire balance sheet of the central bank (as well as of its off-balance-sheet commitments) and fix the value of equity at that level of Value at Risk, thus ensuring that negative equity will be a rare enough event.

The last item on the liabilities side is current accounts, which we assume identical to reserve requirements, the minimum size of which can be determined on the basis of monetary policy implementation needs. The relevant empirical parameters here are the variability of the exogenous factors in the balance sheet, which determines the variability of aggregate current account holdings, as well as the payment technology, which in turn determines the variability of individual banks' current account holdings, notably their uncertainty about their end-of-day position. The minimum level of reserve requirements is the one that ensures, for a chosen level of confidence and given these two parameters and the operational framework for the implementation of monetary policy (including the desired frequency of monetary policy operations), that banks will, in aggregate, be able to absorb liquidity shocks without causing variability in very short-term interest rates. Whether reserve requirements should exceed this minimum level depends on how the central bank trades off the first two criteria. For instance, from the perspective of operational efficiency (the first criterion) one may argue that larger reserve requirements are desirable, because they make it easier for both commercial banks and for the central bank to manage liquidity. On the other hand, from the perspective of efficient allocation of resources (the second criterion) and depending on how the central bank invests the financial resources stemming from reserve requirements, smaller reserve requirements may be preferable.

Overall, even though the arguments just presented show that the central bank may, in the medium to long term, have some limited degree of freedom in determining the size of reserve requirements and equity, it is clear that a central bank that pursues monetary policy implementation by targeting a short-term rate of interest cannot really control the overall level of liabilities on its balance sheet, which will be basically determined by demand.

However, on the assets side, as already pointed out, the central bank has more freedom.

Notwithstanding what was said above about the difficulty of the literature on optimal foreign reserves reaching conclusive results, one may establish, either on the basis of conceptual reasoning or past experience, an estimate, or at least a range of estimates, of the minimum amount of reserves a central bank may need for institutional purposes, first of all to be able to finance foreign exchange interventions. The criterion of efficient allocation of financial resources implies that the holding of international reserves beyond this minimum could be discussed, in comparison with alternative uses. This follows from the fact that foreign exchange reserves, the investment of which is dominated by safety and liquidity considerations, normally have a relatively low financial return and entail a large foreign exchange risk, thus requiring a relatively high amount of equity.

The item denominated 'net residual can be considered exogenous, often depending on factors beyond the control of the central banks. In any case, as seen in Table 17.1, this item is usually very small.

The two remaining items on the asset side, namely temporary operations and the domestic asset portfolio, are the most difficult to determine on the basis of the two constraints and the three criteria identified above. As reported in Section 2, arguments can be developed (see Bindseil and Würtz, 2005) on how to choose the relative size of the two items, but the conclusions are far from definitive. Indeed, this is the most difficult topic in determining the most appropriate balance sheet of a central bank and the one on which further research should concentrate: how should the assets of the central bank be divided between the domestic outright portfolio and temporary operations, taking into account and potentially weighing one against the other the criteria of operational efficiency, efficient allocation of financial resources, and accommodation of government preferences, while at the same time complying with the two constraints, notably the one of independence and credibility? The fact that the resources invested in these two asset categories are very large suggests that the implications deriving from the three criteria and the two constraints should be carefully investigated. We leave this task to a future paper.

17.6 CONCLUSIONS

This chapter attempts to contribute to filling the gap between the importance of the issue of central bank balance sheets and the small amount of economic analysis that has so far been devoted to this topic. It does so by reviewing the scarce literature available, and by proposing a stylized balance sheet and seeing how this balance sheet looks in the case of the 'G3 central banks' (the Eurosystem, and before that the Bundesbank, the US Federal Reserve and the Bank of Japan). The chapter also examines the trends in the Eurosystem balance sheet and tries to interpret the differences among the balance sheets of the G3 central banks, concluding that these reflect historical factors, and related to that, differences in the interpretation of central banks' financial independence. From the differences among the three balance sheets, the chapter draws the conclusion that the objective of price stability can be achieved with very different layouts of the central bank balance sheet. Therefore this objective is insufficient by itself in determining the most appropriate design of the latter.

In the penultimate section, the chapter proposes a highly tentative and preliminary analytical approach determining the most appropriate balance sheet of the Eurosystem. Basically, the approach consists in defining a constrained maximization problem: first, it specifies the constraints on the balance sheet that can be derived from the overriding objective of price stability and, second, it identifies some criteria, which, given these constrains, can identify an appropriate balance sheet. Even if this approach clearly needs much more work and refinement, and as of yet does not reach definitive and complete results, we hope to have taken a first step in identifying a possible path that could lead to the design of an optimal balance sheet.

NOTES

1. The views expressed in this paper are personal and do not necessarily correspond to those of the institution where the two authors work. Comments from Age F.P. Bakker, Denis Blenck, Nuno Cassola, Gertrude Tumpel-Gugerell, Ingmar R.Y van Herpt, Paul Mercier, Ken Nyholm, Huw Pill, Benjamin Sahel, M. Shirakawa, and other colleagues in the Eurosystem as well as data received from colleagues at the Federal Reserve and the Bank of Japan are gratefully acknowledged.
2. If short-term interest rates reach the zero lower bound, the central bank may, however, adopt an additional operating target, possibly a 'quantitative' target for current account balances, as it has been the case for Bank of Japan in the period 2001–6.
3. This obligation may under some circumstances force the central bank to take less profitable positions, for instance if it operates at the zero lower bound.
4. The US Treasury hold an equivalent amount of foreign exchange reserves.
5. During the quantitative easing period the outstanding amount of banknotes also grew exceptionally strongly, implying that the balance sheet of Bank of Japan is even bigger, if its absolute size is measured against other economic variables than banknotes.
6. This is also consistent with the fact that the Eurosystem is at present – in the context of its monetary policy implementation – characterizing all its outright holdings as autonomous factors (see for instance ECB, 2002).
7. In particular, Article 101 of the Treaty prohibits granting 'overdraft facilities or any other type of credit facility' to the government (or government bodies) as well as the purchasing of government bonds in the primary market, while secondary legislation (Council Regulation No. 3603/93) specifies that the purchasing of government debt in the secondary market may not be used to circumvent the objective of this Article. Moreover, Article 102 prohibits the establishment of privileged access by government bodies to financial institutions, unless this would be based on prudential considerations.
8. This was most recently expressed in the Opinion of the European Central Bank of 15 October 2003 on a proposal to amend the Suomen Pankki Act (ECB, 2003).

18. Governance Aspects of Central Bank Reserve Management

Age F.P. Bakker

18.1 INTRODUCTION

Central banks face increasing challenges as demands for transparency and accountability rise. The phenomenal rise of foreign exchange reserves and the attendant risks for central bank balance sheets has highlighted the need to have appropriate governance rules in place. Such rules include *inter alia* well-defined decision-making structures with respect to the management of central bank reserves, adequate risk management frameworks, transparent accounting rules, a clear profit distribution agreement with the shareholder and adequate capitalization rules. In designing these rules particular attention should be paid to the interaction between these governance rules.

For the purpose of this chapter it is helpful to distinguish between external and internal governance rules, by analogy to corporate governance rules. The external governance of central bank reserve management refers to the relationship with the shareholder, i.e. the government, and the transparency and accountability to the outside world. The governance of central bank reserves depends to a large extent on the institutional set-up of the central bank, in particular the institutional arrangements vis-à-vis the government. Of particular relevance is whether the central bank or the government is bearing the ultimate risks on official reserves. Accordingly, the need for adequate capitalization and for financial buffers to cope with risks differs among central banks.

The internal governance of central bank reserves refers to the internal procedures for decision making and risk taking. The responsibilities of governing boards of central banks with respect to the definition of strategic benchmark portfolios and the appropriate asset and risk management frameworks need to be clearly defined. As central banks become active traders in financial markets, high standards for raising Chinese walls are needed in order to ensure that insider knowledge with respect to future interest rate decisions are kept away from the dealing room.

18.2 NEW TRENDS IN RESERVE MANAGEMENT BY CENTRAL BANKS

The exponential growth of foreign exchange reserves, especially among emerging countries and oil exporting countries, has led to sharp increases in central bank balance sheets. Global reserves have doubled over the past five years and are now at over $4 trillion. The growth of foreign exchange reserves has resulted from global imbalances and this in turn has increased the likelihood of shock-wise adjustments with potentially serious consequences for central bank balance sheets.

A general trend among central banks has been an increased focus on raising returns in addition to the traditional considerations of maintaining sound liquidity portfolios. Increasingly, central banks have diversified their asset portfolios in order to seek higher returns. They have added new asset classes and are in the process of diversifying their currency holdings. Although the bulk of reserves still remains invested in US treasuries, there has been a growing demand for agency debt, ABS and MBS and other riskier assets. Central banks have become more active asset managers.

Why are central banks seeking higher returns? The increased focus on transparency and accountability has highlighted the need to get a decent return on what are essentially public funds. In Asian and oil-exporting countries, the enormous increase in foreign exchange reserves has given added flexibility to focus more on return as the need to keep them all in liquid assets has become less pressing. Higher returns can compensate for the costs of carrying these large foreign exchange reserves. In some cases reserve management has taken the character of management of national wealth in separate investment portfolios. The traditional preference for investing reserves in liquid assets has become less relevant as the usefulness of interventions in foreign exchange markets has been called into question in highly liberalized financial markets, particularly for central banks in industrial countries. Finally, profit disbursements from the central bank to government shareholders provide an important source of income.

18.3 EXTERNAL GOVERNANCE RULES

Corporate and agency central bank models

The financial risks central banks can accept may differ according to their institutional set-up as well as on their capital and other financial buffers.

Generally, two main central bank models can be distinguished: the agent and the corporate (or principal) central bank model.

Under the agent model, the central bank serves as an agent of the government: most risks, including foreign exchange risks, are borne by the government and any profits or losses are transferred back to the government. In many cases the official reserves are actually owned by the government and the central bank acts on behalf of the government as an asset manager with a clearly defined mandate. In other cases reserve assets are matched with government liabilities, e.g. reflecting official external debt obligations. The accumulation of reserves is the outcome of interventions in the foreign exchange markets which are made under official instructions in support of the exchange rate policy of the government.

In essence, under the agent model it is the government that defines the risk tolerance of the central bank. Consequently, capital plays a limited role. The Bank of Canada, the Bank of England and the People's Bank of China would fit in this model, among others.

In the corporate model, on the other hand, capital serves as a buffer to absorb losses. All financial risks on balance-sheet items are borne by the central bank and it is the governing board that defines the risk tolerance of the central bank. This model is adopted by the majority of central banks worldwide, including all euro area central banks, largely on the grounds that it supports central bank independence. Under the corporate model, the central bank has clear incentives to manage risks effectively.

For central banks operating under the corporate model the financial relationship with the government, being in most cases the only shareholder, is less clear-cut and needs careful attention. The global move towards central bank independence with respect to monetary policy has led in practice to a redefinition of the financial relationship vis-à-vis the government as well. The focus has been on a clear circumscription of financial independence, as being a prerequisite for an independent central bank, and consequently on appropriate capitalization and profit distribution rules.

Financial independence can be defined as enabling the central bank to act in an independent way and not seeing its room for manoeuvre limited by financial restrictions. Generally, financial independence is understood to imply that the central bank has own resources at its disposal and can generate its own income. This ensures that the central bank is not dependent on government financing its activities, which in practice might undermine its independence with respect to monetary policy making. This would imply, therefore, that central banks are well capitalized and are able to finance their activities from the revenues on their assets. It also implies that the government refrains from interference with the reserve management of the central bank.

Table 18.1 External governance aspects of reserve management

- Responsibility for interventions in foreign exchange markets

- (Re)capitalization rules

- Profit distribution rules

- Application of accounting rules

- Transparency rules with respect to asset composition

- Accountability rules with respect to asset management

Capitalization rules

Central banks operating under the corporate model need adequate capital, including reserves, in order to be able to carry the inherent risks on their balance sheet. Over the past decade in a number of countries the issue of central bank capitalization has received much attention. In particular, for European central banks the establishment of the Euro system and the attendant need to rewrite national central bank laws has focused public attention on the composition of the central bank's balance sheet. The need to capitalize the European Central Bank itself and to establish loss and profit-sharing mechanisms among the participating national central banks, has given a fresh impetus to look at the financial buffers of the national central banks themselves as well.

Usually public attention at first instance focused on the question whether participating national central banks would need the same amount of official reserves, including gold reserves, once they had entered the euro zone. Under the preceding European Monetary System substantial official reserves were needed to defend the national currency at times of tensions in the system. In particular, many European central banks had built up sizable deutsche mark holdings apart from their US dollar holdings enabling them to defend the parity of their currency vis-à-vis the 'hard currency' anchor of the EMS, i.e. the deutsche mark. As the euro would operate under a floating exchange rate regime there might be less need for large reserves.

The first issue that came up during the changeover from the national currency to the euro was whether the deutsche mark official reserve holdings should be exchanged into other foreign currency or should be held in the form of euro assets. A second related issue was whether the combined US dollar holdings of all euro system national central banks taken together were not excessive, given the flexible exchange rate policy of the euro system. Governments and parliaments took an active interest in these issues as they felt that part of these 'excess' reserves could be disbursed to the shareholder. However, it was soon realized that the only component of the balance sheet that can be transferred to the government is on the right hand side of the balance sheet, i.e. capital and reserves, and not on the left hand asset side. This raised the question whether central banks were overcapitalized.

The question of presumed overcapitalization of central banks became more pressing as central banks had been selling substantial parts of their gold holdings, which implied that large revaluation gains were realized. This spurred the debate on whether the proceeds should remain on the balance of the central banks or whether part of the realized valuation gains should be transferred to the government. Many European central banks transferred part of their reserves to the government before joining the euro system. Although efforts were made to quantify as objectively as possible the needed capital and reserves of the central bank it is fair to say that a substantial element of judgment came into play as well.

In practice, levels of capital and financial buffers have been determined by historical factors and different institutional settings. Indeed, can we say anything about the optimal level of capital and reserves for a central bank? Capital adequacy ratios, such as applied by supervisors under the Basle accords, are less relevant for central banks because of their unique balance sheet composition as issuer of bank notes and because of the heterogeneity of public tasks that central banks perform.

A study group on central bank capital, under the aegis of the BIS, has refrained from trying to quantify optimal levels of capital, simply because central banks are too diverse. Different exchange rate regimes, monetary policy objectives and supervision responsibilities may all warrant different levels of capital. Moreover, central bank capital has to be seen in a dynamic context where future flows of seignorage income have to be taken into account.

A more fruitful way of looking at central bank balance sheets is to identify central bank funding regimes that are sustainable, i.e. where the central bank can achieve its long-term policy objectives without its financial independence being impaired. For this it is important to make a risk analysis of all relevant central bank balance sheet items that can negatively affect levels of capital as well as ways to minimize their impact. Also profit distribution rules need to be examined carefully as they can lead to erosion of the capital base over time.

Profit distribution rules and accounting rules

The interaction between accounting rules and profit distribution rules is of particular importance for the long-run sustainability of a central bank. The move towards marked-to-market accounting rules has exposed vulnerabilities in many central banks' balance sheets with large unhedged foreign exchange reserves holdings. The impact of accounting rules is mostly felt by corporate central banks since they bear the risk of volatile income flows themselves.

The new accounting (IFRS) standards are welcome as they enhance transparency in financial markets by promoting the presentation of a true and fair view of the financial activities and positions on which private investors can base their decisions. For central banks transparency is needed as well, but here the objective is more related to the performance of their public tasks and to enhance their credibility. The protection of the financial interests of the shareholder, typically only the government, is only a secondary consideration. Therefore, the new IFRS standard may in certain respects not reach such true and fair view because of the special tasks of central banks. Moreover, central banks need to take a very good look at the impact of the IFRS rules for themselves. If they were to be applied without a change in the profit distribution rules negative dynamics for the financial position of the central bank might ensue.

Many central banks have agreed with the government on *asymmetric* profit distribution rules, meaning that profits are disbursed up to a certain agreed percentage but that losses have to be borne by the central bank itself. Under IFRS, unrealized gains on foreign exchange holdings would have to be recognized in the profit and loss account. This would imply that the central bank would have to pay out additional dividend if the national currency is under downward pressure. This can quickly push central bank capital into a downward spiral if at a later stage the central bank needs to absorb losses on these foreign exchange holdings, if the currency were to appreciate. This mechanism would imply that the bank would eventually run out on its financial buffers and might end up with negative capital.

As well as the treatment of unrealized profits, the treatment of gold holdings also deserves attention. It would seem irresponsible behaviour if by applying IFRS rules gold revaluation accounts would be recognized as a profit and distributed to the government. This would have a serious impact on central bank capital and reserves and would therefore be problematic. Also the required disclosures under IFRS for foreign reserve positions may conflict with the central bank's objectives and confidentiality requirements.

So, what should central banks do? Central banks need to strike a proper balance between the need to be as transparent as possible and at the same time maintain a degree of confidentiality in order not to compromise their tasks, including exchange rate policy. Furthermore accounting rules for central banks should be prudent and preferably avoid undue volatility in the profit and loss account that may undermine the credibility of the central bank. Can central banks, which in their role as supervisor are asking the private sector to apply IFRS standards, make exceptions for themselves? I think deviations from IFRS can be well explained because corporate governance rules in central banks will always differ from that in a private corporation. Central banks pursue a clearly defined policy objective rather than maximize profit.

An alternative route may be for central banks to adopt IFRS rules, while at the same time clearly separating the resulting profit and loss account from the profit remittance rules. Although this would seem to be steering a straight course, in practice there may be political difficulties in achieving such separation of profit recognition from profit disbursement. Political pressures may rise if banks were seen to declare large headline profits under IFRS standards which, however, would not be reflected in actual profit disbursements to the government. Private corporations are not faced with comparable dilemmas because they can modify their dividend policy according to circumstances. In contrast, most central banks function under predetermined, asymmetric profit distribution rules and often there are no automatic capital replenishment agreements.

Central banks differ from private corporations

It is well understood by observers that there are major differences between central banks and private corporations. National central banks are established to achieve clearly defined policy objectives, often defined by law, rather than to maximize profits. In this they differ from private corporations which pursue mainly profit maximization. Of course, central banks can try to optimize returns given the policy constraints they face, and they are in the process of doing so, but monetary and exchange rate policy considerations should always prevail.

A second distinguishing factor from private corporations is that central banks can continue to operate even if their capital has turned negative. Incidental losses by central banks need not affect the credibility of central banks if they are caused by an appreciation of the domestic currency and future seignorage profits will replenish the central bank's capital. The central banks of Chile, the Czech Republic and Slovakia are a case in point, where appreciations of the domestic currency have resulted in substantial losses on foreign exchange holdings which had to be carried forward. Although the negative capital position of these central banks has not yet negatively affected their credibility, prolonged and extended periods of losses are generally not perceived as sustainable.

A final and decisive distinction between central banks and private corporations is the fact that central banks usually have only one shareholder, i.e. the government. This has important implications because profit distribution rules have to be set in accordance with the government, whereas private corporations can decide for themselves what is distributed to shareholders. Moreover distributed profits directly impact on the spending power of the government.

ALM models

Dynamic models such as an ALM model can try to quantify the interaction between accounting rules and profit disbursement agreements and thus increase awareness of the importance of long term sustainability.

In the case of the Netherlands we have performed an ALM study to see whether the bank over time would have adequate financial buffers[1]. The ALM model has been instrumental in understanding how the central bank's balance sheet, the capital and reserves and the profit and loss account would perform under different scenarios over a 10-year time horizon. The model showed that the central bank would incur a loss every six years, implying that the bank's financial buffers would be eroded over time as existing asymmetric profit distribution rules would allow only a very minor recouping of losses (only 5 per cent of profits can be retained). With full application of IFRS, where unrealized profits would have to be distributed as well, the declining trend of capital would have been even more pronounced.

The findings of this ALM model proved instrumental in agreeing with the shareholder to modify the income-sharing agreement by switching to symmetrical profit distribution rules. It was agreed that the Dutch central bank can compensate for losses with profits over the following six years. This means that our capital base, within a certain confidence level, can be preserved over time. In order to decrease the central bank balance sheet risks even further, the central bank has largely hedged its foreign currency exposure. Admittedly this may not be a suitable avenue for central banks operating in a different exchange regime setting than the euro area.

18.5 INTERNAL GOVERNANCE RULES

As many central banks have become more active in reserve management they have strengthened their internal governance procedures. Central banks have applied more sophisticated risk management techniques. Governors and board members of central banks have become involved in setting strategic benchmarks for central bank portfolios and have become familiar with VaR calculations and risk budgeting techniques. Yield and risk considerations have become a more prominent theme in board discussions.

Box 18.1   The Eurosystem accounting rules and IFRS

The European reporting rules for the Eurosystem central banks provide a good example of a common understanding for central bank accounting, which combines many elements of the international accounting standards, including marked-to-market accounting, while at the same time acknowledging the special position of central banks. The overriding principle is prudence and the need to preserve credibility. In order to achieve this, the accounting practices acknowledge the need for financial buffers in order to be able to carry the risk of large foreign exchange positions.

In practice the main difference with IFRS is the requirement that unrealized gains should not go to the profit and loss account and therefore not lead to the distribution of unrealized gains to shareholders. At the same time, all unrealized losses are taken to the profit and loss account. Moreover, netting of unrealized gains and losses across currencies or asset classes is not permitted. Further sensible deviations would include the treatment of gold revaluation accounts and realized profits from the sale of gold.

Although these rules are intended to apply to the ECB itself and for consolidation purposes of the Eurosystem books, national central banks that form part of the Eurosystem are not obliged to use Eurosystem accounting rules for their own reporting uses. At De Nederlandsche Bank we fully comply with the Eurosystem accounting rules.

Under the corporate central bank model major governance issues come out most clearly. The reputation risk of the central bank is a two-edged sword; there is a reputation risk if central banks are being seen as taking too much risk on board, but there is also the risk of too low a rate of return on the assets. Central bank reserves are essentially public funds and central banks should be seen as careful and prudent but not overly conservative investors.

How can central banks mitigate the reputation risk? Here good governance comes into play. The decision-making procedures within the central bank should be clearly spelled-out. In many central banks governing boards have become much more involved in the management of the assets of the bank. Traditionally governing boards of central banks have focused on monetary and exchange rate policies and they have refrained from acting as bankers themselves. The implications of monetary and exchange rate policy decisions for the balance sheet were considered as being of secondary importance, as was the financial result.

Table 18.2 Internal governance aspects of reserve management

Transparent decision making structure

-    governing board decides on strategic benchmark portfolio

-    investment committee decides on tactical position

-    asset managers decide on active position

Appropriate risk management framework

-    VaR calculations

-    stress tests

-    ALM scenarios

setting of risk budgets by governing boards

Chinese walls between monetary policy and financial markets departments

---

The changed environment in which central banks now operate has made it imperative that governing boards of central banks take an active interest in the management of their balance sheet. Governing boards of central banks should consciously determine the tolerance level they have towards risk-taking and take decisions on appropriate risk budgets. Therefore, governing boards need to ensure that an appropriate risk management framework is in place and board members should familiarize themselves with techniques to set strategic benchmarks and value at risk calculations.

Any discussion of central bank reserve management should not only focus on the asset side of the central bank balance sheet, but should equally take into account the composition of the liabilities side of the balance sheet. Decisions on the appropriate risk/return trade-off need to be based on the availability of adequate financial buffers, which are to be found on the right-hand side of the balance sheet. Governing boards should assess on a regular basis the adequacy and the sustainability of financial buffers since they can function as a shock absorber and compensate for losses. Adequate financial buffers would also ensure that monetary policy decisions are taken regardless of their impact on the central bank's balance sheet.

18.5 CONCLUSION

As official reserves have risen and accountability considerations have become more important, the governance of reserve management has become a more important issue. Clear and transparent governance rules, both for external and internal purposes, can be instrumental in mitigating the reputation risks as central banks apply more modern asset management techniques.

Risk management techniques have become much more important for central banks. Governing boards should on a regular basis identify risks and seek how they should be managed. Many central banks have revised and updated their accounting and reporting techniques over the past years. The information that central banks nowadays provide on their websites and in their annual reports has been greatly upgraded. Accountability and financial independence go hand-in-hand and this can enhance their credibility in the public sphere.

Accounting rules should support good risk management and sustainable buffer planning. If central banks are in the process of adopting new accounting rules, such as IFRS, it would seem advisable to have beforehand a clear understanding with the shareholder, i.e. the government, on profit distribution rules. Ideally these rules should be symmetrical, e.g. central banks should not only be obliged to hand out profits but should also be allowed to make up for losses. Ex ante recapitalization rules could serve this purpose, or, as is the case of the Netherlands, profit distribution rules which, after losses have been incurred, would allow the retention of earnings in subsequent years in order to preserve a certain level of capital.

It seems advisable that on the basis of a risk evaluation the central bank and its shareholder agree on an appropriate level of capital and financial buffers. A comfortable level of capital need not be perceived as providing a soft budget constraint as long as the central bank is fully transparent on its operational costs. To sum up, in a world full of risks, strong central banks need a strong financial position which is sustainable over time, so they can carry the risks without their credibility being impaired.

NOTES

1. See Bakker et al (2006)

19. Too Much of a Good Thing: Reserve Accumulation and Volatility in Central Bank Balance Sheets

Hervé Ferhani[1]

19.1 INTRODUCTION

The last decade has been witness to a remarkable increase in world reserves, with the trend being particularly strong in emerging markets, and more recently, the energy exporters[2]. In quite a few cases, the magnitude of reserves accumulated has resulted in stocks that clearly exceed most adequacy benchmarks, (import coverage, external debt coverage, others), by a non-negligible margin.

The macroeconomic benefits ensuing from high reserve holdings are well known, including most importantly, the greater ability to cope with domestic and external shocks, thereby increasing market confidence, consequently reducing the likelihood of an economic crisis. The most significant positive externality for economic growth lies in the lower borrowing costs to the public and private sectors of the country that this often yields.

However, rapid and sustained reserve accumulation may also carry significant costs. This is reflected in the increasing public debt burden related to sterilization of inflows, in the absence of which the economy could overheat through a credit boom and a widening current account deficit, which leave it vulnerable to a sudden stop and reversal of inflows. The cost of sterilization could be substantial, and is most immediately reflected in the spread between the interest paid on domestic debt and the rate accruing on investment grade reserve assets. This negative carry associated with inflow sterilization-cum-investment of reserves in AAA-rated, sovereign foreign assets, worsens the public sector balance sheet, may generate crowding out, thereby lowering domestic investment and growth, and may even yield a sudden stop and capital flow reversal.

As countries increasingly feel the pinch of these *problems of plenty*, there has been considerable interest, therefore, in looking at alternative reserve asset classes to short-term, investment grade, sovereign securities, in order to generate superior returns, albeit with correspondingly higher risk, and avoid the negative carry problem. The choice of the investment horizon and a suitable risk–return trade-off for the reserve portfolio is a question of reserve policy, and hence, to be addressed at the highest level. Operationalizing these policy choices involves the strategic issues of the choice of portfolio duration, investible asset classes (including a currency composition), engagement of external asset managers, and the (ability to) negotiate *fair* mandates with them. At the same time, it also involves choice of suitable institutional arrangements, including the role of the central bank in reserve management, attenuating the associated risk to its balance sheet, and the related question of profit distribution to the shareholder (i.e. the government).

This chapter first explores the question of challenges to reserve management operations in an international environment of rapid reserve accumulation and greater mobility of capital flows. It subsequently focuses attention on implications for central bank balance sheets, concentrating on the consequences of heightened volatility in central banks' financial statements. Some potential ways on dealing with volatility in distributing dividends to governments are discussed. It may be stated upfront that there is no 'silver bullet': not all central banks are alike, and certainly the political economy varies widely across countries, requiring a fair degree of judgment as to what solution to apply in a specific set of circumstances.

19.2 RESERVE MANAGEMENT STRATEGY

Looked at from the broader perspective of the country as a whole, what do higher levels of reserve adequacy rationally imply for the way reserves are managed?

Although reserves serve different specific purposes in different situations, their primary function is to provide a liquidity buffer in foreign exchange in times of balance-of-payments crises. As such, reserves buy time for the country to adjust its policies to remedy the situation and stop the outflow of foreign exchange.

Viewed from that perspective, reserve management strategies were traditionally geared toward safeguarding the value and immediate availability of this liquidity buffer in the short term. This implies that the currency composition is geared toward the composition of likely outflows, to stabilize the value of reserves in terms of these potential outflows, and that there is generally little appetite to engage in higher risk investment strategies to generate additional returns over the longer run.

As said earlier, higher reserve levels carry higher costs, focusing stakeholders' attention on the financial returns from investing reserves.

Higher levels of reserve adequacy imply that there is more certainty that a part of reserves will be there in the longer run. As the average expected holding period is longer, this means that the horizon for evaluating the balance of risk and return of the investment of at least part of reserves should also be longer.

In effect, as part of reserves is less likely to be called on in times of foreign currency liquidity crises this part is arguably a more structural foreign currency asset of the overall government. It therefore makes sense to decide on the risk-return profile of this part of reserves in conjunction with that of government's foreign currency liabilities, with the aim of improving the risk-return profile of the government's balance sheet overall.

The extent to which reserves can be used for that purpose depends largely on the size and likelihood of future reserve draw downs, in other words on the level of reserve adequacy. This is by no means an exact science, as drawing forward-looking balance-of-payments scenarios *and* attaching probabilities to these scenarios obviously involves a high degree of judgment.

Improving the risk-return profile of the government

At first sight, it seems logical to use reserves in excess of an adequate level to pay down the government's external debt, as this immediately saves carrying costs of reserves. However, one has to keep in mind that, although higher, reserves could still be called on in extreme scenarios. In such scenarios, market access to finance foreign currency liquidity shortages will most probably not be available. As the likelihood of such extreme scenarios is virtually impossible to pinpoint exactly and the cost of not having foreign currency liquidity available will arguably be very high, it is advisable to hold a safety margin in reserves above what would constitute an adequate level of reserves on the basis of generally used benchmark measures (for example, reserves-to-short-term external debt of the public sector).

In any case, a decision to buy back debt has to be based on a thorough cost-benefit analysis, weighing on the one hand saved carrying costs of reserves against, on the other hand, implications for the costs of new external debt and the potential macroeconomic costs of having less of a liquidity buffer for crisis situations. A more conservative option is then to hold on to reserves, but match the composition of the part of reserves in excess of an adequate level to the composition of government's external debt.

Of first-order importance is then to match the currency composition of overall government debt, as cross-currency movements can expose the government to large financial risks. This calls for coordination between debt managers and reserve managers, as they have to agree on who should do the matching.

Secondly, the maturity profile of external government debt can also be matched, to mitigate the interest rate risk arising from the mismatch between generally longer maturity external government debt and usually shorter maturity reserve assets. Here it generally makes sense to assign this role to reserve managers, as shortening the maturity profile of debt to match the profile of reserves would lead to increased roll-over risk of debt.

When reserves are even larger than the sum of an adequate reserve level and government's external debt, reserves in excess of that level can be managed to increase risk-adjusted returns over longer horizons.

For both options to work, it is of vital importance that in evaluating risks and returns, the focus extends beyond the short-term implications on the central bank balance sheet. Therefore, care should be taken that the length of the financial reporting cycle, in most cases one year, does not automatically become the investment horizon. Investment profiles that seem low-risk over a one-year horizon, such as short duration portfolios, can actually be more risky over longer horizons. This is because failure to take the longer maturity profile of debt into account leads to potentially large interest rate risk mismatches in the overall government's balance sheet. More generally, even if one were to ignore the mismatch with the profile of external debt, shorter duration investment profiles imply higher exposure to reinvestment risk. As the horizon gets longer, this element of interest rate risk gains in importance compared to the more immediate price risk (duration risk) of bonds. Longer investment horizons should thus lead to a greater focus on locking in interest income over the longer run, reducing the volatility of central bank's future income stream. This points to an increase in duration to reduce interest rate risk[3].

When there is sufficient appetite and adequate risk buffers are in place, the central bank can consider extending duration further to capture the expected term premium in the yield curve, and seek diversified exposure to other risks, (credit risk, prepayment risk, and others), to improve risk-adjusted returns.

Institutional Arrangements

Implications of higher reserves for central bank balance sheets

The rapid accretion of reserves in recent times has been accompanied by a continuous drive towards greater central bank transparency and accountability. This is crucial for central bank credibility, and therefore, enhances central bank independence, as does of course, an adequately capitalized central bank balance sheet. As regards central banks' financial reporting, transparency implies that fair value-based accounting standards are applied, entailing marking-to-market of central banks' assets and liabilities.

For countries that lack credible national accounting standards, this generally means that international accounting standards, notably IFRS, are adopted. The latter prescribe not only marking assets and liabilities to market, but also taking foreign exchange valuation gains and losses and, depending on how assets are classified, also asset price valuation gains and losses to the profit and loss statement.

Higher reserves and more rational reserve management strategies, aimed at generating adequate returns over the longer run, obviously lead to higher financial risk on the central bank balance sheet. It is important to note that this is due to both the higher exposure to exchange rate risk implied by higher reserve levels, and also higher investment risk when measured over the annual financial reporting cycle.

This argues for endowing the central bank upfront with more capital to be able to carry this risk without having to ask for additional capital after losses have materialized. The latter could come at significant cost to central bank independence.

Under fair value based accounting standards, these higher risks come more clearly to the surface in the form of higher volatility of central bank capital and higher volatility in reported central bank profit, depending on to what extent valuation gains and losses (due to both exchange rate movements and asset price movements) are taken to the profit and loss statement.

Implications of volatility

Higher volatility is, generally speaking, poorly understood by the general public and even by the government (i.e. Ministries of Finance). As such, it can easily be interpreted by stakeholders as evidence that the central bank is speculating with public resources. This may be despite the fact that it is in most part a necessary consequence of the pursuit of the latter's functional objectives (i.e. holding adequate reserves for crisis situations), and for another part, a consequence of good stewardship by the central bank to manage the countries wealth (i.e. improving risk-adjusted returns over the longer run). Poor understanding by central banks' stakeholders should not, however, lead to attempts to hide volatile valuation gains and losses by applying non-transparent accounting practices. Taking this route goes against the general trend of more central bank transparency and poses significant risks for central bank credibility.

At the same time, attempting to minimize volatility in valuation gains and losses by investing very conservatively, (i.e. by investing in portfolios having a short maturity profile), can be highly counterproductive, as it leads to high opportunity costs and, as pointed out earlier, can increase risks over the longer term. Similarly, trying to minimize balance sheet volatility by appropriately managing the exchange rate, or minimizing exposure to exchange rate risk by holding less (than adequate) reserves is obviously even worse, as it directly flies in the face of central banks' functional responsibility.

This is not to say that central banks should ignore the reality of their (political) circumstances and pursue more rational investment strategies for reserves without regard to these circumstances. In the absence of sufficient understanding and acceptance by stakeholders for the (short-term) return volatility of more rational investment strategies, one should realize upfront that investments will likely have to be terminated in adverse market circumstances. This makes it a recipe for locking in losses, regardless of the soundness of the investment over the longer term.

Consequently, it is important for central banks to expend energy on educating stakeholders on the reasons for volatility in annual financial statements and should try to persuade stakeholders that adopting more rational, longer-term oriented reserve management strategies carries high rewards for them in the longer run. One possible strategy of nurturing this understanding would be disclosing the structure of the currency and investment benchmarks and shedding light on the rationale behind them. Reporting of investment performance could be structured over trailing multiyear periods in order to strip out volatile annual valuation gains and losses, and could be compared with returns on alternative, more traditional asset allocations. Even if this educational exercise is successful, volatile annual income creates real problems when it is used as a basis for determining annual dividends: first of all, since profit remittances are generally treated as above-the-line items in the budget, their volatility might spill over to the budget and lead to erratic spending patterns. This is especially a concern in emerging market countries, where reserves are generally larger as a percentage of GDP, thereby making income from reserves a bigger item in the budget usually.

It also leads to inconsistencies in fiscal accounts. For example, valuation gains on government debt are not seen as income and do not have consequences for the budget. This inconsistency is most apparent in case of outstanding government debt denominated in foreign currency.

Lastly, distribution of valuation results leads to asymmetries in sharing results with the government: extraordinary central bank gains are transferred to the government, but extraordinary losses have to be buffered by central bank capital. In the absence of adequate capital maintenance charges to profit, this can over time lead to erosion of central bank capital.

Distributing foreign exchange valuation gains

Valuation gains and losses can derive either from exchange rate movements or from movements in asset prices (bond prices). Foreign exchange revaluation gains are the result of depreciation of the domestic currency. These could be dubbed bad gains for they are often a consequence of bad macroeconomic policies and management. If, as is sometimes the case, overly expansive fiscal policy is part of such policies, the distribution of foreign exchange gains can actually exacerbate the initial problem by fuelling additional fiscal spending. When corrective policy action is taken and the exchange rate depreciation is (partly) reversed, the net result is an expansion of domestic liquidity at the expense of central bank capital.

Distributing asset price valuation gains

Including valuation gains due to increases in bond prices in distributable income leads to a change in the direction of remittances that is ultimately unsustainable. The lower current interest rates that caused the valuation gains will ultimately feed into lower reinvestment income of reserves and lead to lower future central bank income. Distributing current bond price valuation gains thus merely raises current distributions at the expense of future distributions, much like borrowing against future income. If distributed, it should, therefore, ideally be treated as below-the-line in fiscal budgets.

Moreover, if bond price valuation gains and losses are significant enough to result in net losses (i.e., valuation losses that exceed interest income), they lead to the same asymmetry in sharing returns with the government as is the case for foreign exchange valuation gains and losses and might erode central bank capital over time.

Should central banks distribute only realized gains?

Accounting separates realized gains and losses from unrealized gains and losses. Frequently, this distinction also plays a role in determining distributable income in the sense that realized gains are seen as distributable, while unrealized gains are not.

Does this really help in solving the problems associated with distributing valuation gains and losses? The answer is no. As regards foreign exchange valuation gains, it only shifts the moment of distribution of gains to the moment of intervention, which is just as bad. More generally, the distinction between realized and unrealized results for determining distributable income frequently seems to be based on the notion that realized gains are more real than unrealized results, which of course flies in the face of the rationale for fair value accounting. It implicitly assumes that by realizing gains the underlying risk exposure is erased and that therefore the gain is non-reversible. Obviously, this is generally not the case for central banks. To take just two examples, the regular trading of bonds by central banks is generally done while maintaining portfolio durations, and the sales of foreign reserves in support of a country's exchange rate are generally followed by an increase of reserves when calm is restored.

The only time such a distinction is relevant is when authorities decide that they can do with less foreign exchange reserves in the future. Such a decision would free up part of central bank capital (depending on whether the central bank is adequately capitalized to begin with) and it could be considered to agree with the government to give back (part of) this capital. This part, however, is not necessarily the same as the size of the realized foreign exchange gain. Obviously, any transfer should take the form of a below-the-line transfer in order not to destabilize the fiscal budget.

Finally, basing distributable profits on the distinction between realized and unrealized gains and losses also opens the door for manipulating central bank profits. Assets can be selected for turnover with the aim of increasing or decreasing realized profits. This leads to opacities in the relation with government and can undermine efficient investment management of reserves.

Two fundamental solutions

There are basically two groups of solutions on how to deal with valuation gains and losses in distributing income.

One is to adjust accounting rules such that it results in a profit concept that is close to a desirable basis for dividend determination. As an example, bring all valuation gains and losses (included those realized) directly to revaluation accounts in the balance sheet.

The other is to clearly separate the determination of annual profit, by application of the relevant accounting rules, from determining annual dividends.

A problematic feature of the first solution is that it makes the accounting rules completely subservient to income distribution purposes, whereby it runs the risk of violating other objectives of accounting, most notably giving a transparent picture of the central bank's financial health by using credible accounting standards. As it is not in accordance with IFRS accounting standards, it will also not be a feasible solution for a lot of central banks that for good reasons aim at adhering to IFRS rules. We will, therefore, subsequently focus on the second set of solutions.

The first option within this class is the Operational Income Model. This works by routing valuation gains and losses through the profit and loss statement, but subsequently removing them entirely to arrive at distributable income. The latter then basically consists of interest income net of operating expenses. The attractive features of this model are: (1) dividends do not risk fuelling fiscal expenditure at times when fiscal restraint is called for; (2) dividends are fairly smooth through time and the direction of change is in accordance with central bank's future earnings potential (hence sustainable); and (3) there is no potential to 'game' annual income[4]. However, there are some important caveats and conditions, including (1) although the risk of gradual erosion of central bank capital is mitigated by the fact that central banks retain extraordinary gains to help buffer subsequent extraordinary losses, capital obviously has to be at a fairly comfortable level to begin with; (2) a capital maintenance charge should be retained to maintain the real value of capital over time; (3) there should be sufficient flexibility to suspend the distribution rule when capital falls below a level that is deemed to be a minimum to support central bank credibility and independence; and (4) the rule should be adjusted in situations where the domestic currency is expected to systematically appreciate. A more correct and slightly more sophisticated version of the model is to base dividends on the average 'purchase yield' of the reserves portfolio. For example, for a portfolio with an average maturity of four years, dividends in any year would be based on the average of market interest rates for the relevant maturity spectrum over the last four years. The rational is that the portfolio will have been (re)invested in the past at approximately these market rates.

The second option consists of averaging fair value income over a given window of the past years. Its major advantages lie in generating a smoother income distribution without opening the door to 'income gaming'. However, it also suffers from the same drawback of distributing bad gains, although in a somewhat smooth and lagged way. In essence, therefore, this option is no different than basing annual dividends on annual profit including valuation results. It only mitigates the distorting effect of valuation gains and losses on the fiscal budget and lessens the risk of gradual central bank capital erosion, as more annual extraordinary gains are withheld to buffer extraordinary losses. It is also worth noting that under this method, the smoothing of dividends is entirely backward-looking. As such, therefore, structural changes at the level of future central bank profitability, for instance due to changes in the level of interest rates, are not reflected in current year dividends. To the contrary, the direction of change in dividends owing to interest rate movements is unsustainable and therefore still leads to unnecessary dividend volatility.

The last option is to adopt some form of a Capital Maintenance Model, targeting a given level of central bank capital and treating dividends purely as a residual. This is particularly appropriate for central banks that have a clearly inadequate level of capital, such as institutions with a combination of a low level of nominal capital, relatively high operating costs and high carrying costs of reserves. As a consequence annual profit will generally be structurally low, leaving very little cushion to buffer losses. In these cases, capital accumulation must take precedence over other objectives. As there is in any case hardly anything to distribute, it does not make sense to be overly sophisticated on how to time distribution of remaining income. Obviously, in these cases it would be ideal to negotiate a structural recapitalization of the central bank, not in the least to remove inadequate capital as a constraint on rational investment strategies for reserves. However, this might not be feasible in all situations. For cases where structural central bank profitability is more comfortable, the solution is not so straightforward. Central banks in this category could actually operate with significant negative capital, without their balance sheets becoming unsustainable. This is because the present value of their future net profits present a large amount of 'goodwill' that is not reflected in reported capital. On the other hand, potential losses can be particularly high for central banks in comparison with commercial banks, due to the nature of their business. It therefore becomes very difficult to agree on what level of capital to target when determining annual dividends. In these cases it therefore makes sense to apply a model along the lines of the first option.

19.3 CONCLUSION

In sum, alleviating or at least mitigating as much as possible the political and institutional constraints on a rational strategy of investing reserves can pay high dividends to society.

First and foremost, this involves education of stakeholders by the central bank. Obviously, the central bank then has to first have its story straight on how to motivate rational strategic asset allocation choices and how to explain the consequences of this allocation to the outside world.

Secondly, it also involves careful crafting of profit distribution rules that are transparent and lead to understandable results for the fiscal accounts, support central bank independence, and do not distort incentives to efficient investment policy.

As should be clear by now, there is no 'silver bullet'. That said, any solution should take account of the specific political and institutional environment prevailing in a particular country. The perfect theoretical solution will break down if the will to adhere to the rules is lacking. Central banks therefore generally have the inclination to be on the cautious side in distributing income if they can help it. However, hoarding too much of the profits will ultimately backfire, as it risks 'raids' on central bank capital and can be as harmful to central bank independence as giving away too much. Consequently, this is a balancing act that requires a fair amount of judgment. Finally, any solution should be supported by a strong governance framework, clarifying the roles and responsibilities of various bodies and mitigating the risk of any party breaking the rules.

NOTES

1. Paulus Dijkstra, Christian Mulder, Kenneth Sullivan and Jay Surti contributed to this work. It greatly benefited from discussions with Peter Stella.
2. Between 1998 and 2005, world reserves more than doubled, increasing from $2 trillion to $4.3 trillion. Over the same period, emerging market reserves increased from $0.7 trillion to $1.7 trillion.
3. This is analogous to debt managers' focus on stability of debt servicing costs over the longer run (refinancing risk) as a risk measure, instead of focusing on potential changes in market value of debt (duration risk) over shorter horizons.
4. This is not strictly true as income gaming is still possible to a limited extent through (for example) choosing low coupon bonds which actually structurally lower dividends to the benefit of capital.

References

Aizenman, Joshua and Jaewoo Lee (2005), 'International reserves: precautionary versus mercantilist views, theory and evidence', paper presented to Federal Reserve Bank of San Francisco conference, 'External imbalances and adjustment in the Pacific Basin', 22–3 September.

Aizenman, Joshua and N.P. Marion (2003), 'The high demand for international reserves in the Far East: What's going on?', *Journal of the Japanese and International Economies*, **17** (3), 370–400.

Andres, J., D. Lopez-Salido and E. Nelson (2004), 'Tobin's imperfect asset substitution in optimizing general equilibrium', Banco de España Working Paper No. 409.

Arora, V. and M. Cerisola (2001), 'How Does U.S. Monetary Policy Influence Sovereign Spreads in Emerging Markets?', *IMF Staff Papers* **48** (3), 474–98.

Bakker, Age (2006), 'Central Bank Balance Sheet Risks and Capital Issues', Speech for the Governor's Forum on Reserve Management, Washington DC, 23 September, mimeo, www.dnb.nl (Research and Statistics / Personal pages of researchers).

Bakker, Age, Han van der Hoorn and Leonard Zwikker (2006), 'How ALM Techniques can Help Central Banks', mimeo, www.dnb.nl (Research and Statistics / Personal pages of researchers).

Bank of Canada (2003), *Bank of Canada Annual Report 2003*, http://www.bankofcanada.ca/en/annual/2003/ar2003.html.

Bank of Japan (2004), *Bank of Japan Annual Review 2004*.

Ben-Bassat, A. and D. Gottlieb (1992), 'Optimal international reserves and sovereign risk', *Journal of International Economics*, **33**, 345–62.

Berg, Andrew, Eduardo Borenszstein and Catherine Patrillo (2003), 'Assessing early warning systems: how have they worked in practice?', IMF Working Paper No. 04/05.

Berg, Andrew, and Catherine Patrillo (1999): 'Are currency crises predictable: a test', *IMF Staff Papers*, **45** (June), 107–88.

Bernanke, B.S. (2002), 'Deflation: Making sure "it" doesn't happen here', remarks before the National Economists Club, Washington DC, 21 November.

Bindseil, U. (2004), 'Monetary policy implementation, theory, past, and present', Oxford University Press.

Bindseil, U., A. Manzanares and B. Weller (2004), 'The role of central bank capital revisited', ECB Working Paper No. 392.

Bindseil, U. and Papadia, F. (2006), 'Credit risk mitigation in central bank operations and its effects on financial markets: the case of the Eurosystem', forthcoming occasional paper, European Central Bank.

Bindseil, U. and F. Würtz (2005), 'Open market operations – their role and specifications today', paper prepared for the SUERF conference on open market operations held at the Bank of Finland, Helsinki, 22–3 September.

Blake, Christopher, Edwin Elton, and Martin Gruber (1993), 'The Performance of Bond Funds', *Journal of Business*, **66** (3), 371–403.

Blenck, D., H. Hasko, S. Hilton and K. Masaki (2001), 'The main features of the monetary policy frameworks of the Bank of Japan, the Federal Reserve and the Eurosystem', in *Comparing monetary policy operating procedures across the United States, Japan and the euro area*, BIS Papers, **9**, Bank for International Settlements.

Broaddus, J. and M. Goodfriend (2001), 'What Assets Should the Federal Reserve buy?, *Federal Reserve Bank of Richmond Economic Quarterly*, **87** (1).

Bussière, Mathieu, and C. Mulder (1999), 'External Vulnerability in Emerging Market Economies: How High Liquidity Can Offset Weak Fundamentals and the Effects of Contagion', IMF Working Paper No. 99/88.

Bussière, M. and M. Fratzscher (2002), 'Towards a New Early Warning System of Financial Crises', Working Paper 145, Frankfurt: European Central Bank.

Calvo, G (1991), 'The perils of sterilization', *IMF Staff Papers*, **38** (4) 921–6.

Calvo, G. (1998), 'Capital flows and capital-market crises: the simple economics of sudden stops', *Journal of Applied Economics*, **November**.

Calvo, G. and E. Mendoza (2000), 'Contagion, globalization and the volatility of capital flows', in Sebastian Edwards (ed.), *Capital flows and the emerging economies*, Chicago, US: University of Chicago Press.

Cantor, R. and F. Packer (1995), 'Determinants and impact of sovereign credit ratings', *Federal Reserve Bank of New York Economic Policy Review*, **2** (2), 37–53.

Central Bank of Chile (2005), *Monetary policy report (September), Appendix A, Central Bank of Chile's balance sheet, and Appendix C, International reserve management*, pp. 65–8 and pp. 73–81.

Claassen, Emil-Maria (1975), 'Demand for International Reserves and the Optimum Mix and Speed of Adjustment Policies', *American Economic Review*, **65** (3), 446.

Cline, W. and K. Barnes (1997), 'Spreads and Risk in Emerging Market Lending', Research Paper 97(1), Institute of International Finance, Washington DC.

Cuthbertson, Keith and Dirk Nitzsche (2004, 2nd ed.), *Quantitative Financial Economics*, Chichester: John Wiley.

De Beaufort Wijnholds, J.O. and A. Kapteyn (2001), 'Reserves Adequacy in Emerging Market Economies', Working Paper 01/143, Washington DC, US: International Monetary Fund.

DeCecco, Marcello (1974), *Money and Empire: the International Gold Standard, 1898–1914*, Oxford, UK: Oxford University Press.

De Gregorio, J. and J. Lee (2003), 'Growth and adjustment in East Asia and Latin America', Central Bank of Chile, Working Paper No. 245.

De la Grandville, Olivier (2001): *Bond Pricing and Portfolio Analysis*, Cambridge: MIT University Press.

Department of Finance Canada (2003), Treasury Management Governance Framework, http:/ww.fin.gc.ca/treas/Goveev/TMGF_e.html.

Edison, Hali (2003), 'Are foreign exchange reserves in Asia too high?', in IMF, *World Economic Outlook*, September, pp. 78–92, Washington DC, US: International Monetary Fund.

Edwards, Sebastian (2004), 'Thirty years of current account imbalances, current account reversals, and sudden stops, *IMF Staff Papers*, **51**, special issue.

Eichengreen, B. and A. Mody (1998), 'What Explains Changing Spreads on Emerging Market Debt: Fundamentals or Market Sentiment', in S. Edwards, *Capital Flows and the Emerging Economies: Theory, Evidence, and Controversies*, NBER Conference Report series, Chicago, US and London, UK: University of Chicago Press.

European Central Bank (2002), *The Liquidity Management of the ECB*, Monthly Bulletin, **May**.

European Central Bank (2003), 'Opinion of the European Central Bank of 15 October 2003 at the request of the Finnish Ministry of Finance on a draft government proposal to amend the Suomen Pankki Act and other related acts', CON/2003/22.

European Central Bank, International Relations Committee Task Force (2006a), 'The Accumulation of Foreign Reserves', ECB Occasional Paper Series, no. 43.

European Central Bank (2006b), *Portfolio Management at the ECB*, Monthly Bulletin, **April**.

Fisher S.J. and M.C. Lie (2004), 'Asset allocation for central banks: Optimally combining liquidity, duration, currency and non-government risk', *Risk management for central bank foreign reserves*, European Central Bank, **May**.

FRBNY (2003), 'Changes in the management of the system open market account', Federal Reserve Bank of New York, press release, May.

FRBNY (2004), *Domestic open market operations during 2003*, Federal Reserve Bank of New York, January.

Garcia, Pablo and Claudio Soto (2006), 'Large hoardings of international reserves: are they worth it?', in R Caballero, C Calderón and L Felipe Céspedes (eds), *External vulnerability and preventative policies*, Santiago, Chile: Central Bank of Chile, 171–206.

Genberg, Hans, Robert N. McCauley, Yung Chul Park and Avinash Persaud (2005), 'Official reserves and currency management in Asia: Myth, reality and the future', *Geneva reports on the world economy* 7, Geneva, Switzerland and London, UK: International Center for Monetary and Banking Studies and Centre for Economic Policy Research.

Goldstein, M, G. Kaminsky and C. Reinhart (2000), *Assessing financial vulnerability: an early warning system for emerging markets*, Washington: Institute for International Economics.

Graham, John and Campbell Harvey (1997), *Market Timing Ability and Volatility Implied in Investment Newletters' Asset Allocation Recommendations*, NBER WP 4890.

Greenspan, Alan (2004), 'Current Account', Remarks before the Economic Club of New York, 2 March.

Gros, D. and F. Schobert (1999), *Excess foreign exchange reserves and overcapitalization in the Eurosystem*, Ifo-Schnelldienst **19**.

Hauner, David (2005), 'A fiscal price tag for international reserves', IMF Working Paper WP/06/81.

Heller, Robert (1966), 'Optimal International Reserves', *Economic Journal*, **76** (June), 296–311.

Higgins, M. and T. Klitgaard (2004): 'Reserve accumulation: implications for global capital flows and financial markets', *Federal Reserve Bank of New York Current issues in economics and finance*, **10** (10).

Hildebrand, Phillip (2005), 'Recent Developments in Asset Management at the Swiss National Bank', Robert Pringle and Nick Carver (eds): *New Horizons in Central Bank Risk Management*, London: Central Banking Publications.

Ho, Corrinne and Robert N. McCauley (2005): 'Resisting exchange rate appreciation and accumulating reserves: What are the consequences for the domestic financial system?', paper presented to Korea Institute of Finance seminar, Seoul, 6 January.

Humpage, Owen (2003), 'Government Intervention in the Foreign Exchange Market', Federal Reserve Bank of Cleveland Working Paper, 0315.

International Monetary Fund (1993), *Balance of Payments Manual,5th edition*, Washington DC, US: International Monetary Fund.

International Monetary Fund (1998), 'Financial Crises: Causes and Indicators', *World Economic Outlook*, **May**, Washington DC, US: International Monetary Fund.

International Monetary Fund (2004), *Guidelines for Foreign Exchange Reserve Management*, Washington DC, US: International Monetary Fund.

International Monetary Fund (2005), *Annual Report 2005*, Washington DC, US: International Monetary Fund.

Ize, A. (2005), 'Capitalizing central banks: A net worth approach', IMF Working Paper No 05/15, International Monetary Fund.

Kamin, S.B., and O.D. Babson (1999), 'The Contribution of Domestic and External Factors to Latin American Devaluation Crises: An Early Warning Systems Approach', International Finance Discussion paper 64, New York, US: Board of Governors of the Federal Reserve System.

Kruger M., P. Osakwe and J. Page (1998), 'Fundamentals, Contagion and Currency Crises: an Empirical Analysis', Working Paper 98–10, Ottawa, Canada: Bank of Canada.

Lakonishok, Josef, Andrei Shleifer and Robert Vishny (1992), 'The Structure and Performance of the Money Management Industry', *Brookings Papers on Economic Activity* (Microeconomics), pp. 339–91.

Latter, Tony (2003), A reappraisal of the form and functions of the Hong Kong Monetary Authority, the usage of the Exchange Fund, and related aspects of Hong Kong's fiscal and foreign reserves policy', *Civic Exchange*, **July**.

Lee, Jaewoo (2005), 'Insurance value of international reserves: An option pricing approach', manuscript, IMF (earlier version Working Paper no 04/175).

Leibowitz, Martin (1986), 'The Dedicated Bond Portfolio in Pension Funds – Part I: Motivation and Basics', *Financial Analysts Journal*, **1**, 61–75.

Lindsley, D.E., H.T. Farr, G.P. Gillum, K.J. Kopecky and R.D. Porter (1984), 'Short-run monetary control: Evidence under a non-borrowed reserve operating procedure', *Journal of Monetary Economics*, **13**, 89–111.

McCauley, Robert N. (2005): 'Distinguishing global dollar reserves from official holdings in the United States', *BIS Quarterly Review*, **September**, 57–72.

McKinnon, R. (2005), 'Exchange Rates, Wages, and International Adjustment: Japan and China versus the United States', Proceedings, Federal Reserve Bank of San Francisco.

Milesi-Ferretti, G.M. and A. Razin (1998), *Current Account Reversals and Currency Crises:* 'Empirical Regularities', Working Paper 98/89, Washington, US: International Monetary Fund.

Min, H. (1998), *Determinants of Emerging Markets Bond Spreads: Do Fundamentals Matter?*, Policy Research Working Papers Series 1899, Washington DC, US: World Bank.

Nakamae, Tadashi (2003), 'Why dramatic currency depreciation and the resulting market resurgence are Tokyo's only way out', *The International Economy*.

New Zealand, Treasury (2004): 'Operationalising a more active foreign exchange intervention policy', report to the Minister of Finance, 2 March http:www.treasury.govt.nz/release/rbnzeri/t2004-322.pdf.

Plamondon and Associates (2004), *Summary Report Governance Evaluation: Debt and Reserves Management*, http://www.fin.gc.ca /activity/goveval-e.html.

Pringle, R. and N. Carver (2006), *RBS Reserve Management Trends 2006*, London, UK: Central Banking Publications.

Putnam B.H. (2004), 'Thoughts on investment guidelines for institutions with special liquidity and capital preservation requirements, Risk management for central bank foreign reserves', European Central Bank, May 2004.

Radelet, S. and J. Sachs (1998), *The East Asia crisis: Diagnoses, remedies, prospects*, Brooking Papers on Economic Activity (1), 1–90.

Remolona, Eli and Martijn A. Schrijvers (2003), 'Reaching for yield: selected issues for reserve managers', *BIS Quarterly Review*, **September**, 65–73.

Reserve Bank of New Zealand (2004, 2005), *Annual Report*.

Rodrik, Dani (2006), 'The Social Costs of Foreign Exchange Reserves', NBER Working Paper 11952.

Rogoff, K. (1985), 'The optimal degree of commitment to an intermediate monetary target', *Quarterly Journal of Economics*, **100**, (11), 69–89.

Shleifer, Andrei and Robert Vishny (1997), 'Limits of Arbitrage', *Journal of Finance*, **52** (3), 35–55.

Soto, C., A. Naudon, E. López and A. Aguirre (2004), 'Acerca del nivel adecuado de las reserves internacionales', Central Bank of Chile Working Paper No. 267.

Stella, P. (1997), 'Do central banks need capital?', IMF Working Paper No. 97/83, Washington DC, US: International Monetary Fund.

Triffin, Robert (1960): *Gold and the Dollar Crisis*, New Haven: Yale University Press.

Tucker, P (2004), 'Managing the central bank's balance sheet: where monetary policy meets financial stability', lecture delivered on 28 July, marking the 15th anniversary of the founding of Lombard Street Research. US Treasury, Federal Reserve Bank of New York, Board of Governors of the Federal Reserve System (2004), *Report on foreign portfolio holdings of U.S. securities as of June 30, 2003, August,* http://www.ustreas.gov/tic/shl2003r.pdf.

Warnock, Francis and Veronica Warnock (2006), *International Capital Flows and U.S. Interest Rates*, Mimeo, University of Virginia.

Woodford, M. (2001), 'Monetary policy in the information economy', paper prepared for the 'Symposium on Economic Policy for the InformationEconomy' held at the Federal Reserve Bank of Kansas City, Jackson Hole, Wyoming, 30 August–1 September.

Index